GLENDA JACKSON

GLENDA JACKSON

A Study in Fire and Ice

Ian Woodward

St. Martin's Press
New York

Library of Congress Cataloging in Publication Data

Woodward, Ian.
  Glenda Jackson : a study in fire and ice.

  1. Jackson, Glenda.   2. Actors—Great Britain—
Biography.   I. Title.
PN2598.J26W66   1985   792′.028′0924   [B]   85-12526
ISBN 0-312-32914-8

First published in Great Britain by George Weidenfeld & Nicolson
Limited.

First U.S. Edition

10 9 8 7 6 5 4 3 2 1

For Doreen Montgomery

Contents

Part Five: A Star in Collision 139

Part Six: A Star in the Unknown 169

Some say the world will end in fire,
Some say in ice.
From what I've tasted of desire
I hold with those who favour fire.
But if it had to perish twice,
I think I know enough of hate
To say that for destruction ice
Is also great
And would suffice.

Robert Frost

And fire and ice within me fight
Beneath the suffocating night.

A. E. Housman

Into the eternal darkness,
into fire and ice . . . .

Dante

Illustrations

LINE DRAWINGS

Chronology

1936   Born (9 lb 12 oz), 9 May, Birkenhead, Cheshire, first of four daughters of Harry ('Micky') and Joan (*née* Pearce) Jackson; christened Glenda May.

1939   Family move to Hoylake, six miles west of Birkenhead.

1941   Begins primary education at Hoylake Church School.
Attends Sunday School. Plays shepherd boy in Nativity play.

1947   Begins ballet classes.
Attends West Kirby Grammar School for Girls.

1949   Appears as witch in pantomime at the YMCA, Hoylake.

1951   Sees Donald Wolfit as Shylock in *The Merchant of Venice*, her first experience of live legitimate theatre.

1952   Leaves school with GCE O-level passes in Geography, English Language and English Literature.
Works behind the counter at local Boots the Chemist.
Takes elocution lessons in Liverpool.
Joins amateur theatre group, the YMCA Players, in Hoylake.

1954   Wins scholarship and starts attending Royal Academy of Dramatic Art (RADA) in London.

1956   Graduates from RADA.

1957   Professional acting début with the Worthing Repertory Company, Sussex, in *Doctor in the House*.
West End début in *All Kinds of Men* at the Arts Theatre.

1958   Television début – bit-part in *A Voice in Vision* (Associated Rediffusion: ITV).
Marries (2 August) stage manager Roy Hodges at the St Marylebone Registry Office, London.

1963   Bit-part in first film, *This Sporting Life*.

1964   Joins Royal Shakespeare Company. Appears in the Theatre of Cruelty season and scores success as Charlotte Corday in *The Marat/Sade*.

1965   Début at the RSC's Stratford-upon-Avon theatre, as the Princess of France in *Love's Labour's Lost*.

1965   Broadway début, with the RSC, in *The Marat/Sade*.

1969   Birth of son, Daniel, in February.

1975   Forms movie production company, Bowden Films, with business part-
          ner Bob Enders.
          Meets Andy Phillips.

1976   Divorces Roy Hodges.
          Forms theatre production company, Bullfinch Productions, with Bob
          Enders and Andy Phillips.

1977   First Hollywood film, *House Calls*, with Walter Matthau.

1978   Awarded CBE and honorary D.Litt.

1981   Glenda Jackson Season of films on British and US television.
          Father dies.

1982   Helps to form the Women's Playhouse Project.

1983   Forms film, TV and video company, United British Artists, with Albert
          Finney, Diana Rigg, Maggie Smith, Richard Johnson and John Hurt.
          Welsh Labour Party asks her to stand for the marginal Bridgend
          parliamentary constituency.
          Opens the Glenda Jackson Theatre in Birkenhead.

1984   Lectures on drama at Balliol College, Oxford.
          Teaches course in acting at the University of Scranton, Pennsylvania.

Glenda Jackson
in Great and Small.
Gerald Scarfe

Introduction

'You're writing a whole book about Glenda Jackson?' queried an actor who had worked with her during her years with the Royal Shakespeare Company. The tone of his voice was coloured by a momentarily unsettling combination of sympathy and disbelief, and then it grew more grave. 'She's very dour, you know. There are no jokes with her, no fooling around. It's all very serious. She doesn't mix with the social set, the places where anecdotes are forged. A very strange lady. You're going to have to do a lot of digging.'

An American writer came home, having spent an afternoon with Glenda Jackson, and talked to two men about her experience with the English actress. One was a sculptor, and he said, 'Is she tough?'

'What makes you think that?' asked the writer.

'Her bad legs,' he said, 'and her pock-marked face – you have to be tough to rise above physical defects – and her cool voice and her controlled manners.'

'Yes,' said the writer. 'She is very tough.'

The other man was a film producer, and he said, 'I'd love to have her for my next picture, but the part needs a vulnerable woman. Is she vulnerable?'

'Yes,' said the writer. 'She is very vulnerable.'

To suggest that Glenda Jackson is a contradiction may sound trite, but her complex personality makes such an observation unavoidable. She is also a woman who engenders conflicting, often turbulent emotions among those with whom she comes in contact. People either like or dislike her intensely. There are few grey areas in her public and private persona. Audiences or colleagues, their view of the actress is cut and dried. One well-known actor who worked extensively with Glenda in her early days talked to me about her with such virulence that, after a one-hour interview, I was unable to use a single sentence of his diatribe.

Her complexity is her very fascination, and yet she herself seems hardly aware of just how interesting she is. She insists that she does not possess a saleable personality: that, essentially, she is an anonymous person. She is at her happiest when blending into the background, which is certainly one reason why it has always been easy for her to adopt other 'personas' in her acting. 'But God knows,' she said, 'there's nothing so personally intriguing about me that someone would drag themselves out on a rainy night to see my movies.'

I first met Glenda Jackson in a desolate meadow in a corner of the Buckinghamshire countryside. It was 1970. A sharp winter breeze was slicing clean through some bulrushes by a stream; and, close by, a BBC camera crew was filming the outdoor sequences for an episode of her television series, *Elizabeth R.* Quite soon a regular clumpity-clump rhythm, accompanied by hilarious laughter, grew to a crescendo as a noble stallion, with Glenda aloft, drew to a halt just behind the camera.

'*Oohhhh!*' cried Glenda, as the noble steed, all sweat and billowing nostrils, trotted towards me. 'Oh, what a hoot, what a *hoot*!' said she, at the precise moment I was gallantly trying to disengage one of her feet from an awkward stirrup. I helped her down. This was not the picture of Elizabeth I, Virgin Queen of England, which television viewers would eventually see, because after several more 'takes' she had so mastered the art of riding side-saddle that not even your original blood royal would have protested. She negotiated her way through the paraphernalia of camera, lighting and recording equipment, and slumped on a folding chair beneath a large oak. Here was Elizabeth, green eyes twinkling, red hair wind-blown, and you somehow expected to hear a proclamation no less majestic than, 'I am your appointed Queen . . . I thank God I am endued with such qualities that if I were turned out of the realm in my petticoat I were able to live in any place in Christome.'

It occurred to me that, even for an actress renowned for being 'formidable' and 'aggressive', this Elizabeth/Glenda was nonetheless a far cry from the Glenda Jackson of respectable suburbia, or from the Glenda Jackson of the cinema. She had become notable for portrayals of fraught and frenzied women: first, in such productions as *The Marat/Sade* and *Negatives*; later, as the sexually-curious Gudrun in *Women in Love*; as Tchaikovsky's nymphomaniac wife in *The Music Lovers*; as the wretched divorcee Mrs Alex Greville in *Sunday, Bloody Sunday*. But by the following summer when I called at her Blackheath home for tea, she seemed a different person. As it turned out, she had just decided that in future she was going to leave all those neurotics to other people. 'Oh, yes,' she declared later, quite matter-of-factly, 'I've played a lot of neurotics, but I don't see myself like that. Neurosis is so often a self-indulgence. I hope that isn't me.'

What was certain at that time was that in an industry which had been almost completely dominated by male stars during the previous decade, Glenda Jackson had become the first strong feminine personality to rise to authentic stardom since Elizabeth Taylor. So forceful was her advent and so eager were top producers to find suitable projects for her that in the 1970s she almost single-handedly brought stories-for-women back to the screen; and in her wake came Meryl Streep and Rachel Ward. Relating to her roles in a manner which enveloped the screen in sensual vibrations she became, for those with a taste for the creatively erotic, the thinking man's Brigitte Bardot. More than any other actress in films, she captured the epoch's new 'modern woman' and, without really trying, she found herself in the enviable position of being the world's hottest-selling movie queen.

Part One

A Star is Born

From birth to age eighteen, a girl needs good parents. From eighteen to thirty-five, she needs good looks. From thirty-five to fifty-five, she needs a good personality. From fifty-five on, she needs good cash.

Sophie Tucker,
quoted 1953

I

A Cheshire Childhood

If ever a woman could be described as a child of her homeland it is Glenda Jackson. Make a pilgrimage to the sprawling, overlapping Wirral suburbs of Hoylake and West Kirby, the locale of her Cheshire upbringing, converse with the people associated with her youth, observe today's inhabitants, and one unassailable – almost bizarre – detail strikes you over and over again: a certain similarity of physiognomy. The intense, penetrating face of the actress seems to be everywhere. The retired science teacher resembles an older version of her most celebrated ex-pupil. The teenage girl walking in Market Street is Glenda 'as was'. The housewife attending the cash-till of the petrol station on Grange Hill is Glenda straight out of *The Class of Miss MacMichael*.

So it continues. In the pub by the West Kirby Sailing Club, or the hotel lounge overlooking Hilbre Point, or the little supermarket opposite the railway station – *that* familiar voice, with its death-knell brusqueness and candour, is all around you. You cannot escape it.

Stop practically anybody in the street, mention Glenda Jackson's name, and the informant will quickly volunteer, 'Oh, yes, her mother lives in Alderley Road, you know,' or 'Of course, you know, Glenda lived in Evans Road,' or 'Did you know that she went to that little church school over there?' After a while, you *do* know, because everybody keeps reminding you.

Although Hoylake and West Kirby are joined together, they differ in several respects; chiefly, perhaps, in climate. Hoylake, facing north into the Irish Sea, is wide open to winds from the north and east, making it colder and more bracing than its neighbour. West Kirby, the location of Glenda's secondary education, faces west into the great estuary of the Dee and is sheltered from the east by the long sandstone ridge of Grange and Caldy Hills, so it enjoys a much milder climate, especially during the winter months.

Yet it was not in Hoylake or West Kirby but seven miles east, in the great dockland borough of Birkenhead, on the south bank of the River Mersey opposite Liverpool, that Joan Jackson, a daily help, and her bricklayer husband, Harry (known to everybody as Mick or Micky), celebrated the birth of their first child on 9 May 1936: Glenda May Jackson weighed 9 pounds 12 ounces. Over the next seventeen years Glenda would be joined by three sisters: five years later by Gill (who would marry the owner of a chemist shop), a further seven years later by Lynne (who would also marry and become a schoolteacher), and finally, after another five years, by Elizabeth (who would work in a chemist shop and marry a car salesman).

The house in which Glenda was born, in common with most of the other houses in the area, was relatively new, for it was little more than a century since Birkenhead itself was a hamlet of but a hundred folk. Now it is the biggest town in Cheshire. It has become part of the great port of Liverpool; it shares with that city the wonderful enterprise of the Mersey Tunnel; and it preserves its own particular fame in its shipyards and its milling. It was the first town in Europe to have streetcars. It has given England a Lord Chancellor. It was here that the worldwide Boy Scout movement was started.

During the nineteenth century the town's most famous son, after the shipbuilder William Laird, was Sir William Jackson, believed to be a distant relative of Glenda's family. Sir William erected a market, laid sewers and paved roads, built gas works and illuminated the main streets with gas lights, in addition to buying a few hundred acres of marshy ground and transforming it into Britain's first public park.

In 1936 – the year in which Margaret Mitchell wrote *Gone With The Wind*, the BBC began the world's first high-definition television service, and Shirley Temple signed a five-year contract worth £1,000 a week – money was in very short supply in the hard working, high principled Jackson household. It was a regime of near poverty. Micky Jackson, then twenty-nine, and his young wife Joan (*née* Pearce) could not yet afford a place of their own and, when Glenda came into the world, were living at the home of Joan's mother in the heart of Birkenhead.

At this time Shirley Temple was the number one box-office attraction, and the Jacksons considered naming their first daughter after the American child star, then just eight years old and already a 'veteran' of twenty films. But they took one look at the shrieking, bawling creature and said, 'She'll never be a Shirley.' Another Hollywood actress, Glenda Farrell, was also very popular during this period; she began her career as a tough gangster's moll in *Little Caesar* and other crime dramas, but was best known in the 1930s for the numerous light films in which she was typecast as a cynical, wisecracking, man-chasing blonde, often as the best friend of Joan Blondell and later as a determined reporter in the 'Torchy Blane' series. Joan was reminded of the name while reading a film magazine in a doctor's waiting room, and so the Jacksons christened their offspring Glenda after the actress with a penchant for playing hard-bitten ladies and May after Joan's mother, with whom Glenda would eventually spend most of her weekends and holidays.

Their choice of name apart, no one in the Jackson family displayed much interest in showbusiness and certainly no one trod the boards, though in later years the Jackson's second daughter, Gill, became a keen amateur actress.

However, Micky had a talent for playing the banjo and is remembered as 'a regular entertainer, a real character'. He spent his life building sheds and walls – nothing grand – but he was a good, meticulous craftsman. During the war he enlisted in the Navy and served in minesweepers. Glenda was nearly nine when he returned home, a period of separation which would always haunt her. 'I always get a lump in my throat,' she admitted years later, 'when I see a destroyer flying one of those funny little flags I can't remember the name of.'

Glenda was barely out of nappies when the family moved to near-by Hoylake; and it was here, as a young man, that Micky made his mark in the town. He was slim and fairish, a handsome fellow. Hilda Bethell, who still lives in the area, was a wide-eyed teenager in those days. 'Oh, he was very nice, a very quiet chap, but when he had a banjo in his hands he was somebody else,' she recalled. 'He was marvellous with a banjo, a wonderful banjo-player. There used to be gangs in those days, before the last war, young boys in their twenties, and they used to go down to the promenade in groups, and I always remember Mick among them. They used to play in a pub in Hoylake called The Plasterer's Arms. I always remember him singing "In An Old Shanty Town", all the time strumming away on his banjo. Very musical he was. Smart. A great character; but then Hoylake breeds great characters.'

The Hoylake which Micky entertained, and which his daughters grew up in, is a watering-place, a seaside resort with open-air baths, bathing, boating, tennis courts, bowling greens and a fine promenade. Yet the local councillors had managed to avoid the vulgarity so often denoted by the word 'popular'. So here, to this day, you will find no fun fair or pleasure beach, no competing bathing beauties, no fake-auctions to trap the unwary, no touting, no blaring loudspeakers, no souvenir kiosks or questionable postcards. This rather staid, even puritanical, atmosphere is echoed in the severe personality of the Glenda Jackson of later years. Puritanism for her, she would admit – and she freely confessed to a strong puritanical streak – was 'self-discipline, responsibility, a sense of duty'. She showed little tolerance for such human frailties as frivolity, triviality, indolence, vanity, and 'showing off'.

But it would be naïve as well as misleading to suggest that it was environment alone which shaped Glenda's personality, for that would be to ignore the fact that home and family were the matrix of her childhood and blossoming womanhood. Although she did not always see eye to eye with her father – had rows with him, in fact – it was essentially a stable, happy home, the legacy of which would see her through the rockier passages of her career and sustains her still. It is a legacy which, much more than climate or geography, formed the framework for the duality of her personality. Micky was the epitome of practicality, a man who tackled every problem with a straightforward level-headedness. Joan, on the other hand, was always full of nervous energy. 'Looking at them,' said Glenda's agent, Peter Crouch, 'you could just see where Glenda got both her no-nonsense attitude towards life, and her terrific nervous drive.'

While Glenda never really resembled her father – she has inherited, instead, the broad, soft features and perceptive eyes of her mother – she nonetheless possesses her father's voice. Its deep, resonant pitch would come sculling through as he rolled off the Scouse wit at home in Evans Road ... at least, that was where anybody unfamiliar with the Jacksons might have supposed the eldest daughter got it. 'Rubbish,' said her mother. 'She got it shouting. We've always let ourselves go in this house.' She thought for a moment. 'A few years ago, when Glenda had become famous, she told me she used to be afraid of me when she was a child because I shouted. With four of them I had to shout. Any mother knows that. But when she told me this it made me upset. I don't shout any more.'

Number 3 Evans Road, the family home in Hoylake, is tucked away in a sausage-string of neat little red-brick terrace houses, two-up, two-down, in an area of tight-knit matchboxes so beloved of L.S.Lowry as a subject for his paintings. In the 1930s, there was a lavatory in the backyard and a tin tub – the bath – in the kitchen.

Until the age of five, Glenda was very much indulged as an only child; but from the moment Gill came into the world, followed in turn by Lynne and Elizabeth, she assumed responsibility as the eldest. She became almost a second mother to her sisters, and long after leaving school she was still entrusted with the role of baby-sitter-in-chief. In such circumstances it was easy enough to develop a hyperactive sense of responsibility, and possibly even to feel lost in the shuffle. In later life she was not called 'Nanny Jackson' for nothing – while being a loyal friend and ally she is inclined to run your life as well – and she herself blames her 'bossy' nature on her role as deputy matriarch back home in Evans Road. Micky, indeed, soon abdicated his authority to, but not his affection for, an overwhelming wife and four strong-willed daughters. One thing was certain: this was never a forcing-house for wilting violets; quite the contrary. Women came no stronger than the Jacksons. Yet this strength evolved despite, or perhaps because of, a lifetime of near poverty. 'Bringing up four daughters, you know, isn't easy – for quite a lot of reasons,' Micky Jackson once remarked, and he chuckled at his own joke. 'I was never out of work unless the weather put us off, but we didn't get paid much. It was hard.'

To make ends meet, Joan Jackson had to go out scrubbing other people's floors and dusting other people's mantelpieces for half a crown (12½p) a morning. 'I remember once Glenda went shopping for me on my birthday,' said Mrs Jackson. 'She came back with two sixpenny bunches of marigolds, my favourite flowers. She'd spent a shilling – almost half a morning's work. I almost had hysterics. I had to say to myself, "Don't shout ... don't shout."'

But I always had to go out to work. Always. Everybody round here had to work. Nine out of ten women were cleaning other people's mess up.'

Later, when Joan wasn't cleaning, she was either pulling pints as a barmaid or serving behind a counter in a near-by shop. But then all the women in the family were involved in such work; and it was a big, close family. Glenda's earliest recollection is one of being surrounded by relatives, all of whom 'thought we were wonderful'. Her father's parents lived just around the corner, as did her paternal aunt; and her mother's family were only seven miles away in Birkenhead. 'I was totally surrounded by love and affection, and a great deal of spoiling went on, I think.'

Glenda received her primary education at the Hoylake Church School, which was housed in two establishments, both of them still standing. One is a red-brick Victorian building opposite the church on Market Street; the other is just across the road, halfway down Church Lane, a rambling, two-hundred-year-old single-storey structure, its old playground backing on to a cemetery. Glenda was a quiet, solitary child who sometimes displayed a perverse mischievousness. Although an average pupil to begin with, she quickly developed a natural aptitude for reading and writing – yet it was never channelled to any particular end – and by her penultimate year her marks had earned her a first place in class IVB, plus the headmistress's observation in the school report that 'Glenda is a very clever child'.

As with so many English actors and actresses, Glenda's first brush with acting came when she began to attend Sunday School at the age of five. She participated in a Nativity play, taking the part of a crippled shepherd boy. Her one and only line was, 'A star in the day.' It was not perhaps an auspicious start and certainly she never followed up that appearance with any burning desire to act. Her heart was already set upon becoming a dancer, or, failing that, a missionary in Africa. Missionaries would occasionally talk to the children at Sunday School and Glenda soon fancied her chances as a pro-pagandist for the Gospel. It gradually passed, although she felt it very in-tensely at the time. But she loved Sunday School: sticking brightly coloured biblical scenes in albums and doing religious knowledge exams. She did so well, in fact, that she was awarded a prize, but unfortunately it turned out to be a book she already owned. She never went to Sunday School again. 'I suppose it shook my faith,' she explained. 'I felt God should have *known* I had that particular book, shouldn't He?' While she was not formally religious, in later life her early contact with Sunday School was reflected in her personal credo: 'There is the basic rule for me that you don't do anything to hurt other people. If you really observe it, it's extremely hard and stringent.'

There were other childish passions, daydreams, imaginings. For a time she indulged the fantasy that she was some highly connected orphan left by gypsies on the doorstep; that she was in fact the Queen of England, and at some point would be discovered for what she really was. (When she moved out of that childish fancy and into her teens, what she felt most strongly was that there *had* to be more to life than she was experiencing, and that she was never going to experience it where she was. 'It was less a feeling that I was "remarkable", that I didn't actually belong to my family, than that I didn't belong to that environment where I was living,' she recalled.)

Again, when her father returned from war-time duty on minesweepers, the sailor's nine-year-old daughter decided she wanted to join the women's navy, the WRNS. She liked the uniforms. But then an uncle took her on a ferry to Liverpool and she concluded somewhat traumatically that she would not be a very good seafarer. Afterwards she thought she might like to become a doctor, but she discovered that she could not stand hypodermic needles: could not bear having injections, seeing injections or learning anything about injections. She could be very firm when it came to avoiding the avoidable; and she was strong-willed.

'Our Glenda May was always a clever girl, but stubborn – very stubborn,' said her mother. 'We'd no idea she'd ever end up on the stage, but there was always a lot of the actress in her, you know. I remember when she was nine she went down to the Hoylake beach and fell into the pool. She knew I'd be vexed, so she got her friends to carry her in like the tragedy queen.' The 'tragedy queen', at around nine or ten, also happened to be a robust young lady. 'Oh, she was fat. I mean, she never stopped eating – like a pig. She'd come home from school and eat a full loaf of bread – she put anything on it that was near – and at half past six, when we all had our dinner, you'd think she was starving.'

'I really was a plain, most hideous child, enormously fat and very spotty,' Glenda once told me with little pleasure. 'It's true. I had an enormous appetite and I stuffed myself with chips and cakes and biscuits, so I really was a barrel of lard.'

'She was shorter than most of her classmates, and dumpy,' said Joyce Harley, her form mistress at the West Kirby Grammar School for Girls.

The grammar school is still situated in an area where working-class Hoylake merges with middle-class West Kirby, a long, rambling Edwardian establishment with modern extensions. Glenda was not gregarious by nature and did not make friends easily, so the vastness of the place and the rigid disciplines it imposed terrified her when she attended the school for the first time at the age of eleven. It mattered little that she arrived there with a commendation from the Church School headmistress, who wrote that she 'ought to do well'. Within a few months the former head teacher would be proved right; but, in the course of time, her qualifying 'ought to' would prove touchingly percipient.

In the meantime, Glenda was still consuming food as if in readiness for some impending siege, and would invariably have one hand foraging in the biscuit tin and her head in a book. There were few books at home but her thirst for literature was seemingly unquenchable. One afternoon, having been entrusted with the care of baby Lynne, she wheeled her sister in her pram to the library, and found a particular book so engrossing that it was not until she arrived home that she realized she was alone. Lynne was still parked outside the library.

She also occupied herself, after school hours, by applying mind and body to the ballet classes started soon after her eleventh birthday. But although she was proficient enough at passing her 'grade' examinations, she could never overcome the weakness stemming from a training which had started six years too late. She came to realize that she would never be adequately prepared or strong enough technically for the tough demands of a professional ballet career – 'besides which, I suddenly shot up from being a dwarf at the age of fourteen to being very tall, virtually overnight, so ballet bit the dust'.

Other possibilities also bit the dust at this time. With the advent of puberty this quiet and basically attentive girl ('I was very good at school until I was thirteen') went through a dramatic – indeed, a traumatic – transformation. Whereas previously she had been a happy, model pupil who displayed an exceptional intelligence, she now began to hate school and her academic achievements declined. The 'old' Glenda May Jackson would never be the same again. 'I just felt all the time in the wrong place,' she said later. 'But I also felt in the wrong place *inside* myself. So I spent the last three years larking about and locking myself in cupboards and thinking it was a great joke. I think adolescent girls are probably worse than boys. I just hated school and couldn't wait to leave.'

There was no short or simple explanation for Glenda's radically changed personality. Puberty alone was not to blame. There was, for instance, a profound deepening of a life-long obsession and dissatisfaction with her physical appearance: 'I was a very fat child, and very short – about four feet tall when I was fourteen. And I was terribly, *terribly* spotty. I had *awful* acne. And, well … yes, I was just *ugly*.' There were no boyfriends: 'It was all my fault because I was, as I am now, a bit anti-social. I didn't find it easy to join clubs or social groups.' There were arguments at home: 'She didn't get on very well with her father, I don't think,' said one woman who knew Glenda at that time. And great inroads were being made into her private hours, since it was her job to look after her sisters when her parents were out working: 'I always got on better with the two younger sisters, Lynne and Elizabeth, simply because of the age difference,' she explained later. 'But with Gill, the sister next to me in age, I used to fight like cat and dog.'

It is almost certain that if it had not been for her dancing lessons, Glenda's life would have lacked purpose and definition. It was the one pursuit she deeply loved and at which she excelled. One year her ballet school appeared in a pantomime at the Hoylake YMCA. As the show's wicked witch, Glenda was in her element, and, according to one eye-witness (her friend, Mrs Aldridge), 'she was absolutely fantastic – she stole the show'.

Despite such happy diversions, the tough, flinty, formidable persona of Glenda Jackson was already developing. It was a quality you would have expected to find in a crofter in the Hebrides or a coal-miner in the Midlands rather than in an adolescent girl in the Wirral. She gave the impression of continually steeling herself – but for *what*? She seemed to be angry with herself, angry with the world, and – more particularly – angry with the school. Certainly, her teachers could not ignore, let alone condone, her self-appointed role as the form's principal trouble-maker and chief wit. 'She just seemed to delight in being a nuisance, in going against the authority of the school,' recalled Mary Handy, Glenda's physical education teacher. 'You never got through a lesson without knowing that Glenda was there. She wasn't the sort of girl who did something good in order to be praised: she'd make a special "stance". It was as if she was seeking attention all the time.'

More than one teacher complained that if Glenda had channelled her reserves of liveliness into academic pursuits rather than insurgency she could have gone far. 'She had boundless energy, which I felt was wasted as regards physical education because she didn't always point it in the right direction,' observed Mary Handy. 'She could have been a team player if she'd chosen to put her mind to it, but she was much more interested in distracting somebody in the background. It's possible that her younger sisters were getting more attention at home than she was and that she was therefore trying to seek attention at school. But she could have had that attention very easily by getting into school sports teams. She was quick and lively. She had the ability, the energy – she was basically very good at sports – but she lacked the dedication. She was always the ring-leader rather than a follower; I think if she didn't have that in her she wouldn't have got where she is today.'

Moreover, not only did Glenda invariably look scruffy but, according to a consensus of opinion, she *delighted* in looking scruffy. She seemed positively to enjoy being in constant trouble. A great deal of her recalcitrant behaviour, however, could be attributed to her self-proclaimed plainness. While Glenda was almost reconciled to her little raisin eyes that disappeared when there was any fat on her round face, she could never forget that she was the possessor of a 'funny snub nose'. But nothing bothered her as much as the fact that her face was in a constant and frequently violent state of acne vulgaris. It went beyond being a normal physiological response to puberty, for it would plague her well into adulthood. The emotional implications of prolonged severe acne are often considerable, and young individuals may become depressed and withdrawn – or, as in Glenda's case, adopt an obstreperous demeanour. So she was mad with the world, or with somebody or something, for inflicting on her physiognomy what she considered was the ultimate miscarriage of justice: her plainness – her *spotty* plainness.

'Oh, I did go through agonies over my looks as a teenager,' she remembered. 'I almost became totally round-shouldered, bending over so much to hide my bad skin. I never expected anything would be given to me because of the way I looked, and it never has been. I was always the plain friend; so the social burden on me was to listen quietly and be ignored.'

Years later she told me, 'I was nobody's delight. If you think of yourself as plain – and I certainly did; in fact, I tried to think about my looks as little as possible because they were so non-promising – you tend to try and distract from it by sprouting in other directions. Well, I became the form's chief wit. I was always the one who could make people laugh, but always, I remember, as a means of compensating for what I lacked in looks.'

Inevitably, there came a time when the laughing had to stop. In the term preceding her last full year at school it was unanimously agreed among the staff that, in order to curtail Glenda's now intolerable skylarking – and thereby re-establish some semblance of normality in the lives of her teachers – she, the 'thorn', would have to be separated from her rebel cronies. The solution was almost brilliant in its simplicity: she would be promoted into a higher stream. And so, instead of accompanying the remainder of her class from 4C to 5C, she joined the cleverer 5B.

Nevertheless, Glenda's notoriety preceded her into the fifth form and few of her new teachers relished the prospect of her company. 'She came to me, you see, with this *awful* reputation for being disobedient,' said Myra Kendrick, who taught English language and English literature and who, three decades later, could not forget her former pupil. 'The change of stream clearly unsettled her. I remember this dark, sullen girl; I could hardly get a spark out of her. Not being with her friends any more, not being with her gang of baddies, she'd landed high and dry in new territory and was disoriented.'

Yet unknown to Miss Kendrick – unknown, indeed, to any other teacher – Glenda's favourite subjects, alongside history, were English language and literature; she still consumed more books than chocolate biscuits. Although it was a secret she chose to keep to herself, her very ability in these subjects finally gave the game away. 'As I began to look at her work, I thought, "There's something about this girl ...",' recalled the English teacher. 'She wrote good essays, particularly when they were based on literary subjects. At that time, for instance, we were studying *A Midsummer Night's Dream* and Glenda wrote about the play very sensibly, far more sensibly than the other girls in that stream. It made me think, "Why wasn't this girl working in a higher stream before?" All I know is that her literary essays were always worth reading and that I was lucky enough to see the best of Glenda in her last year at school.'

Apart from her brief Sunday School appearance in the Nativity play, and her appearance in pantomime, Glenda had never again set foot on stage as an 'actress'. The only live theatre she attended was the annual Christmas panto-mime. When, how or why she first became fascinated by the impact of thea-trical acting even Glenda cannot precisely recollect. But the seeds were probably sown when, in the fourth form, she was taken with a school party to Liverpool to see the great English actor–manager Donald Wolfit play Shylock in *The Merchant of Venice*. It was certainly the first legitimate theatre she had ever seen, and it was equally clear that the experience left a profound impression on her. At school at that time she was reading Shylock as the villain of the piece; but now an overwhelming attraction for Wolfit's sym-pathetic reading of the Jewish money-lender found Glenda emerging from the theatre secure in her mind that she had just witnessed 'an incredible piece of magic'.

For an entire year that 'piece of magic' lay dormant, locked – but not lost – in Glenda's subconscious, with no obvious outlet; there were few school plays. However, in the fifth form Glenda's English teacher made one further discovery about her pupil. 'She was a natural public speaker, by which I mean she knew how to act,' said Miss Kendrick. 'When we were reading the *Dream* aloud in class, her interpretation was always infinitely better than the other girls', who stumbled and fumbled. In the end, rather than have all this stumbling and fumbling, I used to get Glenda to take one of the roles and we'd read the play together as a sort of duo. I always felt that she was unlucky in the period that she was with us, in view of the fact that mimicry and drama were so obviously her strength. It was a period of post-war austerity, and the school was very limited in what it could do in the way of school productions. Another decade and Glenda would have been in her element – and, I think, a far less troublesome child.'

In the final reckoning Glenda left the West Kirby Grammar School at the age of sixteen years and two months with O-level passes in Geography, English Language and English Literature, and with such a consummate disaffection for the school that a feeling of enmity would never forsake her. When she walked out of the school gates at the end of term in July 1952 – 'with practically no particular goal in mind, least of all acting' – she never wanted to see the place again. In her mind, the institution symbolized some of the unhappiest moments of her life. 'I really hated the last two years of school ... and I've never regretted not having been to university, though I do regret not having been taught how to think logically,' she noted. But she would get by.

2
Amateur Dramatics

Life on Merseyside had already made Glenda a socialist, and it was not long before she became a card-carrying member of the Labour Party. So what would she do now? Her background had sufficiently instilled in her the notion that everything you had, you had to earn. She could never forget that her parents were poor, because the Protestant work ethic was very strong in the Jackson house. 'I grew out of an era where you *had* to have a job,' she would later tell people. 'If you didn't earn money, you didn't eat. It was as simple as that. If you didn't like it, hard bloody lines. It's something you don't discard easily.'

Apart from a short spell with Woolworth's, she spent the next two years working for Boots Cash Chemists, dealing with prescriptions on the bilious attack and laxative counter: 'They kept me out of the birth-control department; not old enough, I think.' Her great ambition was 'to get over to the other counter where they sold make-up and scent and pretty things', because it seemed so much more glamorous selling soap than laxatives. She did not succeed. She then saw herself as the first female director of Boots, 'but they weren't having *that*, though if only I hadn't been bored so easily I'd have been a marvellous cosmetics assistant'.

However, something else was already beginning to stir. 'There was a young married couple in our street who were in the local YMCA theatre group,' Joan Jackson explained, 'and they persuaded our Glenda to do some dancing in their productions. That was her first taste of the stage. It was much later, when she was working for Boots, that another woman called Joan Banks – the wife of a local laundry owner – who was very interested in the amateur theatre, got her to take night elocution lessons in Liverpool; then she took fencing lessons to give her balance ...'; and, before she fully realized what was happening, Glenda was a committed member of an amateur theatre group in Hoylake, the YMCA Players.

'I thought, "This will be good fun," but I did quite well,' recalled Glenda. 'I don't think I knew what being an actress was like then, though I'd always suspected it wouldn't be at all glamorous and thrilling in the romantic sense.'

Her acting ability came as a revelation. Prior to joining the group she had approached the Hoylake Amateur Dramatic Society with a view to appearing in one of their productions, but had been turned down. 'She was either not good enough, or not "adult" enough in her approach,' explained someone who knew Glenda at that time.

On reflection, the fact that Glenda now revelled in her new pastime at the YMCA was not really surprising. It may have been only three years since she first became enchanted by the 'magic' of live theatre, and yet, as a dancer, she was already a seasoned performer. Moreover, literature had always been a strong interest, and it was a short step from the printed page to the spoken word: she had amply demonstrated a natural facility at school for uttering the words of Shakespeare. Yet there is a final clue, possibly the most important of all, which helps to explain Glenda's new-found enthusiasm for acting: her love of the cinema. Many years later she would disclose, 'I remember listening to a group of black Americans talking about their cultural links with Africa and I thought "What a load of rubbish!" Your cultural background is shaped by the environment and circumstances in which you grew up. *My* cultural heritage isn't Shakespeare; it is Hollywood and the radio. They were the biggest influences on my young life.'

Glenda not only drew from the films of the 1940s and 1950s her initial knowledge of the art she eventually chose to serve; she was also left with a genuine affection for the Hollywood movies of the period. 'I'd go and watch Maria Montez and all those cobras and it was marvellous,' she recalled of the exotic lady known affectionately as 'The Queen of Technicolor'. Another favourite was Esther Williams. Once, in Hoylake public baths, Glenda tried to emulate the then famous aquatic actress's apparent ability to smile broadly while swimming under water – and nearly drowned.

At that time there were three cinemas in Hoylake, each showing two films a week. This meant that, if she could get the permission and the money ('they only charged sixpence'), she could see six different films a week: 'It didn't happen often, but I tried!' She used to horrify her family, in fact, by going to all the 'adults only' films and begging the grown-ups in the queue to take her inside. Her adolescent idols – Bette Davis, Katharine Hepburn, Barbara Stanwyck and Joan Crawford – soon became her ideals. In their films they clawed their way to the top and paid a terrible price for it. 'They were wonderful actresses because they managed to turn some of the most boring, rubbishy scripts into something you could believe.' Her veneration of these somewhat awesome ladies has never abated. She sees the roles they portrayed as practically indistinguishable from their real-life selves: they all clawed their way to stardom. She could not help drawing a parallel with her own life. She always knew that opportunities would not be offered to her on a plate. If necessary, she too would have to scratch and scrape to make her dreams come true.

In years to come she would proclaim, 'I was the archetypal fat and spotty teenager, suffering the tortures of the damned because I wasn't like all those model girls in the magazines. You *had* to look a certain way then to be acceptable; people didn't do their own thing. I had lank, greasy hair, too. I was the antithesis of what was then regarded as an attractive girl. I minded very much; in a way, your confidence stays a bit dented for ever by years like that. But I think now the realization that my looks would never earn me a penny was a blessing. I knew early on that I'd have to work, work, work if I wanted to amount to much; plums don't drop into plain girls' laps.

'Oh, I wouldn't want to be an adolescent again,' she added. 'I think up till I was about twenty-two was possibly the worst period of my life. I think if I'd been pretty, I'd simply have done what all pretty girls did then, which was to have a job and then get married and have lots of children. Possibly good looks could have been a disadvantage to me; it's very hard to know. But certainly, if I'd been pretty and popular, I'd probably not have felt the need to move out, move on, do things.'

Her first significant move was to join the YMCA Players, who were based in a small rehearsal room at the YMCA building on the corner of Market Street and Hoyle Road, just two hundred yards from the seafront. These amateur actors, under the inspired but imperious direction of the late Warren Owen, staged two plays a year, plus a Christmas pantomime, and were well supported by the local community. Rehearsals were held between two and four on Sunday afternoons and one or two evenings a week. For her baptismal performance, the highly professional Warren Owen agreed to give Glenda a try-out in the small role of the maid in Agatha Christie's *Murder at the Vicarage*. He was impressed from the very first rehearsal, as was another youthful member of the company, Jill Luscombe, whose father was responsible for the Players' make-up, and who was a year younger than Glenda. 'I remember her voice on that first read-through was very loud, very deep, very strong and resonant,' Jill said. 'Warren Owen was constantly imploring us, "Try to make your voice *carry*," but unlike the rest of us, Glenda didn't really have to try. She didn't speak – she shouted.'

'She had rather a raucous voice,' recalled Hilda Bethell, another member of the Players. 'You know, "Don't you bloody well . . . !" I can see her now on stage, shouting "Godamnit, no . . . !" She wouldn't half let herself go if she got in a temper over something, and I used to think, "I wouldn't like to be on the wrong side of *her*." She could stick up for herself, could Glenda. But when she came in for the first rehearsals, she knew her lines word perfect; you never had to jog her memory.'

But what her colleagues at the YMCA did not know was that, during the day at Boots, Glenda would practise her lines with great gusto – in the lavatory and elsewhere on the premises. 'I remember one tea break when there were the most terrible screams and groans coming from the stockroom,' recalled former Hoylake assistant, Ann Birch. 'It was Glenda doing her "dying" bit.' Glenda was lying on the floor, holding a script. 'I bet that fooled you,' she said.

In the course of time her 'word perfect' proficiency was held up to the other players as an example of 'how it should be done'. While they grappled and floundered over the perfection of some particular stage business, she would invariably get it right the first time. 'Why can't you all be like Glenda?' Warren Owen would grumble, brow-beating the assembled cast in moments of desperation. 'I just tell her once and she does it.' The girl concerned 'died' slowly inside. She hated being used as an example to others.

She was being noticed. Explained Hilda Bethell: 'She used to get very good reviews in the local paper. She over-acted, really. Probably that was a good thing – showed that she had it in her.'

Warren Owen's widow, Phyllis, said, 'Warren was always tremendously impressed by Glenda's willingness to do absolutely anything during rehearsals if it was in the best interests of the play. He used to say, "There's nothing that girl can't do or won't do, should I ask her. You tell her to do it, and she does it."'

Jill Luscombe recalled: 'She was always what they call "into the part". When she was playing the maid, you'd think she *was* the maid. She was in a black and white outfit, with a frilly hat. She was a very *bossy* maid. Her impact was "big". When she was on stage, you *knew* she was on stage. She wasn't one of the stars, yet she stood out when she was with the other actors. You couldn't ignore her because of her strong, booming voice and her very purposeful walk.'

'She used to get a bit fed up sometimes,' Hilda Bethell observed. 'She'd be late for rehearsals and she'd say, "Sorry, I had to baby-mind." Glenda's youngest sister, Elizabeth, was born soon after Glenda joined the YMCA Players. She was just an ordinary everyday girl, with a good hearty laugh. At rehearsals we used to joke with the boys, though she didn't go out with any of them. She wasn't really interested in boys. She didn't mind them when they were in mixed company, but I don't think she liked them on their own.'

As Jill Luscombe saw it: 'There were a lot of lads in the group, but none of them seemed to go for Glenda. But then I don't think she was interested in them either. She wasn't a good mixer. While we were all in a crowd, laughing and joking, Glenda would be sitting alone in a corner. You hardly noticed her – except when she was on stage, and then she really stood out, there was no doubt about that. She had no time for tomfoolery; she just got on with the job. Very brusque. If she said anything, she didn't mince words: she said what she meant. She was the most serious girl in our group, even morose in a way. She took her acting very seriously, that's what it was, because the amateur dramatics were definitely a focal point in her life. I think for the first time in her life she felt fulfilled. Playing a part in a play was one way of expressing herself, of getting something *out* of herself, of getting away from one aspect of herself which she was not fond of. When she acted, for instance, her plainness was transcended. At the end of her two years with us, after appearing in *Anastasia* and one other thriller, she had really changed from someone with no obvious ambition to someone with a burning determination in life ... and she was going to make something of it.'

One evening, as Glenda walked off stage after appearing in *Anastasia*, Owen called her over. 'When,' he asked her, 'are you going to give up all this nonsense at Boots?'

'What do you mean?'

'Well, this is what you should be doing, girl – working professionally as an actress. It's what you were born to do. You're just wasting your life at the moment. Why don't you try to get into one of the London drama schools? It's not too late.'

She was eighteen. It hardly needed Owen to entice Glenda away from the prescriptions counter; her own conscience had already made that decision for her: 'I knew there had to be something better than the bloody chemist's shop.' But the amateur producer's encouraging words prompted Glenda into taking some immediate action.

Events moved fast. Within a week she had written to the only drama school with which she was vaguely familiar, the Royal Academy of Dramatic Art (RADA). A month later she was auditioning in London at the Academy's Gower Street premises, though not without some trepidation: in fact, the prospect of travelling to London made her more nervous than the actual auditions: 'I had never been away from home before and I was totally ignorant. But the ignoramus aspect of it was in a way helpful because I just went along, presented myself, did the auditions and left immediately.'

The first audition, which was held on a Monday, won her a place in the school. She was thunderstruck. The second audition, the following Wednesday, brought her the hoped for scholarship, which provided for tuition but not living expenses. However, the school was sufficiently impressed with the raw material it had seen to write to the Cheshire Education Committee on the candidate's behalf and, in those balmy days of munificence, the local authority agreed. So, with the promise of a 'very sizeable' grant to see her through two years at drama school, Glenda was able to start the following term, January 1955. 'I only applied in the first place out of a sense of boredom and not from any driving ambition,' Glenda said later. 'I've never been stagestruck by the glamour of it all. If RADA had refused me, I'd have gone back to Boots.'

When the news of her RADA achievement filtered back to Micky Jackson, he was outraged. The thought of his daughter gallivanting around London filled him with horror, and his natural impulse was to put a stop to it. Showbusiness meant little to him, and twelve years later, after Glenda had become the toast of Broadway, he was still reluctant to accept her success. 'He's totally unimpressed,' said Glenda at the time. 'The only occasion he ever got excited was when I told him I'd met Sammy Davis Jr!'

Years later, when Glenda had been fêted, old Micky Jackson began to mellow in his regard for his daughter's chosen profession. But he would never, or perhaps could never, boast about her achievements. 'When you're a brickie and you have a daughter like our Glenda, it's a nice feeling,' he said. 'You know she's the best, but you don't go round bragging about it, do you? Not round here, you don't.'

At number 3 Evans Road, meanwhile, the whole Jackson household had become uneasy about Glenda's imminent departure for London and her new life. Joan Jackson, the night before, supervised the packing of her daughter's two small suitcases in a mood of mild depression, while Micky sat grimly by the fire in the front parlour wondering if it still wasn't too late to call a halt to the girl's 'craziness'. Lynne, now six, was crying; Gill, thirteen, was brooding, deep in thought; while one-year-old Elizabeth, asleep in her cot, was blissfully unaware of the turmoil.

'It caused great heartache when I left home,' Glenda said simply. 'We were fairly close knit.'

3
Drama School and Dereliction

Glenda arrived at the London home of the relatives with whom she would be staying during her first term at RADA very unsure of herself and grateful to be with people who were 'family'. Tough and strong-willed as she appeared on the surface, she maintained that she was really 'a coward' inside. 'I'd love to be the sort of girl who travels alone across Russia on the Trans-Siberian Railway,' she told people. 'I'm the kind of person who admires hitch-hikers, because in matters of independence I'm basically a coward. I have to know where I'm going and who's going to meet me at the other end.'

Later, complaining that she needed more privacy for her studies, she found new digs in Kew. It was a propitious move. Her landlady, Mrs Hill, took such great care of her new charge that she became like a second mother. And the girl with whom she was sharing digs, a Canadian, inspired Glenda to 'work' on her appearance. She started to use hair conditioners, and to clean her face with something other than soap and water. 'Until then,' Glenda confessed, 'I'd always thought that as long as I was clean and neat, that would be about as much as I'd ever accomplish.'

Gradually, the confused, unsure girl from Hoylake began to realize that life in London could be enormously adventurous. For the first time, at drama school, she was mixing with a group of people much the same age as herself, all interested in the same thing. This was a novel situation. 'Of course, you think you know everything at that stage and the sort of "swingeing" criticism everybody went in for was very stimulating.' She put her head down and worked hard; but she was always amazed to discover that there were people who *didn't* work hard. Eventually, she would be in for a rude awakening. 'I mean, the social life of RADA was something I only learned about years afterward. Friends would say, "Do you remember when so-and-so did such-and-such at some party or other?", and I would have to say, "No, I wasn't there." I wasn't even aware of the intrigues.'

Glenda, in fact, was always far too engrossed in her studies to notice anything or anybody, let alone the school's social calendar. Her routine was literally all work and no play. At weekends she earned a little extra money by serving in coffee bars, and in the summer holidays she returned to

Hoylake with holes in her shoes and worked in Woolworth's. She was still well-rounded, filled out, well-fed: 'I used to be a terrible comfort-eater. At drama school, I ate Crunchie bars by the boxful.'

Those who knew her in those days would later talk of the plump-faced girl who bored the other students with incessant tales of woe on the theme of 'I'll never be properly employed as an actress until I'm about forty-five'. There was some justification for these forebodings, since her tutors rarely lost an opportunity to remind her that they saw her almost entirely as a character actress, adding that she simply did not possess the right sort of face, physique or personality for the *ingénue* parts required in the theatre at that time. 'Girls my age,' she said later, 'were expected to be blonde – home counties, that sort of thing.'

'How well I remember her, a dumpy little thing, sitting with her knitting when we took acting classes together,' recalled a fellow student. 'She only seemed to play housemaids in those days.'

'It's true,' said Glenda. 'I was always given the roles of maids, charladies and zanies at RADA. Terrible type-casting.'

It was a period in the theatre when all the best roles for young actresses went to pretty, busty blondes, and Glenda was certainly none of these things. But what she lacked in physical 'eye appeal' she compensated for with enormous energy and commitment. She was fond of telling her classmates, 'One takes out of drama school what one is prepared to put into it.' She certainly found her two years at RADA tremendously hard work: 'There was just no *time* to get into a clique, or anything.' She once reflected on her period there, 'You study the technical things, how to be heard and seen by everybody, but just what makes a performance more than a technical reading is a mystery. You never know if it's going to be there or not, but that's the risk that makes it interesting.'

She attended RADA just at the tail-end of a 'golden period': 'I was there just a year behind all the golden lads like Albert Finney and Peter O'Toole ... at least we kept being told they were going to be the golden lads, although our year went to watch their year doing plays and were highly cynical about their chances. But we seem to have been proved wrong and the only one from my year to do any good so far is Jack Hedley. Still, I liked RADA.'

But not until her last term could she be certain that RADA liked *her*. In moments of melancholy she told herself that hard work alone would not bring success: some extra physical spark was necessary: 'For two years in London I hadn't aroused any notice. I was trying so hard to be attractive, and to be popular, that there wasn't enough of the real *me* left for anyone to notice.' She was wrong. In her last months at RADA she began to win prizes for the strength and colour of her acting, and her efforts were finally rewarded by being cast as Eliza Doolittle in the end-of-term production of *Pygmalion*, which brought her many laurels. Theatrical agent Peter Crouch thought she was well cast when he saw Glenda in the Shaw play, and he has represented her ever since.

'She'll have a long wait,' he prophesied at the time, 'but one of these days she'll be a big star.' In fact it would be nine years before she landed her first decent part.

A yellowed, dog-eared newspaper cutting shows a picture of a group of young RADA students on graduation day. Of the class of 1956 the caption states, 'After six terms at RADA, these youngsters have been turned out into the hard world of showbusiness to fend for themselves.' One of them – Glenda Jackson – is rather cursorily dismissed as 'plump, and with teeth that need straightening; no raving beauty'. And yet, of all those faces shining with belief in their own talent, perhaps for only Glenda – who graduated with honours – would reality live up to the dream.

For all that, her propulsion into the theatrical market-place was not without its tenor of gravity. Her worst fears were confirmed on graduation when the school's principal, John Fernald, a man with two decades' experience of directing West End plays, took her to one side and casually informed her, 'You know that, essentially, you're a character actress?'

'Er – yes,' answered the discomposed graduate.

'In that case,' he continued, 'don't expect to find much work till you're forty.'

Glenda was floored, but in time she was sufficiently rational to admit, 'When I left RADA in 1956 the British theatre was still mainly commercially oriented. There was male and female lead, male and female juvenile lead, male and female character and male and female juvenile character – and I didn't fit into any of those categories. So it was a fairly accurate assessment of my employment prospects when I left.' She was in her twenty-first year. Not really the most appropriate age to play the sort of parts most producers thought best suited to her – such as forty-three-year-old charladies. 'There were no plays for a spotty girl,' she observed with stoic resignation. But this was no time to feel heavy-hearted. Acting, for the bricklayer's daughter, was not 'art', but 'work'. She embarked on what she later called 'the traditional English round: repertory and unemployment'.

It was a mundane and often depressing treadmill that was to occupy the next eight or nine years of her life, a period when, theatrically speaking, she was unemployed far more frequently than employed. In her repertory years she appeared in some two hundred productions and was called upon to do a wide variety of other things. Often she would have to do a new play every week, comprising seven shows, plus morning and late-night rehearsals for the following week. She also doubled as assistant stage manager (ASM), which meant sweeping out the theatre at night, scrounging props and stage furniture, painting scenery. Those years were to leave their mark.

'Whenever we were filming,' recalled George Segal, one of her later co-stars, 'I noticed that Glenda had a particular habit of picking up matches which had been thrown on the studio floor. Or she'd light a cigarette and tuck the match behind an unused match in the pack, or, if it was a wooden match, put it back in the box. I asked her about it once and she said, "Well, I used to do this when I was an ASM. You always picked up matches; you couldn't leave them lying around: too dangerous."'

Her span in the cold-water-one-room-flats world of the provincial repertory company, that drab, tough training ground that is the heart of the English theatre, had such a profound effect on her that, a decade later, she was heartily sick of stage work: 'Invaluable as it was, it made me loathe the theatre. I neither want to act in it any more or watch others.' It was to be more than just a life of fetid bedsitters and breakfasts of tacky eggs and weak, stewed tea, more than just the feckless plays and the frantic rehearsals; there were those demoralizing fill-in jobs, such as filing clerk, waitress, receptionist and shop assistant, which inevitably followed the end of a short season. Glenda was constantly down to her last penny. To this day, having money still means being able to buy a packet of cigarettes, instead of emptying ashtrays and saving butts. Hope and holed shoes were to be her lifestyle now. 'Any job was valid; two lines as a maid would do,' she declared later. 'It sounds ridiculous, yet my only ambition on materialistic things was to be able to afford more than a pie and chips from Lyons.'

Before she embarked on this grim period of her life, she enjoyed a spell of Mum's home-cooking back in 3 Evans Road, because the only work she could find was a job in the local branch of Woolworth's. But her life of pie and chips was already on the horizon; within three weeks she was in digs in a West Sussex seaside resort famed for its tomatoes – appearing with the Worthing Repertory Theatre as a walk-on nurse in a tatty production of *Doctor in the House*. Stepping in front of a paying audience for the first time made for 'a very potent sensation', though she was deeply distressed when they did not ask her to stay and become a permanent member of the company; it was back to waitressing.

A job then came up with the adventurous Queen's Players in Hornchurch, Essex, whose theatre, the Queen's, had been opened only four years earlier by Sir Ralph Richardson. As theatres go it was small and drab, the seats uncomfortable and the visibility poor, yet its fortnightly rep inspired great affection and loyalty in its devoted band of followers. Not that the customers took much notice of Glenda's modest contributions. Among her roles was the student Jean Stratton in *Separate Tables* and, inevitably, the maid in *The White Sheep of the Family*. Blink and you would miss her. 'She was rather plump and very quiet,' colleague Gwen Watford remembered. 'She was a bit in awe of everything: watching everybody and learning from watching. In every way she was just a youngster, trying her wings, very much feeling her way. When you're in fortnightly rep like that, the pressure is enormous, the learning, the rehearsing, the playing. She struck me as being rather shy. She didn't speak very much.'

Yet Glenda spoke with sufficient conviction to find herself further employment just when she most needed it. Within four weeks of being told by the Hornchurch Rep that her services were no longer required she was making her professional London stage début at the tiny but influential Arts Theatre in Great Newport Street, where the standard of production was so high that it was known affectionately as 'Britain's National Theatre in miniature'. She played good-time-girl Ruby in a short run of *All Kinds of Men*, a three-hour melodrama by Alex Samuels about a marriage that was on the rocks as a result of the couple's baby having been run over. While *Plays and Players* noted that the show 'would make an excellent Hollywood heart-throb', Glenda remained as keen as ever to learn from her acting colleagues, among them Wilfrid Lawson (Hollywood's first Alfred Doolittle in *Pygmalion*) and Miriam Karlin, then all the rage on television as strike-prone Paddy in *The Rag Trade* series.

But it was the play's director, Robert Mitchell, on whom she ultimately focused most of her gratitude. He was about to leave for Cheshire to take over the directorship of the Crewe Repertory Theatre, situated in a town just forty miles from Hoylake, when he asked Glenda to join the company. It was to be another stint – six months this time – of combining acting with ASM-ing. She needed the work. The town itself (population 50,000) was nothing to write home about, being one of the country's busiest railway junctions and having some of the world's largest railway workshops: 'Of all the Godforsaken places to meet someone special,' groaned Glenda.

It was just before the end of 1957 when she arrived in Crewe and was told to report to the company's stage manager, Roy Hodges. 'I'm your new assistant,' said Glenda by way of introduction.

'There's the brush,' he replied, pointing to a worn-out broom propped against the side of the stage. 'Get sweeping!'

'I promise you,' exclaimed the girl in the faded jeans and moth-eaten pullover, 'that I'm the worst ASM the world has ever seen.'

'I've got a surprise for you,' added her boss, 'so am I. Probably the worst actor the world has ever seen, too.'

The verbal horse-play amounted to a sort of emotional 'camouflage', each trying to make it impossible for the other to know what was really going on. But from that first meeting there was a mutual attraction and, within a few days, neither was able to disguise the fact. They were in love. 'For some reason we hit it off straight away,' Roy explained. 'Two weeks after we met I suggested that we should either live together or get married. Glenda wanted to get married, and so that was that.'

'Of course, Roy and I could have lived together without getting married, but I personally wouldn't want that,' Glenda insisted soon after. 'In spite of the fact that my father is a bit of a Left-winger, I *did* have a conventional upbringing. The people to whom I'm emotionally attached would have been shocked, and it seemed needless to hurt them. I have friends who tell me that marriage is obsolete and that if you try to limit it with a legal document it will fail. But I don't agree.'

So, despite her fat, her acne and her greasy hair, here was somebody who wanted her for himself, forever. The extraordinary thing was that Roy was her first boyfriend. Men always came very low in Glenda's scheme of things: 'It's my laziness. I'm always like that. I could never be fagged to make a lot of fuss about men.' Some years later she was asked if she really liked men, and the question stopped her in mid-sentence. 'Well, I don't think I do basically,' she replied thoughtfully. 'Well, sexually, yes. I recognize we certainly can't do without them. But I find men such a . . . well, they need . . . they're so . . . so sensitive about others, particularly the women in their life. And you have to spend so much time pandering to their egos, when you know you could do whatever they're doing in one-half the time and a hundred times better. It really does get so bloody boring, doesn't it?'

Part Two

A Star in the Making

Morale is the state of mind. It is steadfastness and courage and hope. It is confidence and zeal and loyalty. It is *élan, esprit de corps* and determination.

George Catlett Marshall,
Military Review, October 1948

4
Wilderness Years

Roy Hodges, a fellow RADA graduate, was a good-looking ex-actor nine years Glenda's senior, the son of a storekeeper who was 'in concrete'. They were brought up just thirty miles from one another, though Roy liked to describe his childhood upbringing in the Lancashire industrial town of Warrington as being 'much grittier' than Glenda's Hoylake, which he regarded (not a little tongue-in-cheek) as 'the smart country'. Once, like Glenda, he too had been an embryonic actor. In common with most actors, he was stage-struck: he enjoyed the life, the team work, the company spirit. But he was never particularly good. 'He was a very *bad* actor,' proclaimed Glenda, 'but he knew that. So he slid out of it and turned to stage management.'

He had little choice. 'Roy was a curious chap,' observed Peter Graham Scott, at that time a senior drama producer at Associated Rediffusion. 'I tried to use him once as a barman in a TV play with the late Eric Portman. But after the first day's rehearsal Eric came to me in a disconsolate mood. He said, "Can you please not have this man playing the barman, because I can't work with him. He upsets me." So we had to replace him.'

Roy and Glenda only once appeared on stage together, in *Jane Eyre*. She, too, found the experience an unsettling one. There was nothing she could do to stop herself laughing other than stab pins into her hands to induce the most intense pain. 'He had to say, "Come away with me, Jane; I will show you mountains, flowers ..." and all that rubbish, while the set was changed behind us,' said Glenda. 'I used to go on with an open brooch in my hand and force the pin into the palm, and stare at a certain spot until I was blind, because if I'd looked at him, I would have had hysterics, *hysterics*. I said afterwards, "Never again."'

At her lodgings in Crewe, not far from the theatre in Heath Street, Glenda's most prized possession was a portable record-player. There was also a pile of records, including one of Ella Fitzgerald singing 'It Never Entered My Mind', an acid little song which Glenda and Roy played constantly during their lightning courtship. Thirteen years later the song was one of her choices when she became Roy Plomley's 1,089th guest on BBC radio's *Desert Island Discs*, and Roy Hodges would delight in telling their friends, 'I really only married her for her gramophone ....' He would then add, 'There's always something mercenary in a man's attitude to marriage.'

The marriage ceremony in London, on 2 August 1958, not many months after their first meeting, was a simple affair at the St Marylebone Registry Office. It was entirely in keeping with the personality of the bride: quick and to the point. Her sister Gill and Roy's best friend were their witnesses, and later in the evening their theatre pals organized a wedding party. Following the ceremony, Roy went to Euston Station to pick up his parents, who had come down for the ensuing celebrations, while Glenda got on a bus by herself to help her friends with the food arrangements. Sitting across the bus from her was an Iranian student, who proceeded to chat her up and ask if she was busy that night.

'Oh, thank you, but I just got married two hours ago,' she told him.

He bowed. 'Please – my congratulations, madam,' he said.

'Can you *imagine*!' she exclaimed later to a bemused fledgling husband. 'I'd been in London for two years before this afternoon and no one ever made a pass at me. On my wedding day I finally get picked up!'

They were a poor, almost destitute couple, with little left from the £5 they had borrowed from a friend to help them through the big day. 'I know what it's like to be hungry,' the bride recalled. 'When Roy and I married we had five bob [25p] between us.'

In those early days after Crewe, Roy fared rather better than Glenda, though that was not hard to do. They seldom had enough to eat or decent clothes to wear, and Glenda admitted later that they were sometimes really desperate for food. Their first flat was so inhospitable – it was fit for little more than storing their few personal possessions – that they spent their nights in an enormous four-poster bed centre stage in the London theatre where, as stage manager and ASM, they were rehearsing a touring production of *A Girl Called Sady*. The bed was one of the props. An understanding carpenter would bring morning coffee when he awakened them.

On tour, Glenda abhorred everything about *A Girl Called Sady*. She referred to it as 'gruesome', 'pretty awful' and 'this dreadful, dreadful play'. Her job was to understudy the role of the sixty-five-year-old grandmother. But it was not an ecstatic ASM-cum-actress who, having donned a long nightie and a cotton-wool wig, eventually stepped into the role. Her displeasure came to a head one day when the delighted author-impresario told her she was the best granny who had ever played the part.

'Is that so?' she responded quietly. 'Well, I think it's probably the worst play ever written.'

She was promptly sacked, and Roy resigned in sympathy.

On her return to London, Glenda's agent sent her to audition for an Associated Rediffusion television drama called *A Voice in Vision*, a play inspired by the life of the Scottish-born pioneer of television, John Logie Baird. The possibility of working for television had never occurred to her; she was not, she felt, 'that sort of actress'. 'She came into my office, this young actress who'd never done any TV work before, and her strong, uninhibited personality completely filled the room,' said producer Peter Graham Scott. 'I mean, she was no beauty, but she had a very arresting face, very striking eyes. And I said, "All you have to do is scream." So she opened her mouth and you could have heard the scream three miles away, because Glenda – even then – was not one to hide her talent. She was North Country, blunt, and so when she screamed during the production's live transmission, it was horrifying, blood-curdling.'

When the screaming stopped, so did Glenda's work as an actress and for nearly three years she did not perform the job for which she was trained. Roy was similarly affected. The only steady work either of them could find was waiting on tables, working in factories and pubs, filing invoices and answering telephones, and serving behind the counter in large chain stores.

Although she was resigned to the fact that she might never work again as an actress, she was anything but 'resting': 'Because I had no qualifications and no training that I could sell,' she disclosed, 'I did a series of dreadfully soul-destroying jobs which were awful at the time, but I became quite good at lying, pretending I'd be there for the rest of my life.'

One of those soul-destroying jobs was working as a Bluecoat at Butlins holiday camp in Pwllheli, North Wales, where Roy was already in-stalled as a Redcoat. Whereas the main occupation of the Redcoat was to mingle, that of the Bluecoat was purely clerical – and it drove Glenda to despair: 'It meant being in charge of reservations and having to tell all the happy holidaymakers who wanted to be in York House that they were in Windsor House, so there. Not an experience I'd care to repeat.'

It was while working at Butlins that the rounded, slightly overweight Glenda Jackson, now in her twenty-third year and still playing the real-life role of 'the plain friend', changed her shape quite dramatically. She developed acute sinusitis, which made all food taste so vile that she did not eat for ten days. Of course, she regained her appetite as she recovered, but she could never again cram down the quantities which she had been used to since childhood.

'She was so thin,' said Roy, 'that she looked as though she'd snap.'

'Maybe it was also a case of me and my body generally growing up at last and settling down,' Glenda reasoned. 'Anyway, I did become slim, and my weight hasn't varied much since. I am 5 feet 6 inches; as a rule, I'm a pound or two either side of 9 stone 3 pounds. I would loathe to be fat again.'

Glenda's professional psyche was formed by these wilderness years, when food was scarce and the theatre ignored her. Even after adding two Hollywood Oscars to her collection of trophies, she still found difficulty in hiding her insecurity, still constantly reminded herself that she was once unemployed far more than she acted, adding, 'If that goes on for long enough you get a sense that if you're not in work, you'll never work again; and I don't think I'll ever lose that threat hanging over me.'

She looked back on these dark years as a terrible but, in some ways, invaluable period, her philosophy being that if you could come through professional rejection, you could come through almost anything. 'There's no point in considering acting unless you have the ability to bounce back,' she is fond of telling people. 'Acting's tough. The only thing you ever learn is that you don't know how to do it! You can learn the craft, but what produces the x ingredient which turns a reading into a performance is a complete mystery.'

It was no mystery to Glenda's agent, Peter Crouch. From the moment he saw her student performance as Eliza Doolittle, he was convinced that she had been endowed with the x ingredient. It was the 'animal' in her temperament that first attracted him and compelled him to recognize her star potential – though it was a gut instinct which he, and he alone, nursed for nearly a decade before others began to share his conviction. It was something indefinable, he said, something linked with personality, not technique. 'What she has,' agreed film producer Sidney Cole, 'is what Simone Signoret had in my picture *Against the Wind*: it is sheer personality and has nothing to do with looks.'

But in moments of despair, when producer after producer told her that she had nothing to offer them, she began to fear for her sanity. She felt that if she did not find work soon, her personality would be irreparably damaged. In many ways, this was precisely what happened. Her inherent Hoylake grittiness was consolidated by an even greater toughness of character; from this time onwards she was always sharp as razors under the cosy mateyness: articulate, opinionated and a bare-knuckle fighter with anybody who presumed to argue the toss. Roy always found her 'an exhausting person to live with'. One acquaintance has described her as 'a bone-crushing bitch, one of those Thurber ladies who turns into a house; she asks no mercy and gives no quarter'. She was submitted to so much professional neglect and disregard that she would never, *could* never, be the same again.

In London, Glenda had previously befriended a perceptive woman of the theatre who, along with Peter Crouch, saw in the young actress an embryonic talent. Miriam Brickman was the casting director of the Royal Court Theatre which, in earlier years, had provided the setting and opportunity for the dramatic development of George Bernard Shaw, and she rarely lost an opportunity to promote the professional interests of 'my Glenda'. Producers holding auditions would be told in advance of Glenda's special talents, but she would always come away without a job. And then one day the casting director received a frantic call from Anthony Page, director of the Dundee Repertory Theatre.

'I need an extra female – any suggestions?' inquired Page.

'Well,' said Miriam Brickman, 'why not take my Glenda?'

'Okay, why not?'

Thus the unpredictable and often illogical world of the actress, for in the end it was not essentially Glenda's talent, but one theatre director's desperation, which provided Glenda with her first acting job in nearly three years. Momentarily, she was a new woman. She had always found it difficult, returning to her small flat each evening after working at British Home Stores, to tell herself constantly "I'm an actress" when she patently was not. But now, in Dundee, she was back in the theatre – 'and a very happy time it was for me'. Oldham, Watford, Perth and other short-term repertory assignments followed. Work hardly poured through the front door, but she could honestly say she was once again an actress. The thought of it bowled her over. 'When I got to the point where I was being offered work I found it quite remarkable,' she said, 'and I still can't get used to it now . . . .'

Nevertheless, her ability to hold down an acting job was still not proven. It was a critical moment in her theatrical development, a period when she most needed some tangible form of hope to cling to – and the man who provided this was Vladek Sheybal, a Polish actor who had been in England barely four years. Like Glenda, Vladek Sheybal had suffered, had sought hope: having been caught carrying Molotov cocktails through the German lines during the Warsaw rising, he survived a concentration camp and later came to England, where he has become a much sought after character actor in films (he later appeared in two with Glenda). They met for the first time soon after Glenda returned from Perth, at the third-floor apartment of their mutual friend, the Royal Court dramatist Donald Howarth, with whom Sheybal had been working on the translation of a Polish play.

As Sheybal recalled: 'The front doorbell rang and Donald opened the window and looked down to the pavement and said, "It's Glenda Jackson with her husband, Roy. Do you mind?" And I said, "No." He threw down the key and they came up and stayed for tea. I immediately thought she was stunningly fascinating. There was something in her face which was unusual, a sort of vulnerability, which she was doing her best to cover up by adopting a crisp and clipped way of talking. Roy had a very strange voice, too, and he was mad about her. They seemed to be a very strange couple. Roy kept saying, "She was fantastic in this play, she was marvellous in that play, she was stunningly beautiful in this," and all the time Glenda was telling Donald that she didn't have any work. Donald then explained that I was a television director, because I'd just started to direct television; and, of course, as an out-of-work actress, her ears suddenly pricked up and she said, "Oh, are you?", and she was ready to impress me. She was very slim, and she had a very long neck, and very full lips and the eyes, quite literally, of a frightened deer. It was a very uncertain creature I saw that afternoon.'

Later, over a bottle of wine, Sheybal turned to Glenda and told her, 'You shouldn't worry about anything, you know, because I think you will become a big star. You have fantastic star quality.'

Glenda was overjoyed. 'Well, look,' she said, addressing Roy, 'he's a foreign director and he sees something in me, so there must be something in me, even though they don't see it in England.'

Some years later, having established her reputation with one of Britain's national theatre companies, she met Sheybal at a Christmas party held by their mutual agent, Peter Crouch. They had not seen each other since their initial meeting, but Glenda recognized the Polish actor immediately and they started talking. 'I shall never forget what you said that afternoon at Donald's place,' she confided, 'because it kept me alive for several years. I used to tell myself, "If this director from the continent can see something in me, then perhaps I'm not just a lost cause."' She kissed his gaunt forehead.

'She knew that what I said was completely genuine,' Sheybal reflected later, 'because I didn't have any reason to be false. After all, I come from a different culture to hers – and she was clinging to that.'

Glenda's luck began to change in 1962. As the proud and independent Alexandra in a stage adaptation of Dostoevsky's novel *The Idiot*, presented by the experimental new Ikon Theatre Company at the Lyric Theatre in Hammersmith, she elicited some favourable notices. Glenda was part of a nucleus of permanent players who, during a six-month London season at the Lyric, performed a wide variety of plays, old and new. In one of them, Maria Lehmann's *Come Back With Diamonds* – another Russian drama – Glenda was cast, humbly as ever, as one of five neighbours.

Although her life was still not devoid of waitressing and answering telephones, such periods were becoming more infrequent and, before the year was out, she was back at Associated Rediffusion as a bit-part player in the live ITV television drama, *Dr Everyman's Hour*. It was produced, like her first television appearance, by Peter Graham Scott, who recalled, 'I'd heard that Glenda was around, though I hadn't seen her since *A Voice in Vision*, and then one afternoon I came across her in the corridor at Rediffusion. She said, "I've just auditioned for a telly play, but I don't think I'll get it." So I said, "Would you mind being a jury woman in my new production?" All the way through the trial scenes we had to cut to selected jury people, and it was quite marvellous because when anything went wrong one could always cut to Glenda. She was always so alive, she was always acting, always reacting – she acted her way through the entire ninety minutes of the trial. In the jury-room scene she had one or two lines, but the important thing was that in the courtroom there was always this face registering every fact. It saved our day on more than one occasion.'

Yet despite the 'magic' which her face registered on the screen, it was still not obvious to Scott that Glenda was a potential star. 'What *was* obvious was that here was a powerful actress who never wasted a moment of her professional time,' said the producer. 'She was terribly confident, polite and friendly to the crew, but in no way flirtatious. She kept herself to herself. She didn't waste any time in rehearsals; she came very well prepared, and she *listened*, watching everything that was going on around her with a concentration of hawk-like intensity.'

This same capacity for concentration later won Glenda a minor role in her first film, *This Sporting Life*, an account of a tense affair between a rugby player (Richard Harris) and his widowed landlady (Rachel Roberts). This grim film, with its kitchen-sink realism revealing brutal sexuality, was based on the novel by David Storey and directed with tremendous histrionic detail by Lindsay Anderson. Although it offered Glenda little more than 'two days on top of a piano in a party hat', it gave her her first experience of working in front of a movie camera; and producers, at least, were beginning to take notice – though their interest in the twenty-seven-year-old actress was still largely confined to casting her in tiny, often insignificant roles.

It was in such a role, in the summer of 1963, that Glenda opened in *Alfie* at London's Mermaid Theatre. Bill Naughton's regional sex comedy, originally heard on BBC radio and at that time yet to be made into a major film, starred John Neville as an unscrupulous Cockney lecher, boastfully proud of his amorous conquests – one of whom was a girl called Siddie, played by Glenda. The play was a great success and later transferred to the Duchess Theatre in the West End, where Michael Medwin took over the role of Alfie: impresario Peter Saunders, despite enthusiastic encouragement from all sides, refused to cast a non-star named Michael Caine because 'I had never heard of him'. Of Glenda, he said, 'I was so glad to see this unassuming girl do so well.' The 'unassuming' Glenda, meanwhile, grew dispirited in what she described as 'this god-awful thing called *Alfie*'. As she said later, 'After three months I almost died.'

Royal Shakespeare Company

Alfie ran for 194 performances and, perhaps because of that – and despite her misgivings – Glenda was able to utilize the time very much to her advantage, working at her characterization, perfecting it, in a way never previously open to her. Certainly, she made a considerable impression in the relatively small role of Siddie, to such an extent that it brought her to the attention of Peter Brook and Charles Marowitz, who were organizing a season of experimentation at the private theatre club attached to the London Academy of Music and Dramatic Art (LAMDA). Meeting these two influential directors was a watershed in Glenda's life.

Marowitz was a young New Yorker fast making a name for himself in England and was soon to establish what became London's leading experimental theatre, the Open Space. Brook, London-born and nine years Marowitz's senior, was already, at thirty-nine, a theatrical colossus. His 1946 production of *Love's Labour's Lost* was a theatre legend, and in the 1950s and early 1960s he had continued to flourish strokes of great inventive genius with versions of *Titus Andronicus* (with Olivier), *Measure for Measure* (glorious Gielgud) and *King Lear* (a dynamic Scofield), all for the Royal Shakespeare Company (RSC), of which he had become co-director with Peter Hall in 1962. Only Tyrone Guthrie equalled him in inventiveness in the British theatre, one critic describing Brook as 'this greatest explorer among our directors'. And so it was that, with Marowitz, he discovered Glenda. 'I was aware of a disconcerting presence,' Marowitz remembered. 'Here was something inaudibly but palpably ticking, something capable of "going off".'

Glenda revealed this 'disconcerting presence' for the first time at an audition in London conducted by the two directors. They were putting together a season to be known under the generic title of the Theatre of Cruelty, an Artaud-inspired experiment sponsored by the RSC to explore the limits to which the human body could go in sound and movement. At this hair-raising audition, the like of which she had never experienced before, Glenda came armed with a prepared reading of a Dorothy Parker short story.

'Fine,' said Brook. 'Now do that same piece again, but this time you're a woman who's just been committed to a mental asylum by her husband; and, in fact, she's not *really* insane and she's trying to convince the people who come to take her away that she is not insane, and, you know, you're in a straitjacket. Now, let's see you do that.'

When she concluded this new reading, Brook and Marowitz glanced at each other and seemed to be almost in a state of shock. Never had they been confronted by such gusto from an actress, certainly not at a first reading. But was this what Brook, in particular, wanted? When the moment came to make their final selection for the season – eight actors and four actresses were required – and Glenda was nose-to-nose with an odds-on favourite for the final place, Marowitz found himself mounting a frantic campaign on her behalf. 'My fervour was so uncharacteristic,' he later recalled, 'that Peter wondered if I had sexual designs on the girl. I assured him that that wasn't the case and, when asked to state my reasons, found myself explaining lamely that she was beautifully screwed up and that, during a four-hour audition work-out, I had developed the impression that she was, in some inexplicable way, mined.'

Marowitz remembered the first interview he had with Glenda in some woebegone room (an almost obligatory setting for rehearsals in England), 'watching her stark, nutty eyes shifting slowly in her head like arc-lights; feeling that behind that studied stillness was a cobra ready to spring or an hysteric ready to break down; choosing my words carefully and getting back short, orderly answers that betrayed the very minimum both of feeling and information; perpetually conscious of a smouldering intelligence rating both my questions and her own answers as she shifted her focus from within to without, suggesting the mechanism of a hypersensitive tape-recorder that could fast-forward or rewind with the flick of an invisible switch.'

Marowitz had no way of knowing at the time that, banked up behind that confabulation, were several years of anguished unemployment and soul-destroying poverty. But eventually Glenda was chosen to join the company of twelve for a six-month contract at £12 a week, during which her dry, acerbic, languid demeanour – which was certainly not to everyone's liking – implanted itself firmly on the character of the group.

The three months of training which preceded the work of the Theatre of Cruelty represented a kind of basic training. 'Each day Peter Brook and I would put the actors through a series of acting tests and exercises,' explained Marowitz. 'Unlike conventional rehearsals in which, from the start, actors are given roles in scripted situations, these involved interminable improvisations and games in which the actor's personal imagination was being constantly nudged, wooed or flagellated into acting. In circumstances such as these, one sees the centrifugal talent of each person in clear, unmistakable terms. Glenda's choices were staggering. Invariably unexpected, often tinged with sarcasm or perversity, occasionally droll, with a hard, urbane kind of humour which was three-quarters irony and one-quarter absurdity, a complex sensibility spiralling up out of labyrinthine depths.'

During this training period, one of the group's least talented actors watched Glenda 'in action' for a few minutes and then complained to a colleague, 'God, she's so negative – so destructive.' Without realizing it, he was really protesting against Glenda's innate loathing for lame and easy effects. 'Oh yes, Glenda *radiated* disgust in those days,' Marowitz affirmed, 'but its object was the sloppy, ill-defined, un-thought-out mugging which passed for acting in the English theatre and, particularly, the appearance of those characteristics in herself. Whenever she worked, one could hear her built-in bull-detector, that most delicate of all precision instruments, ticking in the background, and the actors who resented her most were those whose execrable effusions were being scrutinized and judged in the glare of those cold, sleepy, cruel eyes.' Marowitz said he had vivid memories of Glenda lounging around the rehearsal room 'looking like a scrubwoman, her face not only un-made-up but seemingly scrubbed raw as if to obliterate her features, emitting great waves of languor tinged with *ennui*; a softly pulsating indictment of everything crude, crummy and unworthy in our work.'

The first evidence of this work was seen in January 1964 when the group presented a kind of surrealist revue at the LAMDA theatre club. The public was not invited to the first performance, but anybody who was anybody in the theatre world was there, including Laurence Olivier, Edith Evans, Kenneth Tynan, Christopher Plummer, Harold Pinter and John Osborne. The vaudeville entertainment, comprising brief pieces by a wide variety of authors, such as John Arden, Paul Ableman, Alain Robbe-Grillet, Ray Bradbury, Jean Genet and Shakespeare, caused a furore, in the centre of which was Glenda enacting a short collage-piece written by Brook. The five-minute item, called *The Public Bath*, made her the most hotly discussed young actress in London. She came on as the London society prostitute Christine Keeler and was seen first whipping a client, then standing trial in the courtroom and finally languishing in prison, where she proceeded to strip naked, take a bath on stage and change into prison clothes. The bathtub was then turned upside-down to become the coffin of John F. Kennedy (this was just two months after the American President's assassination), where-upon Glenda was transformed into Jacqueline Kennedy accepting bishops and politicos at the Kennedy funeral.

Although nakedness was familiar in strip clubs, it was almost unknown in Britain's straight theatre, which was then still under the laws of censorship; and it was only because it was performed 'privately' in a theatre club that Glenda's nakedness avoided prosecution. In the process Glenda earned the dubious distinction of being the first serious actress to take off her clothes on a British stage. Glenda later claimed to have felt no embarrassment whatever. 'I was just cold,' she said matter-of-factly. 'I've done a lot of harder scenes than that.' So her puritanism did not apply when it came to appearing naked in public; and, indeed, she went on to play many more nude scenes when the plot situations made them 'valid', although, in time, she came to deplore the fact that nudity was being used so heavily for erotic purposes, missing what she considered its prime quality of vulnerability. Public nakedness as such did not bother Glenda, nor has it ever. All that concerned her was whether the act of stripping was justified or not.

'Before it actually came to the final stripping rehearsals,' said Marowitz, 'Peter and I wondered whether Glenda would refuse. Remember, these were the heady, pre-*Hair* days when the Lord Chamberlain was still exercising censorship on the British stage and the Age of Permissiveness was as un-thinkable as a world without the Beatles. When it came to the delicate, last-day rehearsals and the stripping had to be rehearsed, I remember Glenda's dry, undramatic resignation – accepting not the embarrassment of appearing nude, but the necessity of the act in regard to the play. Whatever convoluted thought process and emotional wrenching may have paved the way, the decision itself, like everything else in her life, was brisk, clear and decisive. It was the role, not her directors, which had persuaded her, and that was the only authority she ever obeyed implicitly.'

When the LAMDA experiment was over, Glenda went around telling people that meeting Peter Brook was 'like finding an oasis in the desert; no – more than that – it was like going to heaven, actually.' Later on, certainly, Brook became the yardstick by which she judged every other director, whether consciously or otherwise. It has meant that very few directors have measured up to her particular ideal, a fact which caused quite a few of them to curse the day their paths ever crossed hers.

Brook was Glenda's god, her professional ikon, and when in January he invited her to join the Royal Shakespeare Company, it was an ecstatic actress who accepted the offer. Financially, as well as professionally, it was a turning-point. Overnight she went from a sporadic £12 a week to a regular weekly salary of £30. 'Going into films,' she observed later, 'meant nothing compared with that change in my life.' There was also the irony that on three previous occasions she had auditioned for the RSC and been turned down ... and now Peter Brook, no less, had actually *begged* her to join the company.

Although the preliminary work for the season at LAMDA was anarchic, tatty, confused and often pretentious, it was undoubtedly a seminal event with consequences bold and far-reaching. It acclimatized Glenda and other actors of the RSC, then celebrating Shakespeare's quatercentenary, to the shock tactics of the Theatre of Cruelty proper – a series of London-produced theatrical pieces which came to be christened the 'Dirty Plays' season. The most notable of these was Brook's production of Peter Weiss's harrowing *The Persecution and Assassination of Marat as Performed by the Inmates of the Asylum of Charenton under the Direction of the Marquis de Sade* (later shortened, mercifully, to *The Marat/Sade*), which, between 1964 and 1968, won no less than seven major awards from British and American critics.

Glenda's first official appearance on the stage of the RSC's London home, the Aldwych, came with the August opening of *The Marat/Sade*, although she made an unrecorded début there a month earlier in a production of Pinter's *The Birthday Party*, directed by the author. She, along with Freddie Jones, Henry Woolf and Timothy West, was understudying the play. 'We used to sit in Glenda's dressing room with a bottle of wine, hear each other's lines for one act of the play and then chat till it was time to go home,' West recalled. 'We looked forward to *Birthday Party* nights and wished it had been scheduled for more performances, but only one of us ever had to go on – yes, Glenda – and she was extremely good.'

The RSC management at the Aldwych was meanwhile procuring its pound of flesh by making Glenda understudy not just the Pinter play but also several other productions, as well as casting her as Charlotte Corday in *The Marat/Sade*. This extraordinary play's full title explains much about the complexity of its theme: in the bath-house of the asylum at Charenton the Marquis directs the inmates in a re-enactment of the murder by Charlotte Corday of the French political revolutionary Marat. It is both play and play-within-a-play, just as Glenda's role possesses elements of role-within-a-role. One moment she is a pathetic lunatic inmate; the next, the obsessive, murderess noblewoman Charlotte Corday.

One of the most effective, if disturbing, moments in the frequently violent play-within-a-play comes in the flagellation scene during which the patient playing Corday whips de Sade (Patrick Magee) with her own two-foot long hair. Everyone raved about Glenda's savage intensity. The production itself, which examined afresh the public's conception of sanity and lunacy, of sexuality and violence, of revolution and reaction, totally overwhelmed audiences, and it became the highlight of the Aldwych season. It was brilliantly acted down to the most minor role, each actor – including the embryonic talents of Ian Richardson, Michael Williams, Elizabeth Spriggs, Freddie Jones, Clifford Rose, Clive Revill and Timothy West – presenting a detailed study of a particular form of insanity.

Glenda endured Charlotte Corday for two years on the London and New York stage as well as on film. It was the nearest she will probably ever get to going mad. In the end her everyday perceptions began to mesh with her stage role, which frightened her. 'My daily life was like living in a lunatic asylum,' she said later. 'It occurred to me one day that everyone I had talked to that day was insane.' She found the events being enacted on stage so extraordinary and terrifying that she could not eat for weeks during rehearsals, while the performances themselves were so physically punishing that by the end of the day she could only collapse into bed.

Her mother, who was perhaps not a typical member of the *Marat/Sade* audience, took the agony of Glenda's performance for granted, and commented only on Charlotte's bitter and plaintive little song. 'When you started to sing,' said Joan Jackson, 'I started to cry and kept crying and didn't see much after that. You're not a very good singer, dear.'

Singer or not, the London *Evening Standard* noted that she was 'the most exciting new face to emerge from the current Aldwych season', and the American theatrical newspaper *Variety* observed that 'a fairly inexperienced young actress, Glenda Jackson, rises to heights', while *Time* magazine lauded her performance as 'one of the truly curdling experiences in contemporary theatre'.

During the next sixteen months, between the London opening of *The Marat/Sade* and its Broadway première in December 1965, Glenda came to be regarded as one of the most compulsively interesting actresses on the British stage. In London, following Peter Weiss's madhouse, she played the relatively tranquil courtesan Bellamira, with whom Ian Richardson's Ithamore was in love, in Marlowe's *The Jew of Malta*. Although her performance was not in itself distinguished, Glenda was already beginning to make her presence felt behind the scenes. 'I have suggested that we shouldn't dress Bellamira so that she is the conventional all bosom and jewels,' she informed a visitor to the rehearsals. 'I've looked up a book on the Renaissance and it seems they liked their courtesans to be intellectual and a bit wrapped up. It might not work out and perhaps I'll have to play it with a dress gashed to the navel.' She got her way.

Glenda's reputation as a young woman who detested pretension, a dramatic tigress who firmly believed in calling a spade a spade, was rapidly gaining momentum. It came to a head during the run of Bertolt Brecht's Marxist revue-like comedy *Puntila*, in which she gave an amusingly stylized performance as Roy Dotrice's spoilt tomboy daughter, Eva, petulantly flushed and flouncing – resembling, argued critic Penelope Gilliatt, 'a girl in a Gainsborough film from the late 1940s, heavily lipsticked and huffy'. The play concerns the relationship between masters and servants, between the landed and the workers; but, despite her own critical laurels, and those won by Michel Saint-Denis's often jolly direction, Glenda detested every minute of the production.

'People used to come backstage after the show, and Glenda would award points according to how honest or dishonest they were in their remarks about the play,' said Penelope Keith, who shared a dressing room with Glenda. 'If someone came in and said, "Oh, it was wonderful," Glenda gave them nought. If they said, "What an interesting evening," they were awarded two points. One night our lovely actor friend Charlie Kay came round and said, "What an absolutely *awful* evening," and Glenda immediately gave him ten marks. We all knew it was an awful production.'

Another characteristic of Glenda's professional temperament, which was maturing by the day, was displayed at Stratford in John Barton's respectful, if not always enjoyable, production of *Love's Labour's Lost*. While she played the

Princess of France with a loping adolescent gaucheness that was both touching and true, there was more to it than that. Said *Plays and Players* magazine of
her portrayal: 'There is a certain hard, almost metallic edge to her delivery of
verse which at first seems uncalled for but which it is soon evident is an
essential quality of her stage personality and which distinguishes her work
from twenty other young actresses who might tackle the role with equal
competence.' What the critic stumbled upon, almost by accident – and he was
possibly the first to do so – was the aggressive and at times masculine quality
which was beginning to colour Glenda's acting and which has become its
predominant distinguishing feature. Already there were those among her
RSC colleagues who, while admiring her as an actress, could not like her as a
person. The men in the company, especially those who appeared opposite her
in a play, felt uncomfortable, even fearful, in her presence. It was as if they
sensed the male spirit, the masculine ego, inside the undoubtedly female
container.

'If she'd gone into politics, she'd be prime minister,' Roy declared. 'If
she'd taken to crime, she'd be Jack the Ripper.'

'But Margaret Thatcher is also masculine, and yet she's very feminine,'
countered Vladek Sheybal. 'I just thought Glenda was a vulnerable, uncertain little girl who tried desperately to be masculine, because this was the
only way she could survive the *reality*.'

'I remember when she first joined the RSC,' recalled Ian Richardson, who
appeared with Glenda in *The Marat/Sade* and played her 'love interest' in
Puntila and *The Jew of Malta*. 'I've never reckoned her very highly as a
classical actress; I didn't then, and I've had no cause to alter my opinion. But
that's by the by. Shakespeare's women may often be tomboyish, but, at the
same time, they're always essentially feminine – and femininity, curiously
enough, I've never found to be one of Glenda's strongest features. I think it's
no coincidence, when one thinks of her work output, that she has had a
lifelong admiration of Bette Davis – and, indeed, became a friend of Bette
Davis as a direct result of announcing on a radio show or somewhere that one
of her ambitions was to meet the great Bette Davis. I don't think this ambition
to meet such a "tough" Hollywood actress was an accident on Glenda's side,
because a lot of her acting owes a great deal to the "Bette Davis school". It's
big, it's bold and it's brash ... and it's slightly masculine.'

Her power, even then, stemmed from the aggressive manner in which she
used her gender. One distinguished critic began to suspect that any man who
had Lady Macbeth as his elder sister would experience the same dread at her
display of female will-power. Her eyes, certainly, always seemed to be challenging, 'Give *me* the daggers.' This power – indeed, this masculinity –
found its most blatant expression in Stratford's 1965 season, in Peter Hall's
deliberately austere production of *Hamlet*, with David Warner in the title
role. So overpowering was Glenda's portrayal of Ophelia that it prompted

Penelope Gilliatt to suggest in a review that Glenda should have played Hamlet, while another critic proposed that the production should have been billed as *Ophelia*. In a staging described by one reviewer as 'contemporary as the Rolling Stones ... and, finally, just about as attractive', Glenda deliberately set out to play Ophelia against the traditional grain of a soft and swoony daughter repressed into the refuge of madness by the cruelty and hypocrisy of the court and her family; this girl was strong, determined. 'It's almost always the strong-minded people who go mad,' she reasoned.

Glenda's mother and aunt, who came up from Hoylake together to see *Hamlet*, reacted in different ways. After Ophelia's death, Mrs Jackson dropped off gently to sleep. Aunt Esther, on the other hand, was convinced that her niece was really dead and started screaming. Also in the audience was the Irish playwright Hugh Leonard, who commented, 'One can only yammer in admiration. This was a regular man-eater: a highly-sexed young woman, cracking under the strain of a disintegrating love affair. Unlikely? Perhaps. But it works. Never has a character been portrayed so completely despite such a minimum of material as in this instance. While watching Miss Jackson, one could hear the click of numerous minds snapping shut all over the auditorium. I say, the hell with them: this is *acting*!'

This was not a view shared by the newspaper critics; apart from a glowing notice in the *Observer*, Glenda's performance was hacked down like so much diseased elm wood, the *Daily Express*'s description of her characterization as 'unlikeable' being about the most complimentary. But none of this deterred Tony Page, her old boss at Dundee, who was now artistic director of the English Stage Company at the Royal Court. On the contrary, he was bowled over by Glenda's controversial conception of Ophelia, though what he was about to suggest merely acknowledged the existence of those masculine qualities in her acting which many people were beginning to regard as her 'trade mark'. He was keen to stage a production of *Hamlet* in Iran, he told her, because he felt the political intrigues in that country directly paralleled those in Elizabethan England. Would she care to join the team? No, not to play Ophelia. He wanted her for the title role.

What she would have made of that challenge the world will never know, for her commitments (and her contract) to the RSC kept her busy for the best part of the next two years.

6
Lullaby of Broadway

Peter Brook was still an integral part of Glenda's professional life; and it was because of Brook, following the *Hamlet* season, that Glenda returned to the Aldwych for the brief London run of *The Investigation*, in which she and Penelope Keith portrayed all the women witnesses in Peter Weiss's courtroom drama about Auschwitz. 'It was very moving, an extraordinary experience,' Miss Keith remembered. Which was more than could be said by any member of the cast for *The Marat/Sade*, which was back in the repertory in readiness for transportation to the United States.

Consequently it was as Charlotte Corday that Glenda made her Broadway début on 27 December 1965 at the Martin Beck Theater. She hated the play; America loved it, and her. 'Her performance scared the Jesus out of me,' said George Segal. She had scored what the English decorously call a 'personal success'. 'Personal success!' exclaimed the American writer Martha Weinman Lear. 'I was *there*. I saw the play soon after it opened; and what I saw was this young woman whom nobody had ever heard of utterly electrify the audience, stun it with such a raw portrayal of madness as few of us – certainly not I – had ever seen before.'

Glenda became the talk of New York and was courted by the American press for a rapid succession of admiring interviews. She was famous – but at a price. The strain of portraying the murderess Charlotte Corday once again made her anxious about her mental stability. And hardly had she arrived in New York and unpacked than she was telling one reporter that 'the theatre is over-rated, boring, over-priced and often pretentious'. For committing this sin, *The Stage* – Britain's showbusiness newspaper – printed an entire editorial accusing Glenda of 'viper-tongued attacks' on her profession and damning her because she had the audacity 'to cry stinking fish in print'. Glenda's initial reaction was unprintable.

One day towards the end of the play's four-month run – which broke all Broadway box office records for non-musicals – she was dining at Sardi's, New York's celebrated theatrical restaurant. A fellow diner asked her if she was pleased when she learned that David Merrick, the impresario who brought the play over, had extended its run to the end of April. 'God no, I'm not looking forward to it,' she replied. 'I'm in better shape now that my hubby is here with me, but I loathe and detest everything about this production. We all loathe it. We're dying for the end to come so we'll never *ever* have to do it again. If I let myself go, I'd be screaming every night. It's a play that breeds sickness, with no release for the tension.'

She described how the play had wrought havoc among the cast: one actor had rheumatism from wearing a straitjacket every night; another had been crossing his eyes on-stage for so long he was unable to uncross them; several experienced genuine hysterics in the privacy of their dressing rooms. 'At 7.30 every night,' she told those around her, 'I become so terribly frightened that I shake all over. I do everything I can think of to delay the moment when I have to walk into that theatre. If you should wander in before the curtain goes up, you'd be horrified. It's like an asylum. People twitching, slobber running down their chins, everyone preparing to isolate themselves from reality.'

'She's quite impossible to live with after a performance,' said Roy. 'She comes in and I have to leave. I walk around a bit and come back.'

Glenda confessed that the only thing that ruined her trip to New York was 'this bloody play'. But being on Broadway did bring some lighter moments, such as the letters she received at the theatre, written on the same notepaper, addressed simply to 'Assassin'. On one occasion, Patrick Magee (who played de Sade) told her that he had been approached by one of New York's top bookies – a racketeer actually – who said he would give Glenda a fur coat just to meet her. Magee had refused on her behalf, and she was furious. 'Think of that fur coat,' she admonished him. 'And, anyway, it might have been interesting to have been a gangster's moll for a couple of weeks.' There were, however, a few consolations. She spent $140 in as many seconds at the sales, and sent towels home to everyone and still had two trunks full in the hotel room. 'And, you know, we had tea one day with Anita Loos and the most thrilling thing happened – Carroll Baker telephoned from Hollywood. I couldn't believe it. *Carroll Baker*! It made my whole day.'

Star-struck as she was – and, curiously, still is – Glenda was terrified of becoming a star herself. 'People come to see *you* instead of the work you do,' she argued. 'I'd really loathe it if people said "That's a Glenda Jackson role" or a "Glenda Jackson performance".' Alas, alas . . . .

By the end of the year *The Marat/Sade* had won New York's Drama Critics Circle Award and four Tony awards, Glenda receiving a Tony nomination and winning a *Variety* poll award as the most promising new actress of the Broadway season. Pleased as she was, awards have never made Glenda glow. 'No one gives a performance thinking, "If I do this a little bit more I might get an award,"' she commented. 'You give the performance you give in that moment of time. It's absurd to create this pecking order – who's good, who's bad, who's indifferent. It's hard enough to act without having that hung around your neck.'

For the moment, *The Marat/Sade* refused to leave her life. After New York, and a brief season in Paris, the play was filmed with the original cast and released by United Artists. What she saw on the screen she did not much care for: 'I loathed what I did but I suppose, in a way, it was inevitable. You do the same part for two years and you get locked in a terrible groove. We didn't have enough time to pull ourselves out of it. I gave an over-the-top performance. Much too much.'

Brook and his lighting cameraman, David Watkin, worked lovingly – beyond the call of duty – on Glenda. Ian Richardson, who played the Herald in the stage version, and who was promoted to the role of Marat in the film, used to sit in his bath-tub on the set each day and watch with fascination as Glenda's face was transformed into a thing of beauty. 'It was perfectly obvious to me that if, at the end of shooting, Brook had not made a new movie star out of Glenda Jackson, well, my God, it would not be for want of trying,' said Richardson. 'He captured all her best moments. He flattered her with lighting and the best angles when flattery was essential to what he was doing. He created a love affair between the camera and Glenda, which was wonderful for her, because Glenda, like most of us then, had virtually no cinematic experience.'

When America's syndicated columnist, Rex Reed, saw the film, he agreed that Brook's work on Glenda had been little short of miraculous and suggested that her performance was worthy of an Academy Award: 'Trembling across the sweat-stained floorboards, her face swollen and cracked from the terror of sleeping sickness and melancholia, her head bobbing like a rotten cabbage on a stick, Miss Jackson gives the kind of performance that should send every American member of the Screen Actors' Guild back to drama school.' Most critics seemed to like the film, though not without such qualifying statements as 'not for weak stomachs', and 'You might need a strong drink in your hand as you watch.'

Up to this time, Glenda had never really thought of herself as working towards a career in films, though after completing *The Marat/Sade* she found much to commend it. She was fascinated by the immediacy of the medium, the fact that you could make a discovery about a part in a minute – whereas in the theatre this might only come after endless rehearsals and even more endless performances. 'What I want now, more than anything, is to go into films,' she declared. 'It seems an intriguing world to me. It seems that there is much greater freedom of approach somehow. It seems there are lots and lots of small independent producers who have ideas and are doing things and coming up with interesting results.'

'No one was less surprised than me when, as a result of the *Marat/Sade* film, Glenda moved into movies proper, only coming back occasionally to the stage,' explained Ian Richardson. 'Even she must have realized how much the camera "loved" her.'

But Brook and the theatre – and even more touches of seeming insanity – continued to dominate Glenda's life. In Brook's next production in London for the RSC, *US*, an angry examination of the role of the United States in Vietnam based on documentary sources and presented in the form of a revue, Glenda harangued the audience with a hysterical outburst against war, bloodshed and inhumanity; she tearfully demanded those 'out front' to *understand*, to imagine the true, brutish horror of that war touching their own safe English Sunday mornings. This time, coming after Charlotte Corday, no one was quite sure if she was crazy or not, but it was obvious to all that she was acting rather strangely. 'I always seem to be in controversial things, and I'm not that sort at all,' she complained wryly of a production which had the critics divided: 'Too often it succeeds in merely vulgarizing the issue,' said one; 'It is a major theatrical landmark,' insisted another.

What did she think of the great man? 'Peter Brook? The Buddha. Ah, the time and effort suffering the boredoms ... but you will never work with a director as remarkable as him. With Brook, anything is possible.'

When the proceedings got bogged down during rehearsals for *US*, Brook turned to the cast and instructed, in a Charlton Heston God-like voice, '*Surprise* me.'

'Okay,' Glenda replied. 'Shut your eyes.'

When the director opened them again, everyone (led by his leading lady) had fled to the pub next door.

Once again, Brook made a screen version of the production, with the new title *Tell Me Lies*. But it did not translate well to film and is of interest today merely as a historical document about Vietnam.

Early in 1967, her three-year contract with the Royal Shakespeare Company at an end, Glenda became an associate member of that august body – 'which means they don't pay me while I'm not actually performing', she said. 'I was really quite relieved to get out of the rep because I don't think I'm basically community-minded. I found it especially grim at Stratford, where you have only actors to talk to.' So she left behind the asylum and the pulpit for Chekhov's Slavonic mood of despair in *The Three Sisters*, which was being revived at the Royal Court. Although she was cast as Masha, the pivotal role among the sisterly trio, the public's focus of attention was not on her nor on Avril Elgar's Olga, but on the twenty-year-old English-born pop-singer daughter of an Austrian baroness, Marianne Faithfull, who had been cast to make her stage acting début in the role of Irina. The newspapers made a great deal of it, because at that time the ex-convent schoolgirl was enjoying a notorious affair with Mick Jagger. Half an hour before curtain-up on the first night performance, Jagger, his entourage and camp followers crowded into the dressing room of Marianne and the other two sisters to hug and congratulate her. This behaviour drew cries of anger from Glenda, who swiftly threw the Rolling Stone and his friends out of the room.

'With all due respect, Marianne!' she thundered afterwards. 'My God, they could have had you on the staircase – why did they all bloody well have to crowd in here?'

Marianne promised it would not happen again. With Glenda on 'sentry duty', it never did.

'You see, Jagger was interrupting everyone's concentration, spoiling their mental preparation,' said cast member John Nettles. 'There's a rule that nobody must go into a dressing room half an hour before the show starts, and Glenda got furious about that rule being flouted. Marianne and Jagger had no idea about such protocol.'

Still, most reviewers regarded Miss Faithfull's acting début as a considerable achievement in an orthodox production by William Gaskill which was notable for its heavy, interminable pauses, but which nevertheless underlined the Russian author's point that life was full of bitter-sweet people nursing broken hearts. As for Glenda's performance, one reviewer echoed the corporate voice of his colleagues when he intimated that 'Glenda Jackson's controlled intensity will always fit her for roles of incipient hysteria, which roles she plays compellingly'.

Her hysteria at this point, however, tended to be not so much incipient as full-blown, though she found a novel change of pace when she accepted a light comedy role as a lesbian crusader against male chauvinism in David Pinner's play *Fanghorn* at London's Fortune Theatre. The show, directed by Charles Marowitz, sets out deliberately to shock, alarm and provoke, and, through offbeat humour, seeks continually to explore those dark and violent corners of the mind that people take care not to acknowledge. Glenda, as Tamara Fanghorn, was greatly drawn to the play because it offered her the opportunity to portray a tempestuous vamp-cum-vampire-cum-lesbian who sported green hair *à la* Cleopatra, who wore a kinky, tight-fitting, black leather dress slit up the front, and who cracked a bull-whip and terrified one and all.

Throughout there are sado-masochistic overtones. In one scene, having previously seduced both the mother and daughter of the First Secretary to the Minister of Defence, Tamara Fanghorn then symbolically castrates him by shaving off his enormous RAF-style moustache. It was all to little avail. The play, having received one of the most thorough critical demolitions in living memory, clocked up only seven performances. The *Daily Express*, nevertheless, concluded that Glenda 'snarled and sneered to great effect', while *Plays and Players* noted that she 'had the authority and intelligence one invariably associates with this actress'.

Glenda's career, at last, was buoyant. She had never been busier and she appeared in several television productions around this time, including a comedy of manners by David Mercer called *Let's Murder Vivaldi*, for the BBC's Wednesday Play slot. Among other activities, Glenda was required to unload her lover, Denholm Elliott. Playing Elliott's wife was Gwen

1
Glenda, in her fifth year, with baby sister Gill.

2
Glenda at eleven: 'I was totally surrounded by love.'

3
Thirteen-year-old Glenda receives helpful support for her *arabesque* during her local ballet school's annual show.

4
Blackpool outing, 1949. Glenda's mother, standing at the back, holds Glenda's sister Lynne, here in her second year. Middle row, left to right: fellow travellers Mrs Lewis and Pam Lewis, with Glenda, aged thirteen. Front row, left to right: Glenda's sister Gill, aged eight, and companion Judy Heslop.

5
Ready for the dance. Glenda, at seventeen, resplendent in white tie and tails, displaying early theatrical charisma in a production by Hoylake's amateur YMCA Players: 'She wasn't one of the stars, yet she stood out when she was with the other actors.'

6
Number 3, Evans Road, the two-up, two-down white-fronted terrace house in Hoylake, Cheshire, where Glenda lived during her childhood.

BIRKENHEAD EDUCATION COMMITTEE

Cathcart Street Primary School *Junior.* Department

SCHOLAR'S REPORT

Name Glenda Jackson. *Christmas* Term. 19 4 6.

Class IV B. *Containing* 40. *Scholars* *Position in Class* 1st

Times absent 7. *Punctuality* Good.

SUBJECT	MARKS.	TOTAL	SUBJECT	
English Language	50.	50.	Geography	Quite good.
Reading	10	10.	History	Good.
Spelling or Dictation	43	50.	Nature Study	Good.
Composition	20	20.	Art	
Mental Arithmetic	16	20.	Handwork	
Arithmetic	26	50.	Needlework	

Class Teacher's Report Glenda has all round ability and a pleasant disposition. We shall be very sorry to lose her at Xmas. With hard work she should do very well.

Conduct Good. M. Hooson. *Class Teacher*

Head Teacher's Remarks Glenda is a very clever child, & I wish her well when she returns to her old school

Next Term begins Jan. 6th, 1947. *Head Teacher*

7

Glenda's primary school report for the Christmas term of 1946. In a class of forty pupils, ten-year-old Glenda is top of the form.

8

Hoylake Church School, the first of the two primary schools attended by Glenda between the ages of five and eleven.

9

Glenda's second primary school, also in Hoylake, is now used as a funeral parlour.

10

West Kirby Grammar School where, between the ages of eleven and sixteen, Glenda spent a great deal of her time 'larking about and locking myself in cupboards and thinking it was a joke'. She hated the place.

11
As the mad Charlotte Corday in Peter Brook's celebrated 1965 RSC production of *The Marat/Sade*, which brought Glenda a certain notoriety in the West End, on Broadway and, to a lesser extent, in the cinema.

12
Glenda (*centre*) embarks on further insane behaviour in *US*, again for the RSC – Peter Brook's noisy indictment of America's involvement in Vietnam.

13
Glenda's house in Blackheath, south-east London, in 1972. It is still her home, despite marital turmoil.

14
Below At home with husband Roy Hodges, a former actor and stage manager who, in 1971, was running his own art gallery.

15
As a strong-willed Ophelia, opposite David
Warner's vacillating Prince of Denmark, in Peter
Hall's production of *Hamlet* at Stratford-upon-
Avon in 1965.

16
As Tamara Fanghorn, the vampire-cum-lesbian
crusader against male chauvinism in David
Pinner's *Fanghorn* (Fortune Theatre, London,
1967). With Peter Bayliss.

17
Glenda, at twenty-eight, in a rare non-acting 'glamour' pose. She had yet to be billed as 'the thinking
man's Brigitte Bardot'.

18
Pre-opening-night photo call for William Gaskill's production of Chekhov's *The Three Sisters* (Royal Court Theatre, London, 1967): Glenda as Masha, with Avril Elgar as Olga and Marianne Faithfull as Irina.

19
Below With actress Julie Crostwaite and Charles Marowitz, the theatre director and critic who, along with Peter Brook, most influenced Glenda's early theatrical development.

Watford, who had first appeared alongside Glenda at the Hornchurch Rep eleven years earlier. 'Her technique as an actress had become formidable, absolutely formidable,' recalled Miss Watford. 'To play a scene with her was like playing a game of tennis. You hit the ball towards her in a scene, and she would hit it back at you – by which time she had really built on the original shot. She was an exciting, if sometimes terrifying player to work with, and her personality had evolved along the most powerful lines. This was a *powerful* lady.'

7
An Awesome Personality

Established actors and actresses were beginning to regard Glenda Jackson with a certain awe. Not just 'powerful', but 'tough', 'arrogant', 'bossy', 'cool', 'aloof', 'blunt', 'no-nonsense', 'anti-social' and 'aggressive' were the epithets being used to describe her. Soon the adjective 'formidable' was added to the list. At the beginning of her film career, America's *Saturday Review* critic Stanley Kauffmann worried that Glenda might never become a star because 'she is not an actress in order to be loved but in order to act'.

'Glenda's tough, almost perverse independence is probably what gives her sex appeal,' suggested *New Yorker* film critic Pauline Kael. 'Whatever the role, she's a woman without small talk; she attracts by the sturdiness of her level, appraising gaze – a no-nonsense woman.'

Yet, as a no-nonsense woman, she was wholly unrepentant, admitting that most of her 'awesome' statements to people stemmed from the work itself; consequently, she was labelled 'fierce' and 'formidable'. She realizes today that often when she has been speaking impersonally on some detail associated with work that, in the process, other people's egos have been severely bruised. She not only concedes that she has learned little from that knowledge but confesses that she will probably continue to hurt people – which, she laments, 'is a shame'. Her rationale is uncompromising: she does not take her ego to work and she does not expect other people to.

There is more than one colleague who would disagree with her. One actor with whom she worked at Stratford-upon-Avon believes that behind the simple, unaffected 'our Glenda' image is a thundering secret arrogance: 'She cultivates that Simple Sara look because it protects her from her own carnivorous ego. Her "coolness" and "aloofness" are fundamentally anti-human. She doesn't like associating with people who are inferior talents and, for Glenda, almost everyone is an inferior talent. There is a built-in smugness there which she can't disguise in the roles she plays. I'm not saying she's not a great actress, but I'd hate to find myself on a blind date with her.'

More than one observer noted at this time that, far from being simple and unpretentious, Glenda possessed a personality of great complexity. On a film set, where the prevailing atmosphere could be as blue-collar as a factory floor, Glenda was relaxed and good-natured, 'matey' even, conducting herself like some high-spirited navvy. She preferred to communicate by the jocular insult: for Glenda, it was a sign of affection. The American writer Richard Grenier observed her at work during this period and was struck by the amazing duality of her personality. 'She was kind, considerate and engaging with all the more modest ranks on the movie production – the drivers and hairdressers and stagehands and electricians – just as she was with salesgirls, barmaids and supermarket cashiers, most of whom were in the kinds of jobs she herself held during her unsuccessful early years. But among her peers she became cold and edgy, tended to be rather widely disliked.'

In the straight theatre, with which she was about to break company for several years and where pretensions were greater than on a film set, it was said she 'radiated disgust'. The word 'withering' was used. 'She is a very chilly character,' said someone who knew her then.

'I know I make this impression on people,' Glenda told Richard Grenier, shaking her head, as if the thought of how people got such an impression was a mystery to her.

'But the small smile which played on her lips indicated that she was far from displeased,' concluded Grenier.

Many of Glenda's colleagues nursed a wide range of theories about why people were beginning to feel in awe of her – and why some even despised her. The most likely explanation came from Vladek Sheybal. 'It's to do with her way of being "outside",' he said. 'For instance, if throughout our conversation I never once looked at you, and I sat like *this*' – he stared steadfastly three feet to the left of my eyes – 'you'd become a little bit nervous and uneasy after a time. This trait of hers, of not looking at people *directly*, is her protective armour. But it creates an intense nervousness in people, and so they dislike her.'

When asked if she personally approved of sexually aggressive women, she replied that it was not a question of approving or disapproving. 'If they *are* they *are*,' she said. But was woman as the sexual aggressor an image she liked? 'I'm just trying to think what would happen if a woman tried to be sexually aggressive with me because, presumably, their sexual aggression isn't limited to the male sex,' she went on. 'I think I'd probably find it a little unnerving, so presumably men would, too. But I don't think it is necessarily wrong, or that there's any moral issue in it. If that's a way for them to get whatever their heart desires, and it works, terrific. If it doesn't get them what their heart desires, then they're going to have to box a little bit more cleverly, aren't they? I think women have always been quite clever in that area, really.'

Glenda, deliberately or otherwise, had avoided the point: the question had, of course, been aimed at *her*. She so perfectly epitomized the actresses of the late 1960s, those poised, assured, classless women who usually conveyed the impression of being independent of men. 'I'm lucky in one respect,' she said. 'I have always been surrounded by people who tell me when I'm coming it a bit.' This was not so. Anybody who told her she was coming it a bit would either receive the 'withering' look, or, more likely, some choice verbal fireworks.

One thing was certain, though: Glenda Jackson was the name British film producers were now apt to come up with when they were casting around for someone to play a sexually fraught lady, though American producers were not yet entirely convinced of her pulling power. When RSC actor Peter McEnery suggested that Glenda should be his leading lady in *Negatives*, producer Judd Bernard demurred, 'She's hardly going to appeal to the teeny-boppers in New York, is she!' In the eventual film, a low-budget crime thriller generally panned by the critics, Glenda and McEnery play an unmarried couple living above an antique shop where, for psycho-erotic stimulation, they thrive on outrageous sexual fantasies – their favourite charade being that of wife-murderer Dr Crippen and his lady victim. But she eventually loses him as the World War I air ace, the Red Baron, to a full-sized scarlet biplane anchored on the roof, and, in the event, goes mad and has to be carried away in a basket.

Peter Medak, the Hungarian director who was making his directorial film début, found Glenda 'unselfish, wonderful, cooperative, brilliant, sexy, responsive, willing to do whatever it takes, strong, ballsy, and easy to work with'. Glenda, for her part, adored working with Medak, though her relationship with most of her future directors proved strained. 'She'll be lovely to the other actors, lovely to the technicians, lovely to the understudy, and terrible to the director,' said Timothy West, who first worked with her in *The Marat/Sade*. 'She seems to feel the need for some kind of elected enemy.'

West's theory was that Glenda was searching for another director with Brook's strength and dominating intelligence – in fact, someone bossier than herself. Her apparent abandonment of that search with Medak perhaps stemmed from the fact that she did not regard him as a threat, or possibly because – this being his directorial début – she looked upon him as her 'inferior'. But whatever the reason, the relationship for both was a happy one. 'I remember very clearly when, at Peter McEnery's suggestion, she came to see me in this very small dark office in Wardour Street,' said Medak. 'She wore a dark-brown skirt and a roll-neck pullover from Marks & Sparks, and I remember her hair was very straight and wet. I loved her for the role, as she was (and remains) very strong and rough and tough; and I immediately knew she had the kind of face the camera just falls in love with.'

After about ten days of rehearsing at Judd Bernard's home, in a mews cottage behind Buckingham Palace, filming got under way in Hyde Park and Chelsea prior to shooting the interiors at Shepperton Studios, just outside London. There was one sequence in the film where she was to stand in front of a mirror, naked, with a fur wrapped around her shoulders and her front. Eventually she had to drop the fur, turn, and walk seductively towards

McEnery on the sofa, where they would kiss and begin to make love. Medak, the novice director, did not look forward to the filming of this piece of 'business'. 'The closer we got to this scene,' he said, 'the more nervous I got. I just didn't know how to ask Glenda to be naked. She said she was going to bring in various flesh-coloured bras and underpants; and, as she tried them on the next day in her dressing room, she could see by the look on my face that I wasn't happy with any of them. She finally just dropped everything and turned to me and said, "Come on, let's just do it naked and stop screwing about."'

The actress whom the popular press would dub the 'First Lady of the Flesh' has always seemed strangely at odds with Glenda-the-Puritan; but, at this juncture in her career, it was her willingness to embark on a goose-pimply trail of self-exposure on the screen that brought her such wide notice. Her ability to act was something else. So was her sexuality ... and, indeed, her blazing sensuality. She could achieve more male unrest with a deftly aimed glance, on or off the screen, than all Hollywood's well-known bosoms heaving together in perfect harmony.

Since appearing as a naked Christine Keeler with the Theatre of Cruelty, she told people she was willing to act in the nude 'as long as the purpose is not spurious or sensational'. Clothes, she felt, like film sets, often only hampered and distracted from the action. 'You can't equate nudity with sex,' she was fond of saying. 'Actually, the greatest intimacy between two people doesn't depend at all on whether they can lie together naked.' So what did she regard as a convincing way to evoke intimacy? 'Maybe a couple cutting their toenails. No one ever does that in public.' In any event, she was delighted that 'the whole enormous hang-up about sex is well and truly smashed, and a much saner attitude is around'.

Peter Brook made the definitive statement about Glenda. He said, 'You can't look at this woman without feeling you've matured five years.' Note he said 'matured', not 'aged'. What she possesses is that same incredible quality that Marlon Brando projects – a feeling of an unpredictable force about to explode; and that force can certainly come across sexually.

Her physical appearance was another matter. She was neither glamour symbol nor yet strident drudge. It was an odd, enigmatic face, constantly mobile, reflecting with almost painful fidelity every shifting idea, emotion, opinion. Few other faces can so eloquently convey such a marked sense of pain and suffering, an impression which is accentuated on the screen by the fact that her mouth (which is probably too prominent a feature) often looks as if she has just bitten into something acid. There is a touch of Katharine Hepburn about her looks, except that the effect is less spare, less highly-strung, and rather more scrubbed.

At the time one writer thought she looked Scandinavian; another noted that, with her thick nose and slit eyes, she photographed like a Chinese boy;

another referred to her 'broad, vaguely Oriental face'. 'She's flat as a pan-cake, wears no make-up and has lank, unattractive hair, but an actress like Glenda makes you *believe* she's beautiful,' said Glenda's friend Lyn Pinkney, who worked with her in *The Marat/Sade*. 'It's a strong face with extraordinary things hidden in it,' added Peter Medak. One critic claimed that her face was 'so erotically explicit it could be used as a diagram for an advanced sex-education class'. British broadcaster Jack de Manio's remark that her face could 'launch a thousand dredgers' has become legendary. Close behind is film director John Schlesinger's observation that she looked like Tom Courtenay in drag. Glenda once described Audrey Hepburn to me as one of the most beautiful women in the world, explaining, 'I see in her everything I would like to be and am not.' She then ruefully pointed out that her own high cheekbones only emphasized the depth of her dark eyes: 'One brush of mascara and they disappear like little raisins in unbaked dough.'

Gerry Fisher, who worked with Glenda on a couple of movies as a director of photography, indulged in repartee of quite an irreverent nature about the actress's looks. He would pay an early morning visit to the make-up room and ask, 'Where's Glenda then?'

'In these jars, of course – you *fool*!'

'You'll be all right, Glenda,' he would continue. 'I've made a lighting set-up for your close-up which I last used for Elizabeth Taylor.'

Later, arriving on the set, Glenda would fix Fisher with a determined, questioning look, and demand – '*Well*?'

'Sorry, Glenda, it hasn't worked. You still look like you . . . .'

'Bloody insults!'

She said while making *Negatives*, 'I find it terribly boring to have to use make-up. Anyone can *act* being beautiful with sufficient conviction to con-vince the people watching.'

Explained Roy, 'People are always commenting on the fact that she wears no make-up, but when she was younger she wore it half an inch thick. She's got the self-confidence not to now, and I prefer her to be herself at home. But when she wants to she can be magnificent.'

'I've got three sisters, all with *enormous* eyes,' added Glenda. 'A bit unfair of them, don't you think, having these enormous orbs? They don't need them – and I could use them.'

Unlike them, too, her large, capable hands look as if they have done more than their share of spud-bashing, and her feet are broad, big and ugly. She has the rolling stride of a paratrooper in combat boots. Shoes have always been her principal extravagance. She tends to buy a great many in one mad shopping spree, and then just wear one pair until they fall to pieces before working round to the rest. This means she can usually be seen wearing highly unfashionable shoes, although they were high fashion when she bought them. To Glenda, clothes – like shoes – are meant for wearing, not for preening in. 'I'm not anti-fashion,' she maintains. 'I just don't seem to have the aptitude for it.' Her aim in an outfit is to look as good as she can, and then forget about it: 'I hate to be conscious of the dress I'm wearing.'

This workaday attitude to fashion reached its peak when, for a party being given by America's First Lady, Jackie Kennedy, she wore a forty-five-shilling (£2.25p) cotton dress from Marks & Spencer. She confessed later to Sally O'Sullivan of *Woman's World*, 'I do have a couple of grand frocks for the occasional grand evening, but apart from that I stick to good old Marks & Sparks.' About her often downright *ordinariness* – and by any standards, off-screen, she looks ordinary – she used to announce: 'I couldn't care less if people don't like the way I look. If it upsets them so much they can go and talk to someone else.'

Glenda was quite prepared to admit that she was inclined to be on the thin side, had varicose veins, a sallow, translucent complexion scarred by acne, a too-thin upper lip, eyes that are deep set, and badly spaced buckteeth. It became Peter Medak's unenviable task, before shooting *Negatives*, to draw her attention to one particular tooth which was slightly overgrown. After much discussion, she agreed to go to the dentist and have it filed down and capped so that it would look better on the screen. Several weeks later, when the film was shooting at Shepperton Studios, Glenda was holding court in the restaurant when, to Medak's horror, he noticed that the offending tooth which, up until that moment, had looked fine, was *still there*.

'My God, Glenda!' gasped Medak. 'What's happened to your tooth?'

In reply she quietly dived into her bag and pulled out a dental cap and shoved it over the tooth: 'Sorry dear, I'm glad you reminded me. I nearly forgot!'

'That was typical of Glenda,' Medak said resignedly. 'She just wouldn't change herself, permanently, for anyone. Glenda was Glenda, and what had an overgrown tooth got to do with things?'

Part Three

A Star Affirmed

The secret of success is constancy to purpose.

Benjamin Disraeli,
Speech, 24 June 1872

Nothing succeeds like success.

Alexandre Dumas the Elder,
Ange Pitou, Vol. 1, 1854

8
Women in Love

'Out with those varicose veins, Glenda, dear!' The flamboyant Ken Russell is accustomed to his stars bowing without question to his often outrageous demands, even iron-willed damsels like Glenda Jackson, and so cosmetic surgery was promptly arranged for his new leading lady. The controversial, middle-aged English director had already acquired an *enfant terrible* reputation by stunning, delighting and upsetting British television viewers with a series of fictionalized film biographies of famous composers. Now, with *Billion Dollar Brain* starring Michael Caine behind him, he was about to embark on a movie which would transform a great many other people's lives. And he wanted Glenda.

'When she walked into the room,' said Russell of their first meeting, 'I found myself watching her varicose veins more than her face. Our film was set in the 1920s, with a lot of ankle – and a good deal more – in evidence. Glenda, fortunately, was not one to let a few veins stand between her and stardom, and so out they came.'

And international stardom, as predicted, came swiftly to Glenda with Russell's 1969 screen rendering of D. H. Lawrence's celebrated and controversial novel *Women in Love*, about the battle of the sexes and relationships among the *élite* of Britain's industrial Midlands in the 1920s. By casting her as the domineering, emasculating sculptress Gudrun Brangwen – who, amongst other things, liked to dance with bulls – Russell was accorded an Academy Award nomination for his efforts and Glenda won the Oscar itself.

'How could a beautiful, feminine girl like you emasculate a tough, rugged character like me?' Oliver Reed asked her, not a little tongue-in-cheek, when filming started. But he soon discovered that his character, Gerald Rich, the decadent homosexual son of a wealthy colliery owner, is reduced to a state of suicidal depression by the guile and wiles of the formidable, mean-lipped but sexually-curious Gudrun, whom Lawrence is said to have modelled upon the writer Katherine Mansfield. Their relationship becomes a strange mixture of brutality and love, ranging from one to the other until she finally destroys him.

There are many stories about the actual working relationship of Glenda and Reed, some of them no doubt apocryphal. At the end of the shoot, the burly, bull-necked actor–nephew of film director Sir Carol Reed, who for a

while specialized in sullen, scowling, often vicious roles, would go around
announcing, 'I'm articulate on the subjects of horses, dogs, cats, actors,
pissoirs – but not Glenda. And remember: I wasn't in her picture; she was in
mine.'

Their first meeting was at Russell's house, where the cast (including Alan
Bates and Glenda's screen sister, Jennie Linden) had assembled for a preliminary script reading. Before Glenda's arrival, Russell informed Reed,
'You're going to work with an actress from the Royal Shakespeare Company.'
Reed, the erstwhile school drop-out, Soho nightclub bouncer, boxer, cab
driver and former film extra who, with no formal drama training, much less
theatrical experience, had become one of Britain's highest-paid movie stars,
looked half suspiciously at the corpulent director and, in exaggeratedly
'cultured' tones, replied sarcastically, 'Oh, jolly good.'

Glenda then entered the room, and Reed inclined his head towards her
and looked aghast: 'Suddenly this woman sat on a chair on the other side of
the room, and this rather plain truck started to make the air move. So I just
mumbled my lines, because I had no identity towards Glenda. I didn't know
her from Eve; never heard of her. I'd heard of Shakespeare, but not this truck
sitting across the room from me. Unlike her, I wasn't associated with *art*: I
made commercial films. I love motor cars, and you can judge a car by its pitch;
and suddenly I'd met a *truck*, no less, and when its engine started to rev I
began to realize that it had a different pitch to what I'd expected. Glenda was
like a Ford truck with a highly-tuned V8 engine in it. If an engine is properly
tuned, it doesn't care about the road. So, more than making the air move, she
began to eat up the road very quickly, because she didn't care about the
hypocrisy of the old structure of the cinema, the star system and the casting
couch. Glenda didn't take that route. She came straight from the dust of the
theatre, and she began to growl.

'And suddenly the truck met somebody like me. I swear to God, I admired
her for what she was, but I wouldn't budge one inch when it came to putting
my masculinity on the line; and it came to it once, this confrontation, when
Glenda said she wanted to dominate me sexually. Russell and I were trying to
convince her that I should rape her and be the dominant factor in that
particular love scene. She was so aggressive about it, saying no, *she* should
dominate *me*. In the end we had to call in the producers, because this
unknown girl was being so headstrong. It made me wonder whether she'd
read the book, because she thought she had to rape me, had to completely
dominate me, had to climb on top of me and become the aggressor. But she
wasn't experienced enough to know that to be on top is not the be-all and
end-all of the conquest. I don't think she would have compromised had she
not believed that there was still enough superstition left in male vanity to
warrant the leading man, and the director, to think that she should be underneath getting fucked for the things that she said.'

Vladek Sheybal has a quite different view of the 'headstrong' actress. He played the homosexual German sculptor, Loerke, who exerts a disturbing emotional influence on Glenda and Reed in the sequences filmed at the Swiss ski resort of Zermatt. In the trio's first scene together, Reed took exception to Glenda's particular interpretation. 'Oliver was expressing dislike of what she was doing,' said Sheybal, 'but she was completely immune to his heated behaviour and simply disregarded it. I thought, "Poor Ollie!", because he really was jumping up and down with rage, ranting, "This shouldn't be played like that, you know." She just sat quietly, almost immobile, and either looked out of the window at the snow and the Matterhorn, or smiled at me; but she refused to react to Ollie's behaviour, refused to reply to anything he said.'

Why would she choose not to defend herself? 'Because she was still very much the vulnerable girl,' said Sheybal. 'Choosing not to react was her particular defence mechanism. When we first met, after her struggling rep days at Perth, she also sat like that and hardly looked at me. No, not to look somebody in the eyes, not to respond to somebody, was Glenda's ultimate weapon in self-protection.'

Being pregnant, added Sheybal, also seemed to increase her sense of vulnerability during the making of the film. Certainly producers Larry Kramer and Martin Rosen had some unkind thoughts when, a couple of weeks after the cameras started rolling, she announced she was pregnant. 'Roy and I have been trying for ten years to have a baby,' the leading lady sheepishly told her bosses. As it happened, it worked out to everybody's advantage. Glenda's usually undersized breasts achieved a pleasing roundness.

Few people in the unit knew about her pregnancy, but Sheybal was one of them. They were standing in the snow in Zermatt, waiting to be called for another shot, when she confessed her secret.

'You know,' she said, 'when we started the film Ken didn't know I was pregnant.'

'Did *you*?' asked Sheybal.

'I did, and it was a tremendous decision to make, whether to tell him or not to tell him. And I didn't.'

'I think you were very wise.'

'But now I feel a bit guilty, because it already shows. Ken's now having to photograph me in a certain way . . . .'

Explained Sheybal: 'There is a revealing shot in the film which nobody noticed after its release, but which I noticed, when she dances with me in the snow – suddenly you see a bulge!'

Towards the end of the filming, a night-time market scene had to be photographed in Gateshead in which a drunken young miner named Palmer, amid much talk of flesh and thighs, had to force Glenda into a doorway and try to have his way with her. The attempted rape was often violent in the extreme. 'After one of the many "takes" of this struggle in the doorway,' said Michael Graham Cox (who played Palmer), 'Ken Russell took me to one side and whispered in my ear to take it easy with her, because Glenda was pregnant. I was shocked. None of us had any idea. I remember thinking what a trouper she was, working a difficult scene in difficult conditions and not saying anything about her condition.'

'We were filming in Gateshead, and she was putting on a lot of weight, and they were having to let out all her clothes,' affirmed Glenda's stand-in, Geraldine Addison. 'And the producer, Larry Kramer, came up to me and said, "She can eat anything she wants to." So she was able to have steak every day, and her figure became really rounded; and, because her boobs had considerably enlarged, Ken re-shot some nude scenes at the very end of the filming.'

At this time it was initially assumed that Glenda was far too genteel ever to agree to a nude scene for Russell, a notion which was reinforced when, in no uncertain terms, she turned down a photo session with *Playboy* magazine. The truth was rather different: 'The scenes in which I've been nude were scenes about sex and it seemed absurd to pretend that the character I was playing would have sex with her clothes on. There is always a good reason for nudity as far as I am concerned. For instance, the scene in *Women in Love* in which Jennie Linden and I swam naked in the lake was there because in their situation nakedness was the ultimate revolutionary act and the closest you could get to any natural spirit.'

That scene was one of several which made the screen version of D. H. Lawrence's novel daring for its time. (Lawrence, it should be remembered, explored characters so sexually liberated that they caused his novels to be banned, censored and hauled into court for obscenity.) Because of Glenda's practical approach to acting she became one of the first women to show that nudity on screen could be acceptable. 'I wouldn't strip as a general rule,' she said. 'But sex is such an integral part of D. H. Lawrence that you can't film his work without examining that area with as much honesty as possible. I'm not trying to make it sound as if I'm alibi-ing. I took my clothes off for reasons that were of a deeply intellectual nature, though obviously the effect and impact of those scenes is more than purely intellectual. But that was the reason for doing it and that's why I did it . . . because it was right.'

Somebody asked her, rather naïvely, if she could ever appear in a nude scene with her husband. 'Oh dear, no,' she said, 'I couldn't possibly do anything like that with Roy in front of the cameras. I don't believe in acting scenes of this nature with someone I care about, and Roy would be the last person I could ever make love to on the screen. It would be the most ghastly acting because, for me, there would be the inner agony of feeling people were invading a very private domain.'

Unlike her mother, Roy had seen and loved all her performances, and he could find nothing wrong with his wife appearing naked in films. 'No, it didn't put me off her personally,' he said. 'Nothing could do that. Sex is an appetite which you have or you haven't. Glenda on the screen is not Glenda at home. On the screen she is much more powerful than in real life. She's powerful because she's a great actress.' He said he did not care what Glenda did in a film; but he did get teased about some of the things she got up to. 'Blokes say to me, "Saw your wife with no clothes on last night." But somehow these days it doesn't mean anything. Things have changed since the shock caused by Shaw saying "Not bloody likely!"'

Soon after *Women in Love* was released, a rumour circulated that Oliver Reed tried to have Glenda replaced on the grounds that it would be impossible for him to make love to her. Whether or not it was true it was obvious to the crew that the mutual respect between Glenda and Reed was so powerful that, paradoxically, it sometimes bordered on manic antipathy. Each recognized the other's strengths and weaknesses, and they manoeuvred around each other like two powerful motorboats forced to compete in a narrow, dangerous waterway.

Her relationship with Russell was no less ambivalent. When the filming was completed he refused to discuss her, saying enigmatically, 'I'd better not talk. I might say something both she and I would regret.' Glenda called him 'an utter physical coward', because, she said, he always made his actors do extremely dangerous things so that he would not look a coward himself. 'Yes, he's a bloody coward,' agreed Reed, 'and he makes everybody live out the performances that he has in his mind. Ken's a voyeur, of course; but that's his strength. Some like to watch, some like to do it; and there are moments, I suppose, given the freedom, when some like to do a little bit of both, or a lot of both. But that's me being honest; Ken merely shrouds it in Art. Glenda understands that and says, "Fuck it!", and off come the clothes and – *voilà*!'

Both Reed and Russell used the same phrase about her: 'Glenda is no fool.' She was shrewder, and more self-protective, than most people realized. Vladek Sheybal, unknown to Reed, had had first-hand experience of Glenda's guile. It had occurred in the fantasy scene in the Swiss chalet where, in Loerke's bedroom, Glenda and Sheybal dress up as the passionate Cleopatra and the homosexual Tchaikovsky, a game which ends by their spending the night together. 'The whole scene had been suggested by me to Ken Russell, and Glenda was following it,' said Sheybal. 'But when I saw the rushes a few days later I was astounded to discover that Glenda had some close-ups that I couldn't remember being filmed – a lot of reaction shots to my lines, *fantastic* reactions. I said to Ken, "I don't remember making those," and Ken said, "Well, darling, she rang me in the middle of the night and said, 'Vladek did that scene so brilliantly, and I don't have the counterpoint. Could you ...?', and so I accommodated her wishes." She was defending herself as an actress. She wanted to have equal play with me. She was always on the ball.'

Her shrewdness, allied to her full-frontal talent, paid off. The awards, proclaiming her Film Actress of the Year, started to flood in. First it was the New York Film Critics Award, then the National Society of Film Critics Award, followed by the Variety Club of Great Britain Award, and others, culminating in Hollywood's highest accolade, the Oscar – her competitors being Ali MacGraw for *Love Story*, Carrie Snodgress for *Diary of a Mad Housewife*, Jane Alexander for *The Great White Hope* and Sarah Miles for *Ryan's Daughter*. 'She bursts upon the screen like a young, sturdier version of Katharine Hepburn, with all of her animal magnetism,' trumpeted America's *Saturday Review*.

At the ceremony at Sardi's for the New York Film Critics Award, Bette Davis paid tribute to Glenda as 'possessing one of the best acting talents of today'. She added that she hoped Glenda realized what this award meant in America; for although the Hollywood Oscars rated first, the awards of the New York critics carried more professional and artistic integrity. 'I had to wait from 1930 to 1950 before I got mine,' Miss Davis told Glenda. 'If you take your career as an actress seriously, this is the award you want.' In her acceptance speech, Glenda said she had derived as much pleasure in having Bette Davis give her the award as she had in first receiving the news. 'You can't tell me in all seriousness I'm becoming a sex symbol,' she told the friend who broke the news of the award to her. 'How lovely! How bloody weird!'

When the American press started referring to her as 'the intellectual's Raquel Welch', she thought it was the funniest thing since laughing gas. 'Listen,' she said, 'Raquel Welch is Raquel Welch because she is what no man has ... and wouldn't know what to do with if he had. Sex symbols are remote ladies. You don't live with them, don't commit yourself to them. They stay a rather lovely dream. I'm a reality. I'm a blemished, faulty human being.'

None of the awards, including the Oscar, impressed Glenda – they all ended up on the sideboard in her mother's front room – though they certainly unsettled a great many of her peers. Thus spoke Oliver Reed: 'When she came in and swept the Oscar from under the carpets of all those foul goblins and demons and turbaned genies that flew out with all sorts of magic lanterns in the cinema-world sky, I told everybody: "Watch out, world, Glenda's arrived. Here she is – revving up."'

9
Motherhood

Glenda now undertook two new roles, neither of them theatrical: home-ownership and motherhood. 'Our way of life may not have changed but the money has,' she observed. 'We have lived frugally for most of our lives. Now, after twelve years of marriage, we are buying our own house, we have a Triumph Herald car, and we can smoke without me having to go round the ashtrays like I used to, unpicking the dog-ends and re-rolling them in bits of paper.'

The Hodges moved from their modest flat in Hampstead, where Glenda loathed her neighbours, to the fringes of Blackheath, a respectable but hardly fashionable London suburb, its casual greens – once the haunt of high-waymen – bordered by militarily regular rows of staid brick houses. Glenda's new home in Hervey Road was a square, four-bedroom, early Edwardian house with a conventional façade and small front garden: a low paling fence and stark, pruned shrubs; nothing exotic, nothing fancy, a very *un*-film-star sort of abode. It cost a bargain £8,500 and its modest home comforts so suit her temperament that she has never so far found one good reason for moving.

She lives there today with the most important man in her life, her son Daniel, who took his first breath in February 1969. 'She's *crazy* about him,' said Geraldine Addison. 'Absolutely, totally adores him.'

'The highest point of my life was the day Dan was born,' explained Glenda. 'They had to knock me out because he got stuck and I came to on a trolley with drips in my arms and asked, "What did I have?" and they said, "Oh, a boy" – totally unconcerned, you know. Then I came round again, at two in the afternoon, and this little white bundle was brought in for me to see. I felt as though I was just the delivery van that Dan had arrived in.'

For the first four months of Daniel's life Glenda stayed at home to take care of him. She then recorded a half-hour television play and was riddled with guilt for 'deserting' her son. 'It was awful,' she said. 'I couldn't bear to leave him with anybody else, so Roy stayed at home to look after him.' In fact, he did rather better than that: he swapped roles with Glenda to become a house-husband. Roy's 'big break' as an actor never did come and, at a time when it was all suddenly starting to happen for Glenda, his own stop-gap career in stage management (the obscure rep companies, the cheap digs in the provinces) was all but over. So he gave up showbusiness to stay at home with

Daniel. He took care of all the bottle-feeding, nappy-changing and washing, as well as most of the shopping, and generally looked after Daniel and the house, leaving Glenda free to concentrate on her career. It was a situation many men might find intolerable, but it was one that – on the surface at least – he accepted with great equanimity and even, on occasion, much good humour. 'One of us had to be near the baby,' he reasoned, 'and Glenda was already at the top. She might have to fly off somewhere at a moment's notice.' He thought for a moment and then added, 'I'm not at all jealous of her success. Having been an actor, I know how hard it is. I'm just glad one of us made it. I always thought she was great and I'm just surprised it took so long.'

'For many people,' explained Glenda, 'it would be very difficult for the wife to be more successful than the husband. It might have been difficult for us if we hadn't both been unsuccessful together. You see, success has taken a comparatively long time to arrive for me, and I think it has probably arrived at the right time. I can see it for what it really is, and recognize what are the valuable things that have come out of it and what are the rubbishy things.'

Roy, nine years her senior, would have been perfectly content to fit into the same groove as Glenda's father. But, in fact, he was important as a sounding board for her; in the early days, his was the only professional advice she listened to consistently and with respect. Glenda would inform people that, in a man and woman situation, she was not at all domineering, though she admitted, 'I certainly do have a bossy streak, perhaps because I was the oldest of four girls.'

'I remember while we were making *Women in Love*,' said Oliver Reed, 'that Glenda was always asking Roy to go and collect her coffee or whatever, and I could never quite work out whether it was because she was pregnant or because her husband did as she bid.'

In her next movie commitment, *The Music Lovers*, her screen husband would certainly not do as she bid. Not sexually at least. Seven months after having her baby, Glenda was once again baring all for the cameras, this time as the pathetic, mad Nina Milukova, nymphomaniac wife of the homosexual Russian composer Tchaikovsky – played by the tall, blond, clean-cut American Richard Chamberlain, who was still trying to shake off his anti-septic title-role image from TV's long-running *Dr Kildare* series. Ken Russell was once again at the helm of this controversial, idiosyncratic and highly agitated portrait of Tchaikovsky, every minute of its two hours filled to the sprocket holes with flamboyant images, neurotic passions and shaky historical detail. Based on *Beloved Friend*, an early biography of the composer by Catherine Drinker Bowen and Barbara von Meck, the film provided Glenda with one of the most challenging and demanding roles of her career; and, as in *The Marat/Sade*, she would once more end her days in the mad-house. This sort of thing, accompanied by great wedges of bare, writhing flesh, was, said the critics, fast becoming Glenda's exclusive domain.

What was remarkable was not so much that Glenda was naked once again, but rather the purpose behind it, for few actresses could ever have given a greater testimony of their belief in a director. In one scene, following Tchaikovsky's inability to copulate with her, she rolls naked on the floor of a train and writhes herself into multiple orgasms. In another scene, in a lunatic asylum, she bestrides an open grill while greedy male fingers reach up to meander beneath her skirt. Of the latter scene, she told me at the time, 'It was our way, admittedly a slightly surrealistic way, of referring to Nina's nymphomania.' The effect in each case was not sexual or pornographic – it was horrific. 'You see this horrible skeletal figure writhing around and it's enough to put you off sex for the rest of your life,' she added.

Even Roy was shaken on this particular occasion when he first saw the sexually explicit scenes. 'I felt horrified,' he said, 'even though I knew all the technicalities. I just wasn't looking at the Glenda I knew.' She herself justified her actions by explaining, 'It's never Roy's *wife* up there: it's just her outward shape playing whatever the character happens to be.'

From Roy's vantage point, Glenda's anatomy was always something of a joke, as was her 'sex' image. 'Some mornings when she gets up,' he said, 'she looks like the wrath of God. I must admit, I tease her about it. "What's this they're writing about you? *Staggering? . . . Physically extraordinary? . . . Tremendous sexuality?* Darling," I say to her, "they should see you now!"'

The explicit love scenes, first with Oliver Reed and now with Richard Chamberlain, provoked accusations of pornography from some quarters – yet they established new boundaries of cinematic permissiveness. Glenda dismissed her body as 'the envelope I live in'. The scripts she was receiving at that time, though, in which she figured nude on every page, suggested that some producers mistook her professionalism for exhibitionism. She defended herself by explaining, 'I don't feel I've contributed to the "flesh" cinema cult. If I've contributed to flesh taking its rightful place on the screen, then I'm very happy.'

During the filming of the most famous sequence in *The Music Lovers* – the honeymoon journey on the Trans-Siberian train – the scene involved the fully clothed Richard Chamberlain looking down on the naked figure of Glenda on the carriage floor. Ken Russell wanted the carriage lights to wave about frantically as the train hurtled through the Russian countryside. In fact, of course, it was a lonely railway carriage sitting stationary on a film set at Bray Studios in Berkshire. He instructed director of photography Douglas Slocombe to swing the carriage lights about but Slocombe, a purist at heart, objected that carriage lights were usually fixed into the roof. Russell overruled this observation. So Slocombe climbed into the new luggage-rack, which he clung on to with one hand while holding in the other a small light known in the trade as a 'pup'. Meanwhile, camera operator Chick Waterson, hand-holding the camera, knelt precariously on the opposite railway carriage seat.

Outside, all was mayhem as every available crew hand was brought to bear in rocking the carriage from side to side. The magic words were proclaimed when all comes to life: 'Turn over!', 'Mark it!' and, after the snap of the clapper-board, 'Action!' Immediately, over-enthusiastic hands went to work in agitating the little Russian carriage. Glenda rolled from port to starboard with sickening alacrity, while brave Dougie Slocombe, clinging for his life to the luggage-rack, waved the 'pup' about with a frenzy not normally seen in such a gentle person. All was steam, noise and movement. Suddenly, there was a rending sound and a crack: the frail Victorian baggage-rack had given way, and an astounded, naked and prostrate Glenda Jackson received a fully clothed Dougie Slocombe, clutching a red-hot 'pup', on top of her. She was scorched and brought the scene to a halt with a full-blooded shriek. After a second's silence Chick Waterson, the operator, was heard to say to his director of photography boss: "What the hell are you doing in my shot?"

The heated frenzy of this particular sequence was stoked by Russell's penchant for stimulating a performance with background music – in this case a plangent section from Shostakovich's *The Execution of Stepan Razin*, although it was never heard in the completed film. Russell recalled thinking, 'Here's this lady from the Royal Shakespeare Company lying naked like a piece of meat on the floor, being bombarded with this music. I wonder if it's distracting her from what she thinks she should be doing in this scene.'

'Glenda,' he said, 'I know you don't usually work like this. In the RSC, I know it's all hours of intellectual chat with Peter Brook. Would you prefer to do the scene without the music?'

'Christ, if you stopped the music I couldn't do it,' she replied.

'That's fine,' said the director, 'because I'd made up my mind that I was going to use it anyway, whatever your answer.'

He then played it louder than ever. 'After the film,' he recalled, 'I sent her a record of the music, which I'm sure she burned immediately.'

While Glenda found Richard Chamberlain 'smashing to work with', she also discovered that he was 'a very difficult person to get to know; he can protect himself very well'. But, in this respect, she might have been describing herself.

Soon after the release of *The Music Lovers* in 1970 she was asked how she would describe herself on a computer dating application: Gregarious? Neat dresser? Fun on a date? Loner? None of these? She thought for a moment, and then disclosed, 'I suppose I'd have to say I was a loner.'

'On location,' said Vladek Sheybal, 'actors are the gossipers. They like to know things – but how can they *know*, if Glenda doesn't drink with them? I'm an enigma for them as well: what's your private life? No comment, good-bye – I'm going to that bar. And Glenda's the same: keeps herself to herself.'

'While making *Women in Love*, we only saw Glenda for work,' said Oliver Reed. 'Russell and I used to go out together, go to cake shows and aunty's hat shows. No, Glenda was always very private.'

But her private nature had very little to do with the quality of her relationship with Russell. At best it was mutually reverent; at worst, fuelled by an identical arrogance. Oliver Reed talked about 'these two strong-minded characters who made the air move'. A few years after completing work on *The Music Lovers*, the following conversation took place with the American magazine *Viva*:

'Of course, the most controversial director you've worked with is Ken Russell.'

'Yes,' answered Glenda, 'but I just wish he would find a really good scriptwriter he could respect because he needs to be dragged by someone with a talent as large as his own. Then he could get himself out of this fearful rut.'

'By "rut" you mean the excesses in his films?'

'Excesses which are so repetitious now, yes.'

'And so outrageous?'

'Well, they lack outrage, I think.'

'Sacrilegious?'

'No, I don't think so. I think they're quite specious because he's done them so many times that the shock value is gone. They've stopped being what he actually represents them to be and become something called "Ken Russellisms", and what is that exactly? It's very boring and a great waste.'

'Why is he indulging in all that?'

'Why indeed? I wish one knew. It isn't that he hasn't got the talent to support being a bit braver ... he needs a kick up the backside, actually.'

'Aren't you afraid of hurting his feelings, talking so frankly?'

'No. I think the ideal director/actor relationship is one of total trust, which means you can say precisely what you think at any moment. It's the most tedious waste of energy when people get their feelings hurt. Directors should be able to say to an actor anything at all. And vice versa. You're not in this business to make friends and influence people.'

She firmly believed that. 'Be yourself' was a favourite maxim. Even on the screen, Glenda always seems to play the character she knows best – herself. Despite her allegation that 'the me I am' and 'the me I act' are totally separate, there seems to be a striking similarity between the two. She often plays independent-minded women and indeed she is one. Yet her apparent aversion to making friends and influencing people frequently backfires on her. 'Doors are always being opened for me before I voice my opinion,' she observed. 'But once I've opened my mouth, I find I also have to open my own doors. ...'

After *The Music Lovers*, which the critics derided as 'kitsch', 'schmaltz' and 'hokum', Glenda made a decision which clearly upset Ken Russell. The director asked her if she would like to play a hunchbacked, sex-crazed nun in his next film, *The Devils*, based on an account of the apparent demoniacal possession of the seventeenth-century nuns of Loudun. 'Yes, it sounds very interesting,' she said. But, after reading the script, she changed her mind. 'No,' she informed Russell by letter, 'I don't want to do another sexually neurotic lady.'

'That enraged him,' said Glenda. 'So he wrote me a rude letter, and I wrote him a rude letter back.'

Russell's account, according to Charles Marowitz, was slightly more informative. It seems that in his original conception of the film, Russell planned to include the scene in which Sister Jeanne, after her death, had her head cut off, placed in a glass casket and then placed on the altar in her own convent. People would then come, on their knees, to pay homage to the severed head. But in the final script, Russell found it necessary to remove this sequence as it tended to make Sister Jeanne too much the focus of the story. 'When Glenda saw the final script, which ended with the death of the leading man [Oliver Reed], she said, "That's not the way you told it to me," which I had to admit was true,' Russell recounted. 'She'd loved the idea of her head in a casket and everyone worshipping her on their knees. And with all that gone, she'd have just been back in the madhouse again.'

Marriage Lines

Glenda's next film role was in John Schlesinger's *Sunday, Bloody Sunday* (1971), in which she and Peter Finch shared a young man's affections; Murray Head, from the London cast of *Hair*, played the bisexual young man, a kinetic sculptor in his twenties. The action of the drama, which is set in London, spans ten days during the course of which the trio eat, sleep, talk, work, argue and make love. All know it cannot last indefinitely, but, as Finch says at the end, 'You know you only have half a loaf, but that's better than none at all.'

Finch, as the homosexual Jewish doctor, was fifty-three and enjoying a resurgence in his professional fortunes. He had been a rebel and a non-conformist in his time. A ruggedly handsome man with weather-beaten features projecting intelligence, sensitivity and warmth, he proved himself capable of roles suggesting both strength and subtlety; he was particularly noted for his reticent characterizations of publicly successful men whose emotional life was in some way flawed – a notable instance being Oscar Wilde in *The Trials of Oscar Wilde*. When his agent put a call through from London to his home in Jamaica to say that he was wanted for *Sunday, Bloody Sunday*, he was at first guarded.

'I'm not a queer,' protested Finch.

'No, dear,' said his agent, 'but I'd like to see you play one to prove you're an actor.'

Glenda knew what the agent meant, as did Finch later on. 'We had to be so precise,' said Glenda, who found the intelligent, discontented divorcee, Alex Greville, her most demanding role to date. 'Those people have rich emotional lives, but they don't make big emotional gestures. So everything had to be done through inflection and suggestion. The movie's great achievement was showing a homosexual relationship as a loving relationship. But the woman still got punished in the end, didn't she? Couldn't we, just once, get away with something?'

On this occasion Glenda and Finch got on well together – she even called him 'an angel in human form' – but in a later film her behaviour unnerved him to such an extent that his lip developed a painful sore. As for Schlesinger, Oscar-winning director of *Billy Liar, Darling, Midnight Cowboy* and *Far From the Madding Crowd* (Finch's first movie for the English film-maker),

Glenda was initially suspicious of the man. 'I had this vision of him being incredibly intellectual and locked into his head,' she said, 'and there never being a smile, let alone a laugh, on the set.' She found that this was not the case.

Schlesinger was no less wary of directing this 'rather grand' lady from the Royal Shakespeare Company: 'I was terrified at the idea of working with her because I thought she would be very serious-minded.' At least the reality did not disappoint him. Later, he was even delighted to discover in the actress 'a great sense of fun and humour'. His leading lady accused him of being 'the worst bloody giggler in the world', and complained somewhat dryly that he 'wanted to catch every damned flicker of the eyelid: can you imagine how long it takes to light the flicker of an eyelid?'

The English director was attracted to Glenda in the first place because of her 'no-holds-barred sexuality'. He offered her the role the day after he saw *Women in Love*, in part, at least, because 'a certain sort of maternal quality in her pops up to the surface'. But it was one more film where the actress thought, 'Christ, my mother mustn't come to see me in *this* . . . .' Glenda was nude again, though rather more discreetly than of late. 'It's very gentle nudity,' she argued. 'The way people would make love when they're *in* love. Not always biting each other in the jugular vein and all that.'

The film was an unexpected success, being almost universally praised for its depth in exploring human relationships, and even Schlesinger was surprised by its cordial reception. Stanley Kauffmann in his *New Republic* review found Glenda's performance 'beautifully modulated, with humour and sharp slivers of pain and little catlike enjoyments', while Pauline Kael in the *New Yorker* noted that she gave the film a 'needed tensile strength' but displayed 'a slightly repellent hardness' that was not suited to the role. But in Hollywood it brought her an Academy Award nomination as best actress, with Oscar nominations also for Finch, Schlesinger, and screenwriter

Penelope Gilliatt; Britain's Society of Film and Television Arts voted Glenda the best actress of the year, Finch best actor, and Schlesinger best director. 'It's nice to receive something like this from your own country,' said Glenda in clipped tones when she received the award from Princess Alexandra at the Royal Albert Hall.

After the release of *Sunday, Bloody Sunday* she began to react angrily to the world's apparently insatiable obsession with matters pertaining to 'Glenda-the-Flesh-Queen'. 'Some actresses,' she snorted, 'have asked to be naked because they have superb figures. Mine is not impressive. Others need that kind of erotic presentation for their careers, but I don't. If it was an interesting part, then I have taken my clothes off. It's not a difficult thing to do, but there's nothing arousing about it.'

While shooting *Sunday, Bloody Sunday* at Bray Studios, where they made the Hammer horror movies, she found herself naked in bed with actor Tony Britton at 9 a.m. They had never met before.

'How do you do,' said Britton, shaking Glenda's hand. 'I'm a great admirer of your work. How nice to see you.'

'Same here.'

'Come on! Come on!' called Schlesinger. 'Let's get cracking. Positions everybody . . . .'

As Glenda recalled, 'We divested ourselves of our dressing-gowns, climbed into bed stark naked, and two perfect strangers started to make love for the camera. Then it was "CUT!" . . . "Good-bye, Tony" . . . "Good-bye, Glenda." And I'd hardly had time to ask, "With whom am I having the pleasure?"'

Her views on sex, as always, were doggedly down-to-earth. 'Although you would think sex is the most important thing in the world, it actually isn't,' she pointed out coolly. 'It's no more or less important than any other human appetite. The fact that it is wrapped up in love – which is not a human appetite but a human need – creates one of the greatest difficulties in essaying love on the screen.' Later, when Finch, Schlesinger and Glenda had gone their separate ways, the actress from Hoylake took stock of what she had achieved so far in the cinema. It came as something of a shock to her. 'I'm through with the excesses,' she concluded. 'Oh God, I've had enough of those mouth-foaming, rolling-on-the-floor orgasm bits for a while. I've done it all, and I'm really not ready to fall into it all again . . . .'

Glenda still liked to bill herself as the housewife who just happened to make movies. Because in films her face was invariably heavily made up, and in private life she tended to abandon make-up entirely, the general public rarely recognized her as the woman they had seen in the cinema the night before. 'Thank God,' said Glenda. 'But if they do recognize me there is a modicum of surprise in the supermarkets that I should actually be there at all. People gasp and say, "You're *not* Glenda Jackson?" They don't expect a film star to have to do anything that relates to everyday life. How do they think I eat?'

She got away with not being recognized 'mostly because their expectation of me would be of someone miraculously swathed in mink and diamonds ... and all they see is a woman in Marks & Spencer jeans who spends her entire life toting bulging plastic carrier bags full of junk, bearing the butcher's name, because she loses handbags.' During this period she would spend hours in the local launderette, watching her washing go round and chatting to the other housewives, none of whom seemed to be even remotely aware that they had been talking to Charlotte, Gudrun, Nina and Alex. But all that stopped when Roy bought her a washing machine. 'It never crossed my mind to get one,' she said. 'I don't think of things like that.' She was the original housewife superstar. She maintained, 'I enjoy being a housewife. If I had to choose between that and acting, I'd be a housewife.' So she found herself engaged in a ceaseless struggle to live out some semblance of an 'ordinary' life in Blackheath. If she arrived home early, she cooked the dinner, and sometimes cooked it when she got home late.

'Sometimes I have to wait,' said Roy, 'but I don't mind. I'm not a great eater. We get into the car and load it up at Sainsbury's once a week. Glenda chooses everything.'

With Glenda, being *ordinary* in private life verged on the obsessive. Her priorities were pre-ordained. She looked after Daniel, she cooked, watched television, saw friends from time to time, enjoyed gardening, knitting (but not mending: 'What's wrong with safety pins?'), eating apples, and reading Jane Austen. In the garden, she firmly believed in talking to her plants: 'Grow, you buggers.' She said, 'You really feel like God when you pick the peas you've grown in your back garden.'

Soon after the birth of Daniel, Roy took Glenda to Hatton Garden, the precious-stones centre in London, to buy a spectacular emerald ring, but she did not like it. She returned home, much happier, with 75p-worth of green plants. It was only later she discovered the ring had been worth £400. 'Extra-ordinary woman,' muttered Roy. 'Fancy preferring plants to an emerald.' (She was notorious for losing rings. In the first decade of her marriage she was always losing wedding rings in the garden.)

Although a cleaning woman came in three times a week, Glenda still did the 'Hoovering' and housework. 'I *do* do it,' she insisted. 'If there's any housekeeping done over the weekend, it's done by me.' She felt that scrubbing the floors, making dinner or washing the dishes was 'sheer relax-ation' after a hard day or night at work. Whenever possible, she also did her own shopping in the local shops. When a reporter pointed out that her life seemed surprisingly suburban for a movie star, she replied angrily, 'For God's sake! What did you expect ...?"

'I still don't really understand her,' said Oliver Reed, ' – the fact that she relegates almost everything to the fish-pond, including her Oscar. It's almost as though she's *got* to live in Blackheath.'

'I'd be surprised if she lived anywhere else *but* Blackheath,' explained Vladek Sheybal. 'I remember her saying once, which I understand very well, "If I couldn't go to the butcher to buy my Sunday joint, I couldn't be an actress." I absolutely agree. Doing her own shopping, doing her own cooking and cleaning, gives her an injection into life. It's a part of her uniqueness.'

As always, Glenda's reasoning was built on a solid, practical foundation. She insisted, 'If, as an actor, you allow yourself to be cocooned from the boring pin-pricks of day-to-day existence – like standing in a queue at the butcher's or any of the other dreary little events that we all have in our daily lives – you begin to lose your lifeline to what people *are*. And if you lose *that*, you eventually lose the ability to act.'

An American executive visiting her home was taken aback by the sparseness of its furnishings. 'Glenda,' he said, weighing his words, 'I hope you'll forgive me for being rude, but as I throw an eye on your drawing room I find it rather modest for one of the world's highest-paid actresses.'

'Really?' she queried. 'I find it rather comfortable.'

'It is,' replied the visitor, 'but I was expecting elaborate wall groupings, Turkish toss-pillows, fun furs all over the floor – you know, the whole Cecil Beaton number.'

'I suppose I'm rather mean,' she then confessed. 'It must come from the early days of my marriage when Roy and I were finding things a bit bleak. We were very poor . . . .'

Her meanness was well known within the business. She did not go in for expensive items, and never had. She refused to indulge in the luxury of maids and 'gofers' to look after her life: 'I really don't know why people should do things for you that you can perfectly well do for yourself.' Later: 'Oh yes,' she said, 'I'm incredibly mean. I'll be foolishly extravagant and rush out and buy a lot of books, because I reason that they're okay things to spend money on; but it was years before I spared the cash to buy a vacuum cleaner.'

'She was totally mean,' affirmed RSC colleague Patrick Stewart. 'I remember going to a pub with her in a little village outside Stratford. There were six of us, three of whom had gone ahead, and three of us arrived in the pub at the same time. I said, "Okay, what are you having to drink?", and Glenda said, "No, no, we'll all buy our own," and she went ahead and ordered a bottle of Guinness for herself. Oh shit, that's weird! I think that's *off*, really.'

The interior of her house at Blackheath may not be a monument to meanness, but then neither is it a celebration of runaway extravagance. On the occasions I called there, there was always a sense of restrained disorder. White lace curtains billowed mysteriously in the breeze from the open windows, and several pots of slender rubber plants rustled a weird counterpoint.

I detected shades of D. H. Lawrence – which became more tangible as I took in the etchings of the novelist at the top of the stairs, the cinema poster advertising *Women In Love*, the portrait of Lawrence which Glenda had painted while she was filming. The whole 'feel' of the place was of a house that was lived in, not on show. Like the mistress of the abode. 'I'm a great collector of furniture, things, pictures,' said Roy. 'Glenda is a great chucker-out, but we don't argue about *choice*. Of course, we still have rows, although sometimes in the middle of them, when I'm telling her to push off, I do realize it's all hers, the house and everything. Funnily enough, it never occurs to her to say it to me – she has no sense of material possessions at all.'

Roy's love of paintings, and the theatre's lack of interest in his professional skills, inspired the notion that he should open his own art gallery (with Glenda's money) in near-by Greenwich High Street. The Room, as it was called, opened just as Glenda was becoming involved in Schlesinger's cinematic *ménage à trois*, and served primarily as a showplace for new young artists. Having failed in showbusiness, it was important to Roy that he should succeed in *something*, and the world of art seemed as good a place as any in which to make his mark. 'I want to exhibit paintings which I would like to have myself,' he said. 'It's going to be a battle for Glenda and me not to be our own best customers.'

Glenda mustered a tremendous show of interest. 'One tends to get stuck in a theatrical mould,' she told people, 'so now I'm finding it terribly exciting to move into the world of painters and sculptors.'

Roy, a tall, exotic, gaunt-faced man, is no fool. He was well aware that the gallery would not have attracted the same kind of publicity if he had not been married to Glenda. 'That brought people in, which is super,' he acknowledged. But the people did not continue to flood through the door in sufficient numbers to make it a profitable concern. After a splash reopening in June 1972, he was forced to concede that art administration was not his forte and, two years later, he sold the business. It was a bitter disappointment to a man who desperately needed to show the world that he was more than just 'Mr Jackson' – a form of address that was known to turn him white with rage. Failure hit him hard, though both he and Glenda went to considerable lengths to play it down. Whatever rows they might have had in private – 'We fight like hell,' Roy admitted – Glenda always maintained a public stance that suggested that here were two very contented human beings.

'When she earned twice as much as me,' said Roy, 'I was, I think, resentful, jealous and affronted. When she earned ten times as much, I began to turn it to my advantage. Now she earns so much more that it would be ludicrous for me even to think of it.'

What made their marriage work, it would seem, was what Roy referred to as 'our complete freedom'. But this freedom seemed to many people to be rather more in Glenda's favour, through her own sheer talent: she was in demand, free to do as she wished; he was much more severely constrained by a less visible talent and by eking out an existence as 'Glenda Jackson's husband'. She was idolized; he was ignored. She paid the mortgage; he paid the price. She was surprised by everything ... but he was not. 'It's ironical really,' she said, 'because ever since Daniel was born I've been teetering on the edge of giving up work altogether, but everybody suddenly keeps offering me the most super jobs.'

Roy tried desperately to be philosophical. 'Of course I was jealous at first,' he said, 'but now I know I have fourteen years' advantage over any man she meets, and I don't worry about her. But I still find it very flattering that she comes home to me.' In time he would remember those words with more than a touch of irony.

At about this time Glenda made the first of many statements on the theme of 'retirement'. While filming *Sunday, Bloody Sunday* she announced, 'I can't see acting keeping its grip on me for the rest of my life. I'd like to do something socially useful or adopt lots of children.' Hardly a month has gone by, up to the present day, when she has not trotted out that story or some variation on it. But Roy was frankly sceptical: 'She talks a lot about doing social work, but I don't really know whether she'd do it. She certainly wouldn't stay at home – she'd be the lousiest mother and the lousiest house-wife if she had nothing else to do.'

While Glenda was talking about social work, Polish director Roman Polanski was talking about nudity – again. He was planning a screen version of *Macbeth*, with Jon Finch in the title role, and he went out of his way to try to convince Glenda that the role of Lady Macbeth – complete with much bare flesh – might have been written with her in mind. She turned him down flat. 'I don't fancy six weeks on location,' she told him, 'walking through that damned gorse for next to no money.' The part went to Francesca Annis; but the money, for Glenda, was not exactly what counted. It was well known in movie circles that if Glenda really liked a part she would do it for next to nothing – perhaps even for nothing.

Instead, she compromised, and accepted a contract with BBC television to star as England's Virgin Queen in a lavish six-part series, *Elizabeth R*, in which she was required to age from fifteen to sixty-nine ('I looked like an old turtle'). Television was not a medium in which she was vastly experienced, and so it was with some trepidation that she accepted the challenge of the mammoth six ninety-minute segments. But the result ('posh escapism', she called it) was a resounding popular success, both for the series and for Glenda personally, reaping all the major television awards in Britain and two Emmys (one of them Glenda's) in the United States, and becoming the most acclaimed and viewed drama series throughout the world. It even caused a sensation in Peking. The cinema's Queen of the Flesh became television's queen of the year.

Elizabeth I, high-handed and autocratic, was very much Glenda's kind of woman. She was intrigued by the last of the Tudor monarchs who gave her name to an age of outstanding national achievement and who died a childless spinster. 'I like Elizabeth,' she said categorically. 'She's about eighteen people under one skin and she made sure that no one ever really got to the central character.' Yes, Glenda could equate with that. 'She was an arrogant, selfish, flamboyant and thoroughly mean woman,' added the actress about whom similar claims have been made.

To prepare for the role, she took riding lessons from a teacher so smart (she taught the present Queen) that the activity was called equitation, never riding. She also took driving lessons so that she could get to the studio each day. The BBC built her an appropriately Plantagenet nose, and, to duplicate Elizabeth I's enormously high forehead, half of her head was shaved. 'I couldn't look at her at first,' remembered Roy, who accused his wife of being 'imperious' at home during the making of the series. 'It was a shock to see a half-bald head on the pillow in the morning.' And her 'imperiousness' at home? 'She was soon told where she could put that role,' said her husband reprovingly.

Although she rarely missed an opportunity to voice her dislike of working in television – 'It seems to have all the faults of the theatre and none of its advantages, and all the faults of film and none of its advantages' – *Elizabeth R* producer Roderick Graham said that he had rarely met anyone so painstaking in TV. 'Glenda,' he explained, 'has a fantastic sense of danger. You never know what she'll do next. She can go from total woman to total politician in mid-sentence. After six episodes, she now knows more about Elizabeth than I do. If it's part of the role, she'll do it, whatever it is. She's learned to ride, shoot a bow and arrow, play the virginal, dance and do italic handwriting. It was she herself who suggested shaving her head at the front so she would have a high forehead like Elizabeth.'

However, in retrospect, Glenda was far from happy with her performance. She was convinced she had not made Elizabeth extraordinary enough: 'I should have given her a lot more brilliance.' And there were those who agreed with her. 'She could be very uneven as an actress,' said Vladek Sheybal. 'I'm a great admirer of Glenda's work, but I don't think she was good in *Elizabeth R.* She was just average. She had scenes where I thought, "Christ, if only I could have directed her in that, she could have done it fantastically well." Instead, she just acted like an accomplished repertory company actress. Watching it, I thought "Glenda, no, no!"'

II
Just Misunderstood?

One of the consequences of Glenda's international stardom was that she no longer felt able to accept many small *fun* parts in films – such as her cameo in Ken Russell's screen version of Sandy Wilson's empty-headed musical, *The Boy Friend* (1971), in which she played the actress whose broken leg gave Twiggy her break. 'You can't do it that often, that's the sad thing, because people feel cheated,' she said regretfully.

But her next movie, she told people, 'should be a lark'. (Her work on *The Boy Friend* was sandwiched between *Elizabeth R* and *Mary, Queen of Scots*.) She was signed to portray the Virgin Queen once more – this time opposite Vanessa Redgrave's titular role – in Hal Wallis's blatantly 'Hollywood' conception of *Mary, Queen of Scots*, which was subsequently chosen for the Royal Film Performance of 1972. Just six weeks separated the recording of the last episode of *Elizabeth R* from the first day of shooting along the Scottish border for a film which, contrary to history, included a scene in which the two queens came together for a meeting. Glenda asked for a re-write, but Hollywood mentality was obdurate.

In the interests of authenticity, Glenda once again submitted her forehead to daily shavings, and off came a good three inches from her hair-line. 'I could have a worn a plastic wig, but they don't work,' she maintained. 'They're fine for long shots, but when the cameras come close in, it doesn't move like skin. It seems ridiculous to sabotage hours of hard slogging work if people in cinemas say, "Oh look! The top three inches of her forehead don't move!"' Hair stylist Harold Leighton warned her that her hair might not grow again if she repeatedly shaved her head. She didn't care; authenticity was all.

From the first day of shooting, Glenda made it known that she had grave reservations about making the film. Having just played Elizabeth on television, she was bored with the role. There was also a more basic nervousness stemming from the fact that her part was undeniably smaller than Vanessa Redgrave's. 'I'd much prefer Vanessa's part,' she grumbled. Hal Wallis failed to convince her that the role of Elizabeth was worth taking and for a while the project hung in the balance. Universal's Edd Henry later flew over and, after meeting the reluctant actress at her Blackheath home, finally managed to change Glenda's mind. 'But she insisted on doing all her scenes in three and a half weeks, before boredom affected her performance,' recalled a considerably chastened Hal Wallis. 'All her scenes had to be done first, which meant a major reworking of the script. We wanted her, and we had to put up with it.'

Trevor Howard, who played Lord Burghley, complained to director Charles Jarrott one day, 'I've just spent over a year on *Ryan's Daughter*. Now I have to do this picture in three and a half weeks. Isn't there a middle way?' There was not. Glenda had spoken and her conditions had to be met. She declared later, rather coyly, under the circumstances, 'They've been most awfully accommodating at adjusting their shooting schedule to fit me in early.'

Glenda's personality touched members of the cast in different ways. At the party to launch the shooting, Vernon Dobtcheff (who played the Duc de Guise) found she was 'her usual trim and forthright self'. Nigel Davenport – who, as the Earl of Bothwell, had two brief scenes with Glenda – noted that in appearing in front of the camera with her there was 'a sense of speed and clinical efficiency; each scene was completed almost before you realized it had started'.

Yet the film itself, despite all the concessions made to her, soon died on the actress. She looked back on the project with horror and referred to it as the first film of which she was ashamed to be a part. 'One really shouldn't do films like that,' she growled, 'especially if like me you're a silly cow and talk about your artistic principles and then go blithely into productions which you know bloody well are going to make you compromise and betray them.' She lambasted her own performance as 'a bit of a re-hash'.

Whatever her misgivings, Glenda was rapidly becoming a movie actress to be reckoned with, and to thousands of viewers who never strayed far from their television sets, she was a new discovery. Success for Glenda signalled a dramatic increase in press interviews and publicity jaunts; neither activities she enjoyed. Hollywood columnist Dorothy Manners cooed: 'No doubt about it, Glenda Jackson is the premier actress of the year. For my money, she deserves all the plaudits.' The columnist's praise was generously matched by that of Bette Davis, who predicted: 'Glenda Jackson is going to have an incredible career. She makes me think of myself. She hasn't got the motion picture beautiful face, and neither have I. But she cares and is dedicated. That counts.'

Film offers poured in. She was approached to star in a Richard Fleischer property called *The Brontës*, to play Charlotte alongside Mia Farrow's Emily, Hayley Mills's Anne and John Hurt's Branwell. Romanian producer Samuel Bronston, who saw everything on an epic scale (*King of Kings*, *El Cid*, *The Fall of the Roman Empire*), wanted Glenda to play the title role in a monumental production of *Isabella of Spain*; she was the lady, it will be recalled, who hocked all those jewels to enable Christopher Columbus to sail off and

20, 21, 22

Three films with Oliver Reed: (*above*) as country-woman Alice in *The Triple Echo* (1972); (*below left*) as Gudrun in *Women in Love* (1969); and (*below right*) as the idealist schoolteacher Conor MacMichael in an alfresco staff meeting in *The Class of Miss Mac-Michael* (1978).

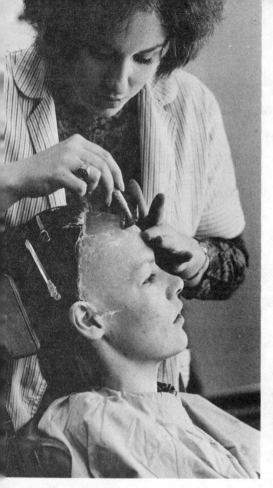

23
Glenda's head receives a close shave for her portrayal of England's Virgin Queen in BBC Television's award-winning series *Elizabeth R* (1971).

24
After a good lather and shave, the finished result – made up and costumed for 'Sweet England's Pride', the sixth and final episode of *Elizabeth R*.

25

At London's Savoy Hotel in 1970 to receive the Film Actress of the Year award from the Variety Club of Great Britain – with Wendy Craig (BBC TV Personality of the Year) and (*right*) Margaret Leighton (Stage Actress of the Year), who worked with Glenda shortly afterwards in *Bequest to the Nation*.

26, 27

Glenda is one of only ten actresses to receive more than one Hollywood Oscar: (*above left*) producer Hal B. Wallis presents Glenda with her Best Actress Oscar, in 1971, for her performance in *Women in Love*; (*above right*) with Oscar number two, in 1974, for her film comedy début in *A Touch of Class*.

28
Glenda, the suburban mother, with two-year-old son, Daniel, at home in Blackheath.

29
Domestic chores are momentarily forgotten as, feet up, Glenda acts the 'glamorous movie star at home' role . . . for this particular film star, an uncharacteristic image.

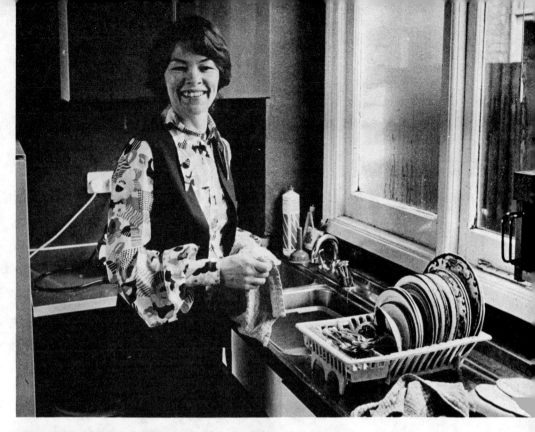

30
Home-lover Glenda feels that scrubbing the floors, making dinner or washing the dishes is sheer relaxation after a hard day or night at work.

31
'I love my garden,' says Glenda. 'I've got some wellies somewhere, but I can't find them – which means I'm ruining most of my shoes.'

32, 33

Glenda comes to terms with two sexually inverted screen lovers: (*above*) as Nina Milukova, the nymphomaniac wife of Tchaikovsky (Richard Chamberlain) in Ken Russell's *The Music Lovers* (1970), and (*right*) as Alex Greville, who is in love with a bi-sexual designer (Murray Head, *left*), who, in turn, is in love with a homosexual Jewish doctor (Peter Finch), in John Schlesinger's *Sunday, Bloody Sunday* (1971).

34, 35
Glenda's movie roles cause pain to two further screen lovers: (*left*) as the tempestuous Lady Hamilton who causes Peter Finch's Admiral Lord Nelson much emotional agony in *Bequest to the Nation* (1973), and (*below*) as Vicki Allessio, who induces more than physical agony in the life of George Segal in Mel Frank's *A Touch of Class* (1972).

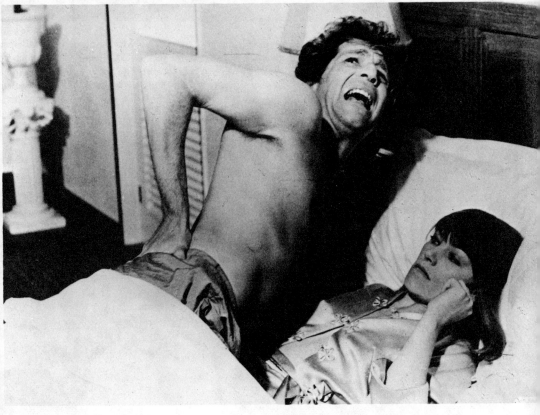

36, 37

Glenda hilarious, Glenda serious. (*Above*) As Cleopatra to Ernie Wise's Mark Antony (*left*) and Eric Morecambe's Octavius Caesar in *The Morecambe and Wise Show*, the 1971 BBC TV production which led to Glenda being cast for her first comedy film, *A Touch of Class*. (*Below*) The socio-politically-minded Glenda in 1973, with showbusiness colleagues Malcolm McDowell, Lindsay Anderson, Michael Medwin and Albert Finney, demonstrating in London outside the Indonesian Embassy in support of political prisoners held in that country without trial.

discover America. Neither enterprise got off the drawing-board. Glenda was bitterly disappointed: the role of Queen Isabella would have been the greatest plum in her acting career.

The cancellation of the Bronston pageant enabled Glenda to devote her unexpectedly free time to a low-budget British film, *The Triple Echo* (1972), based on a novel by the English pastoral writer H. E. Bates. Shot entirely on location in Wiltshire and Dorset, and completed in six weeks, it became a project very dear to Glenda's heart – to the extent that both she and co-star Oliver Reed, together again for the first time since *Women in Love*, agreed to accept 'short' money plus a percentage of the profits. Alas, there were to be no profits. Set in the remote English countryside during the Second World War, it tells of Glenda's passion for Brian Deacon, a young deserter, and her determination not to hand him over to the military authorities who beleaguer her isolated farm. She resorts to disguising the boy as her sister. This subterfuge is successful at first but leads to bizarre consequences as they slowly discover their sexual roles beginning to change and the emergence of new erotic fantasies. The advent of a bull-like sergeant, Oliver Reed, who is completely deceived by the boy's disguise and attempts to seduce both 'sisters', brings about the film's savage climax.

Reed, in fact, very nearly bolted from the project, because the seduction of Glenda *and* a man seemed to be at odds with his macho image. 'In the script it said I had to kiss the soldier while feeling his bollocks, and I said no,' Reed recalled. 'So they said Glenda Jackson was in the film, and I still refused to do it. I said, "Do I have a love affair with Glenda?" and they said, "No, she has a love affair with another fellow – but the fellow is dressed up as a girl." So I said I'd do it if I didn't have to kiss the fellow; and so we made it.'

During the making of the film Glenda and Reed received a lot of bad press about their off-screen relationship, which was put across as being about as cosy as a pair of angry grizzly bears. 'Working with Glenda,' said Reed, 'is rather like being run over by a Bedford truck.' While describing their feuding as 'a myth', Glenda then intimated quite a different picture: 'We're neither the other's favourite sort of person. I mean, I certainly don't hate him ... I neither like nor dislike Oliver on a personal level.' But visitors to the set noticed that Glenda, with a scarf over her 1940s wig and gum boots on her feet, invariably sat alone on a rickety canvas chair between takes, almost cold-shouldered by the other actors and totally ignored by Reed. Actress Judy Loe found her 'very straightforward, very business-like'.

Her 'business-like' manner has been best described as being mean with life's social refinements. She has no interest in pleasantries, no tolerance of evasions. When it comes to verbal intercourse, her philosophy is 'Waste not, want not.' Explains RSC colleague Patrick Stewart: 'There are some stars who can sit down and talk to complete strangers for five minutes and be totally charming, but Glenda was not one of them. She'd never waste time on people in that way.' She enjoyed then virtually no social life, and had no friends outside the profession and not many within. Her main standby was a small group of people with whom she'd been at RADA, none of them famous. She kept her profile so low that it sometimes threatened to fade into oblivion.

'I don't think anyone fully understands Glenda,' said Roy, 'because she is essentially a very private person, even to me.'

Her agent Peter Crouch claimed that only people who knew her could appreciate just *how* private a person she was: 'I remember when she was at Stratford, actors would say to me, "Why doesn't she ever come to our parties? As soon as the curtain is down, she packs up and goes home." Well, that's her way. It always has been. She keeps herself to herself. It isn't meant to be rude and it isn't meant to be cold, and it's very sad if people interpret it that way.'

'She's the fastest "trapper" I know,' said Geraldine Addison. 'When we finish at night, within thirty seconds she's gone from the studios. We just say "she traps fast", goes fast. I sometimes go to her dressing room to say good night, because I've only just left the set, and she's out of costume and make-up, and gone. It's just that her home is so important to her and, when he was younger, she liked to see Daniel before he went to bed. I don't think it's got anything to do with being antisocial.'

But Glenda confessed otherwise: 'I'm *notoriously* antisocial.' She also explained, 'I don't go to work to make friends, and I think a lot of people do. I go to work to work.'

Big gatherings frightened her and, as in her YMCA days as a girl, she always hated being part of a group: 'I find a room full of strangers difficult to deal with.' She automatically refused most of the invitations that were sent to her – first nights, premières, nightclubs, award ceremonies, and, above all, parties. (At cocktail parties she always seemed to fall over. She suffered from poor circulation and if she stood still for any length of time, she passed out.) Not so long ago, while appearing in a West End play, the management held a party in the stalls bar and Glenda strolled in looking as though she had just walked off a building site. She took one look at the gaggle of people – and turned tail. 'If people find that offensive, then there's really nothing I can do about it,' she later declared curtly.

She would accept only invitations that really appealed to her, and which posed no threat to her private life. She enjoyed talking to schools, for instance. But then her ability to get on with children was well known. 'They don't expect you to put on any sort of act,' she explained. She maintained that if your work involved make-believe and illusion, you were wise not to extend it into your private life: 'If you want real friends, then you must lead a "real" sort of life.'

'It's only a guess,' said another RSC actor, John Nettles, 'but I think she regards her private life as being sacrosanct and her professional life as being rather trivial and unimportant. There's no question that she can do the job, it's just that her attitude is different from the attitudes of most other women of her age. She's inaccessible. The face she turns towards her peers, and towards the profession at large, is that of the cold, lip-tight woman. But I think that's the price she pays for preserving some kind of sensitivity in her private life.'

Despite her chronic dislike of parties, Glenda decided to throw a party in Salisbury for the whole unit of *The Triple Echo*. 'What was so amazing about it was that she thoroughly enjoyed it,' noted Geraldine Addison. 'But then she wasn't expected to be anything but herself. It was *her* party.'

When the film 'wrapped', Glenda became increasingly preoccupied with her domestic life. Professionally, she felt she had essentially accomplished what she had set out to do, and she told Roy that she would be ready to quit the day Daniel, now three, said: 'I don't want you to go out, Mummy.' In Hollywood such familiar pronouncements had become grain-of-salt clichés. In England, at the end of the Hervey Road cul-de-sac, the forthright mistress of the house meant what she said. I recall being at the house when she said it. I recall, too, thinking that Daniel tended to have a mind and a will of his own, like his mother. She talked about having another child; she was too old for four, she said, so she would settle for two. She was thirty-five. It would have been a mistake to believe she was being blasé about her career. It was just that she was a very cool actress. Her straightforward conversation showed a remarkable intelligence. It was a mind at home with abstractions but oriented to the pragmatic, the real. It was a mind that seemed to relish the exercise of hard, clear thinking.

Family bonds forged during her childhood were totally unaffected by her success. She still much preferred to go home to Mum and Dad than take the kind of glamorous holiday she could well afford, and up in Hoylake no one made any concessions to her fame. 'If she started getting a bit uppity,' said Joan Jackson, 'we'd soon put her in her place.' And, being a Jackson, she meant it.

12
Feuding

All actors and actresses are ham-strung by the lack of imagination shown by the people who cast films and plays. They are inevitably stuck, for a certain length of time, with what first brought them to the public eye, and Glenda's particular breakthrough was to amaze audiences as a lunatic lady in the stage and film versions of *The Marat/Sade*. It is conceivable that if she had been a sensation playing a bright, frothy lady she might well have been associated ever more with playing bright, frothy ladies. 'People seem to think I'm good at playing maniacs or neurotics,' Glenda sighed, 'but I should hate it if everyone thought it was the *only* thing I can do.'

All this was about to change in her next film, *A Touch of Class* (1972), an amiable farce in which Glenda was transformed unexpectedly into a romantic comedienne in the style of an early Katharine Hepburn or Carole Lombard. She could not dump fast enough all those weighty period plots and costumes to get into the skin of a sophisticated career woman swinging around 1970s London on the lookout for an uncomplicated love affair with someone who would not be 'a pain in the ass when it's all over'. The sharp-faced, hawk-nosed George Segal, as a married American insurance executive on the make, obliged her. 'God, I hope I can do it!' exclaimed Glenda when Peter Crouch divulged that she had been offered a comedy role.

As it happened, veteran American writer-producer-director Melvin Frank, who had made a number of memorable Bob Hope and Danny Kaye comedies, had originally written Glenda's part for an American woman. But then he saw the English actress cavorting on television in a 1971 Christmas show with Britain's best comedy double act, Morecambe and Wise. She was grinding through a musical burlesque of Ginger Rogers. 'I said to myself, my God, is that Glenda Jackson?' Frank recalled. 'She's *funny*; she'd be terrific in *A Touch of Class*.'

Appearing as a guest star on *The Morecambe and Wise Show* was generally regarded as another kind of 'award' or 'honour': you had 'arrived' if the two comics asked you to appear on their show, an accolade, in fact, which was extended to Glenda on more occasions than to any other serious actress or actor. Glenda was delighted that the zany humour of the TV shows did more to change her 'serious' image than any other single factor. She had always wanted to play comedy but had never up to now been considered for it, so when the offer of the Morecambe and Wise spot came up, she was quick to accept: 'I said yes, terrific, of course.'

She was asked if Morecambe and Wise gave her any advice.

'Yes. *Louder, faster.*'

'Good advice?'

'Of course, the *best*. When we talk of Eric and Ern, we're talking about the jewels in the crown. You're not just working with them, you're working with their thirty years' experience, which is something money can't buy.'

So it was an ecstatic Mel Frank who caught Glenda in one of their shows. He was so impressed by her performance that he was on the phone the next morning to offer her the lead role opposite George Segal. 'Yes, yes,' she told him, 'I want to do comedy to see if I *can* do it.'

When the cameras started rolling at Lee Studios, just outside London, Frank described Glenda as 'the most magnificent acting instrument of our time'. He said, 'There are certain actors and actresses who you know exactly what it would feel like to direct. Spencer Tracy and James Cagney, for instance. Well, Glenda is in that class. It's exactly as I expected, like taking the controls of a new Rolls-Royce, gliding effortlessly, smoothly . . . .'

Early 'rushes' soon convinced the film unit that the elegant counterpoint playing of Glenda and Segal would remind audiences of those evergreen screen comedies of yesteryear which starred such performers as Cary Grant, Myrna Loy, James Stewart and Katharine Hepburn. 'It's fireworks all the time on the screen,' said Frank. 'There is this complementing quality between George and Glenda. He is the archetypal American cosmopolite and he can be very, very funny and never lose his sexuality. And Glenda is this curious mixture of things. She has this beautiful gentility that is inescapable, but when she is on screen with George there is a very tangible, raw sexuality. Strangely, when one of them is on screen without the other, there is a vacuum. You are just waiting for the other one to come back.'

Segal, who was already established as a likeable, popular player of neurotic middle-class men, arrived at the studios initially in awe of 'the great Glenda'. 'Here I was, plonked in a foreign country, and it was up to Glenda to make me feel at home,' said the former janitor, usher, and jazz musician from Columbia University. 'It wasn't easy for me. Her staggering TV series, *Elizabeth R*, was still fresh in my mind, and so I couldn't help thinking, "I believe I'm in the presence of one of the great actresses of the world." It was tough to change that feeling of veneration.'

But working with Richard Burton in *Who's Afraid of Virginia Woolf?* had at least prepared him for his session with Glenda, who, he was relieved to discover, was 'a definite T-shirt-and-blue-jeans-actress' at rehearsals. 'They're both consummate actors,' said Segal, 'and neither one ever discusses the work. I come out of the American school of actors who loved to talk about The Work and the process of acting. What both Burton knew and

Glenda knows is that there's no such thing. It's simply showing up and knowing your lines, and it comes right for some reason. This is a much more mystical approach than we have in the States, where we try to analyse every-thing. I've never had an analytical discussion with Glenda in my life, and *A Touch of Class* was consequently filled with a kind of raw energy from Glenda that I'd never really experienced before. Only one other actress whom I'd worked with had that sort of energy, and that was Barbra Streisand. In Glenda's case it wasn't so much the energy, but the *focus* of the energy, which was so compelling, and that's something which is almost impossible to find in an American actress. There's something about the *specific*, the logic of the piece, that delights the English; they've got the logic nailed when they arrive on the set, and the fun is that they do a twist on that, a curve. American actors have a problem just nailing the logic down, and there's a kind of a hope and a prayer that they'll go into something spontaneously. So, with Glenda, there was no way I could prepare for that. In our relationship, she did the prepar-ation and I did the showing up. It made for a conflict of energies. We met as professionals on the field of battle.'

There was always a desire, somewhere in the back of Glenda's mind, to operate in what she referred to as 'an American situation', and she found the experience of working in her first American film – albeit UK-based – extremely invigorating. Segal displayed what she regarded as the best aspects of the American way of work, which was an enormous, direct energy to match her own. 'He doesn't hang about,' she said with characteristic candour. 'You throw something and he catches it and tosses it back. I liked that directness very much.'

Mel Frank was struck by Glenda's ability to bring out the best in her fellow actors – though some of the actors themselves would challenge his point of view. Nevertheless, Frank had this to say on the subject: 'Take after take in one very complicated scene, calling for Segal to go into a complete rage, brought a perfectly matching response from Glenda no matter how much he varied the intensity of his performance. It was extraordinary.' Producer Bob Enders, who became Glenda's business partner and never lost an oppor-tunity to describe her as 'probably the finest and most versatile actress anywhere', had one further theory about her. 'She's so good,' he said, 'she makes other actors look better. Look what happened to George Segal in *A Touch of Class.*'

Playing a frisky divorcee, Glenda further demonstrated that you did not need to be built like Raquel Welch or resemble an early Elizabeth Taylor to hit the erotic bull's eye. Segal's confidential analysis: 'She feels the stirrings of sexuality, but it confuses her and makes her angry.' He added, 'She projects more sexuality than any other actress I know, certainly more than any American movie stars, who do a kind of imitation of it. I found our love scenes were so illuminating, because they revealed sexual areas of which I'd been completely unaware. She played them as if she was playing another Shakespearean role. She came to the bed prepared. I don't mean she was preparing for it each night at home: I mean all the great parts she played before she got to me. Her sexuality made the movie a smash, and it came across more strongly than in any pornographic film. She made it the sexual film of the Seventies. I think "sex" and "sexual" are weak words compared to what it was she projected. She made all the women love me and, in turn, all the men love her. The whole film changed into a sex comedy when her legs went up in our tussle on the bed and you got to see her pantie-hose. It galvanized the audience.'

Segal demolished the myth that, even in the most passionate love scenes, actors are only acting. He was more than once 'turned on' by Glenda's sexuality in the more erotic scenes. 'The first time I kissed her, well, there was all that sexual energy, I guess, that had been held down and kept in check, because we'd been together for a long time by then,' he said. 'It was explosive, and each time I kissed her the passion grew more intense. That's why the movie shimmers.'

It brought Glenda her second Hollywood Oscar (she thought she had only an 8–1 chance to be named Best Actress, with Barbra Streisand and Joanne Woodward the favourites), plus several other accolades: Best Actress in the London *Evening News* British Film Awards and a Golden Globe nomination. Since her mother possessed her first Oscar, Glenda said she would give her the second one as well: 'They'll make a lovely pair of bookends for my mother's sideboard.' She had won the Oscars, she said, because in each case her make-up and cameramen had 'done a lot with my tiny eyes and my rotten skin'.

Mel Frank wanted to capitalize on the commercial appeal of the double Oscar winner by trying to re-team her with Segal in the spoof Western, *The Duchess and the Dirtwater Fox*; Glenda declined and Goldie Hawn stepped into the re-tailored role. Columbia also tried to re-unite Glenda and Segal for a horrendously bad *Maltese Falcon* parody, *The Black Bird*; but Glenda wasn't interested, though her substitute – the French beauty Stéphane Audran – most certainly was. In its first year, *A Touch of Class* attracted $20 million at the box office, and so Glenda was offered dozens of films that capitalized on its success, all with Segal. 'Of course I wasn't interested,' she stated coolly.

Not everybody was impressed by the worldwide adulation of Glenda. Her old sparring partner, Ken Russell, let his white hair down one day in Hollywood in a way he would probably never have done back home in England. 'Lately she seems to have fallen into a clichéd way of screen acting,' he complained to an American interviewer. 'Maybe it's over-exposure, but I thought she was terrible in *A Touch of Class*. Totally mechanical . . . .' Glenda had made a similar accusation in an American publication about Russell's clichéd way of directing; so it was *touché*.

A frequent visitor to the set of *A Touch of Class* was the talented Welsh director James Cellan Jones, whose skill with television dramas was unsurpassed (the worldwide success of *The Forsyte Saga* was largely due to his sensitive handling of the stars, Eric Porter, Nyree Dawn Porter, Kenneth More and Susan Hampshire). He was about to make his movie début by directing a screen version of Terence Rattigan's stage play *Bequest to the Nation*, the story of Lord Nelson's long affair with the tempestuous Lady Hamilton. As Glenda was signed to play the notorious Emma Hamilton – to Peter Finch's Nelson – Jones decided to watch his future leading lady at work at Lee Studios.

Jones had heard rumours that Glenda could be, well, difficult ... especially with directors. He had already watched with growing horror a BBC television documentary about *The Triple Echo*, in which Glenda had been seen to take the film's director, Michael Apted, apart in public; Apted then, as Jones now, was a television man who was making his directorial début in the cinema. Jones's apprehension was not reduced when Mel Frank, after a tongue-lashing from Glenda, told Jones, 'I think you will find working with Miss Jackson an *interesting* experience.'

The film, released in America as *The Nelson Affair*, was shot at Shepperton Studios during the summer of 1972, and Jones embarked on the project with high hopes. He had always believed that the public's view of actors and directors locked in endless temperamental shouting matches was a fairy tale; but his explosive contact with Glenda proved to be anything but an excursion through never-never land. At the helm was the autocratic Hollywood independent producer, Hal Wallis, who insisted that only Glenda should play the blowzy and boozy Lady Hamilton and, because he was so impressed by the 'draw' of the double Oscar winner, he insisted on paying her £70,000 for three weeks' work, which could buy a lot of cigarettes in those days. Rattigan received the same amount for the screenplay, though by this time he regarded Hollywood money simply as 'fairy gold', and he made very little effort to adapt the stage drama. The resulting script, according to Jones, 'wasn't among Rattigan's best, as he was ill at the time'. The film takes up the story when Nelson is already a hero, while Lady Hamilton, no longer the famous beauty of her youth, is seen as an ageing, brandy-swigging, vulgar voluptuary. 'Her vulgarity is *not* something I dislike,' Glenda wanted everybody to know during filming.

But James Cellan Jones was not quite so enamoured of Glenda's physical conception of the part: 'I didn't like Hal Wallis's casting ideas from the start. Finchy wasn't ideal for Nelson, but was a marvellous actor. Lady Hamilton on the other hand, in 1805, was grossly fat and drunken – reportedly fourteen and a half stones – with a tempestuous but warm and outgoing nature. Elizabeth Taylor and Ava Gardner wanted to play her, but Hal was set on Glenda, who, to my mind, was physically and emotionally wrong. I had to go along with it. We started with quite a good working relationship. She was talented, we knew, and usually professional.

'Finchy, though, had a hard time from the outset. When he was nervous a sore used to appear on his upper lip, and it erupted during the first two days' shooting, because of a not very happy relationship with Glenda. It's very difficult to put one's finger on the numerous reasons why she made him so uncomfortable and insecure, but let me hazard some of them: she wouldn't talk to him at all, except when working; she ran to the dressing room as soon as a shot was over; she discussed things of mutual interest only through me; she wouldn't look him in the eye; she screamed when I had to restage in order not to show Finchy's nervous cold sore. All this contributed to Finchy's insecurity and, in the early stages, made him obsessive. Like most good actors and directors, he thought that work should be *fun*, and, with Glenda, it wasn't. Alethea, his wife, was passionately pro-Finchy. When she saw what Glenda's behaviour was doing to him, she went wild.'

The situation came to a head during a day's location shooting in the south Devonshire seaport of Dartmouth. Glenda was not there. Hal Wallis had brought down a lot of smart friends to see the day's filming, and Alethea, an uninhibited Jamaican lady, used the opportunity to put matters right.

'Listen, man,' she said, grabbing hold of the seventy-two-year-old producer in front of the crew and the assembled guests, 'if you don't get that fockin' Glenda Jackson to stop makin' a monkey out of my Finchy, I goin' to cut her fockin' throat.'

Wallis, visibly shaken, was struck dumb.

Back at Shepperton, ten days into shooting, Jones's relationship with Glenda started to sour. He noticed that her accent was becoming 'a little too grand' and told her so. 'Could we have a little more Wirral and a little less Blackheath?' he asked, since Emma Hamilton came from the same part of the country as Glenda. She scowled.

'From that point on, everything went downhill,' Jones remarked. 'She later took exception to a scene she was playing with Tony Quayle and recited it to him, his lines and hers, pouring scorn on the script – which wasn't, I have to say, too brilliant. He was a bit crushed.'

A few days later, while working on a big staircase set, Jones was giving special attention to Margaret Leighton, an actress he much admired – she was a beautiful and touching Lady Nelson – and who was almost crippled with arthritis.

'Hey, you, come here – *now*!' Glenda's voice boomed from the top of the staircase. 'I want to speak to you.'

'Do you mean me?' answered Jones, somewhat nonplussed.

'Yes, you, director – if that's what you call yourself.'

The sound stage went very quiet.

'What do you want?' Jones inquired, *sotto voce*.

'I want to see you in my dressing room at lunchtime. Be there.'

The meeting was frosty.

'I've never been spoken to by a director like that in my life,' screamed Glenda.

'And I've never been spoken to by an actress like that in *my* life,' answered Jones.

The remainder of the shooting was conducted on a highly frigid level, with Glenda refusing almost entirely to take directions. Eventually there was an *impasse* in the star–director relationship which the whole studio realized was unbridgeable. For Jones, the situation was intolerable and it was an extremely glum Glenda Jackson who turned up each day for filming. 'It appeared to be a most unhappy experience for her,' affirmed a member of the cast, Barbara Leigh-Hunt.

One or two other members of the film unit hinted at a more complex facet of Glenda's personality. Director of photography Gerry Fisher explained, 'I've seen her propose her characterization to the director, only to seem ill at ease when he, wilting under the force of her personality, agreed to everything.' But such 'ill at ease' behaviour from Glenda was rare. 'Like most real stars she had a very strong will,' said Peter Jeffrey, who played Philip of Spain in *Elizabeth R.* 'In a showdown with her director or a fellow actor she almost always got her own way.'

Jones later discovered that Hal Wallis had been secretly directing Glenda's post-synch dialogue in the evenings, a cloak-and-dagger operation that incensed him. 'Hal was no director, and the performance he was getting from Glenda wasn't good,' remembered Jones. 'I insisted on re-doing them, and it was a demonstration of her professionalism that, even though she hated my guts, she improved her performance in the dubbing theatre under my direction by a hundred per cent.'

The film was subsequently crucified by the critics, one of whom accused Glenda of appearing to be acting in 'a different film from everyone else'. Another concluded, 'In the kind of part she does best – practical, independent, highly intelligent *modern* young women – she has virtually no peer on the British stage or screen, but for some reason best known to themselves the powers-that-be insist on casting her in costume roles, a species for which vocally, physically and temperamentally she is totally unsuited.' But most critics, while hating the movie, loved what they saw of Glenda on the screen, and so did her director. 'I still think Glenda gave a good performance,' noted Jones, 'in spite of the script and her miscasting.' Glenda, though, felt disgusted and humiliated by her performance and, breaking every rule in the movie publicity handbook, went on British television, as the film was released, to inform viewers that she was appalling as Emma.

There was a furore. Her reputation with fellow professionals was already delicate; now they made their indignation public. A director with whom she had worked at the Royal Court deplored her arrogance in denouncing the film, and many voices accused her of 'unprofessional behaviour'. Her colleagues on the film, in fact, regarded what she had said publicly as nothing short of treason. Finch was furious. Wallis and Jones were apoplectic. Rattigan fumed. 'In the old days,' the playwright exclaimed, 'one's leading lady didn't feel it necessary to say such things, even if they were true. A film is, after all, a team effort. Perhaps it is the new fashion to knock the film you're in. But she has not, so far as I know, returned the cheque.'

'Glenda, sweetheart, will you please stop saying unkind things or no one will go to see the movie,' producer Wallis implored her via a transatlantic cable.

But then she proceeded to bang the final nail in the coffin by not attending the film's Royal Première. So why had she behaved so outrageously? Why had she spoken out so vehemently against the film? '*Why?*' she asked with renewed anger. 'Because what I said was *true*. It was a rotten, appalling performance. Bloody dreadful.'

Rattigan added mischievously, 'In saying she's miscast, I'm afraid she's right. It's a pity we didn't cast Liz Taylor, who would have loved to do it and would have done it for practically nothing.'

Director Charles Marowitz later came to Glenda's defence, noting that her personal candour was a rare trait in a profession in which everyone was hypersensitive about protocol and the necessity to 'keep in' with potential employers. He said he recognized the reasoning behind the action: 'Just as Glenda had never catered to the Hollywood notion of glamour, so she found it impossible to repress her own fiercely critical intelligence for the sake of some imposed sense of propriety.' Others attributed her particular stance to more complex reasons. 'What it seems she couldn't bear,' said an American writer who knew her, 'was that people should walk out of the theatre thinking the great Glenda Jackson was such a self-infatuated fool as to actually imagine she'd been *good*.'

'I like and respect actors,' James Cellan Jones said later, 'but Glenda is the only person I would refuse to work with again. She is talented, and sometimes brilliant, but I wouldn't do it again.'

When he thought the occasion merited it, Terence Rattigan could be as waspish as the best of them: 'Of course Miss Jackson did leave rather a lot out – Emma Hamilton's love for Nelson, for one thing, which is quite important. She played her as a mean-spirited bitch, instead of a great-hearted whore, but I suppose that is her range.' Glenda lost on points.

Part Four

A Star in Turmoil

Think of the storm roaming the sky uneasily like a dog
looking for a place to sleep in, listen to it growling.

Elizabeth Bishop,
Little Exercise, 1946

13
Good Works and Disasters

Towards the end of 1972 Glenda took stock of her life. The nagging thoughts about turning her back on acting had returned and she lay awake at night with worry. 'I'm reaching what is a very difficult age for an actress,' she told an acquaintance not associated with the business. 'You don't get offered the young heroine parts in films – not that I've ever been a glamorous figure anyway – and there's a very long way to go before I can play the part of the old lady. It's a period in a woman's life for which very few good parts are written, and if I were to carry on acting, I can only see the offers getting less and less interesting. There is simply no point in waiting around to start going downhill. I believe every actress has a peak, and my heyday is already past.'

There were many people within the industry who poured scorn on her ability as an actress in the first place. 'Her acting is contemptuous,' insisted American movie star Christopher Reeve. 'Not contemptible – *contemptuous*. It's as if her mind is elsewhere, as if she's only giving a small amount of energy to any given role. Never do I think she *is* the character.' He broke off and then added categorically, 'She'll never be in the same league, say, as Katharine Hepburn, Joan Crawford or Bette Davis, all those great actresses some people compare her with.'

'She's probably won more acting awards than any other British actress,' he was reminded.

'So what?' answered the man who had himself stepped on to the Oscar podium in Hollywood a few times. 'Am I supposed to be impressed by that? Awards breed awards in the same way as success breeds success; but it's got nothing to do with ability.'

Actor John Nettles, who worked with Glenda at the RSC, agreed about Glenda's 'detached' style of acting. 'I formed the impression that she only acted because she knew that that was what she did very well,' he said, 'and yet her heart always seemed to be somewhere else. There was a kind of ironic distancing about her, a kind of "stand back and look" quality, which is very peculiar in a woman. We've all seen a cynical hero – but a cynical woman? That's what gives her that "strange" quality. As an actor, you don't quite know where you are with her.'

'I think she has forced herself to be totally disciplined,' said James Cellan Jones. 'And just as Edith Evans said of herself that she was not beautiful but she could always convince an audience that she was, so Glenda grabs hold of the audience and says, "I AM IT!" Whatever she wants you to believe, you'll believe.'

None of her critics could deny that Glenda was compulsive viewing. The magic came from her mind and soul. 'It's an enormous relief to work with someone who is out to work, and that's it,' said actor Daniel Massey. Film producer Otto Plaschkes described her as 'probably the most professional actress I've worked with'. Oliver Reed said much the same thing: 'Glenda is the most professional actress I've ever met, and I would deem Raquel Welch second. I've worked with them both, Glenda and Raquel, and they are just *there.*'

A casual visitor to a movie set where Glenda was engaged on a new film role soon noticed the 'look' that appeared on her face when she finished a scene and her director called 'Cut!' The word would be instantly followed by an expression of sharp distaste. The eyes darted quickly to one side. The mouth curled sourly. She seemed to smirk in scorn. She repeated it after every single take. 'It's as if she must immediately dissociate herself from the person she is playing, reassert herself and her own values without losing a split second,' reflected the American writer Richard Grenier, who has observed her behind the cameras over many years. 'But toward whom is Glenda feeling such bitter scorn? The character? The movie? All human activities not having to do with social work? One wonders. One feels, of course, that Glenda's values are superior to other people's.'

By now, at the age of thirty-six, with twelve films behind her plus a classical period in the theatre, she was beginning to ask herself if acting still mattered. 'The old besetting urgency is no longer with me,' she confided to a friend. Theatre pangs were once again stirring within her, yet she knew only too well that she could never be happy in a permanent company: 'I used to feel like a floating spare part at Stratford, and there's nothing worse than the unadulterated companionship of other actors.' For the past six years she had not been offered a possible stage play, probably because she had been so busy complaining to the media how *awful* the West End was and how she could not bear audiences who just sat in their seats like steamed puddings. But one night, soon after completing *Bequest to the Nation*, she telephoned Peter Brook at the RSC's London theatre, the Aldwych, and heard all the backstage noises again and knew immediately that she must return at the first opportunity to live theatre.

While she considered the most appropriate vehicle for her return to the stage, film offers continued to drop through her letterbox for consideration. One concerned a Rolls-Royce family left derelict by the firm's collapse, another was based on the family of the suffragette Mrs Pankhurst, and a third was a screen version of Penelope Mortimer's novel *Home*. She declined and they came to nothing. There was also talk of a film about Jennie Jerome, mother of Sir Winston Churchill; it did not materialize. But the film world continued to acclaim her, and she flew to Paris to be honoured by the French Film Academy with the Étoile de Cristal for 'her all-round excellence as a motion picture actress'.

Back home, the Royal Shakespeare Company invited her to play Rosalind in *As You Like It* at Stratford, but other commitments made this impossible. She was subsequently asked to do Samuel Beckett's *Not I* at the Royal Court in the spring of 1973, which she accepted, but the Irish playwright changed his mind about the casting at the last moment and decided he would rather have Billie Whitelaw. This left her free to undertake a new stage comedy by the barrister–playwright John Mortimer. *Collaborators*, on which she had first offer, opened at London's Duchess Theatre in April 1973. The story was a love triangle involving a barrister-playwright (John Wood), his wife (Glenda) and a film producer (Joss Ackland).

When I talked to Glenda during rehearsals, which were being conducted in a basement studio in the West End, she was in ecstatic mood. If the play worked, she said, it would be her first London success in the commercial theatre. With the première of *A Touch of Class* still a month away, she was not yet regarded as a comedy actress, but *Collaborators* had whetted her appetite for the genre. All that worried her as we talked was the possibility that she might not get a single laugh: 'That would be horrific.' Although it was a sad-funny comedy, calculated to confuse its audience with its abrupt switches from laughter to savagery, audiences loved it and came flocking; and, despite less than rhapsodic reviews, it broke the Duchess Theatre's box-office record in its first week. Typical of the notices was Alan Brien's affectionate dressing down in *Plays and Players* magazine: '*Collaborators* is sometimes irritating but never boring, entertaining but rarely moving, often deeply pleasurable but totally painless. We are affected by the laughing gas, but no teeth are ever pulled, and only bared in fun.'

The critics were equally divided over Glenda's contribution to the pro-ceedings. 'Glenda Jackson plays the wife with her special kind of fierceness,' wrote Herbert Kretzmer in the *Daily Express*. 'Her strong presence distin-guishes and somewhat salvages the play's self-regarding style.' However, 'Glenda Jackson is not obvious casting as an earth-mother,' said *Plays and Players*, 'though much has been achieved by performers of her concentrated, spiky talents playing against physical type. But her role is basically that of the squash court wall against which John Wood bounces his balls – not that his balls seem much more than metaphorical.' And again, 'Glenda Jackson, as the wife, retains a set look of cold distaste for her husband which would freeze any man into impotence,' said Milton Shulman in the London *Evening Standard*. 'Even when she breaks into an affectionate dance it is only as sunny as the tinkle of ice cubes.'

Disappointed by the reviews – she desperately wanted to be taken seriously as a funny lady – she was in some way consoled to discover that when America's *Box Office* magazine released its 1973 listing of the twenty-five Top Moneymakers in the cinema, her name was among the eight actresses who made the list (the others were Barbra Streisand, Liza Minnelli, Diana Ross, Ali MacGraw, Dyan Cannon, Goldie Hawn and Jane Fonda).

One of the attractions of appearing in the West End, for Glenda, was that it would enable her to spend more time with Daniel, now four; and it was largely with her son in mind that, in July, when his school had broken up for the summer holidays, she flew to Italy to star in an Anglo–Italian movie of awesome strangeness, *The Tempter*. By allowing Daniel to accompany her, Glenda fulfilled two objectives: she gave him a wonderful holiday, and, along the way, avoided the long separations that film work inevitably dictated. At a time when the chinks in her relationship with Roy were beginning to show, Daniel became more than ever the centre of her life. 'She was absolutely besotted with the boy,' said Geraldine Addison. 'We could only work until 2 p.m., so we had the whole afternoon and weekends off. We used to go to the beach and Glenda and Dan had a whale of a time. There was an incredible closeness between them.'

Glenda and Daniel, along with Roy, moved into a comfortable but plain two-bedroom villa in the Frascati wine country south of Rome. *The Tempter* was the first film Glenda had made completely outside England and, much to her amazement, she fell in love with Italy. 'I've always thought that I could live nowhere but England,' she told the film's director and co-writer, Damiano Damiani, 'but Italy is very seductive.' She also discovered very quickly how popular she was in that country when, following a news conference at which she expressed her 'enormous admiration for Italian directors', she was jostled outside by excited paparazzi. The movie people sprinted to three identical chauffeured dark-blue Fiat 124s, with Glenda in the first, producer Anis Nohra in the second and assistant director Bergeres in the third. On a wide avenue near Rome's Polyclinic Hospital the last two cars pulled to a halt beside a bus, thereby blocking the street while Glenda's car sped off to escape the pursuing photographers. 'My God,' screamed Glenda as she clung tightly to the car's strap-handle, 'I thought all this went out with Fellini!'

She accepted her role in the film, which co-starred Claudio Cassinelli and Britain's Lisa Harrow, almost as if her new frothier direction in *A Touch of Class* had never existed. As a sadistic, sex-starved mother superior given to planting lusty kisses upon the lips of a bust of St Mary in a demented nunnery, she was back among the heavy, doom-laden, hopelessly neurotic women from whom she had said she wanted to escape. Her perverse and often reckless nature never ceased to amaze; but the film flickered through very few projectors in Britain and it was not seen by a large audience until BBC television included it in a Glenda Jackson season eight years later.

After Rome she was to have moved on to Paris for *Good Morning, Midnight*, a film adaptation of the Jean Rhys novel, but this was postponed and, ultimately, shelved. Instead, she returned home to Blackheath and pruned her roses ('I'm not a hobbyist, but if I have a hobby, it's gardening'). She later learned that she had been named best actress in the first reader poll of British film 'bests' conducted by the London *Evening News*. 'How nice,' she said dourly when told of the award.

Before the year was out she opened Wingfield Primary School in South London, and unveiled a portrait of herself in her TV role of Elizabeth I. After the opening ceremony she toured the buildings, watched pupils at work and helped supervise a play session with toddlers. Children and charity work associated with them were now occupying more and more of Glenda's free time. She still spoke of the day when she might work in a field concerned with family and children, though she debated whether she would ever obtain the relevant qualifications. Some insisted that, like Vanessa Redgrave, she protested too much about social conditions in Britain, yet her active concern about under-privileged and deprived children was genuine enough and, unlike certain actresses', without political motivation. It was no publicity gimmick, even though her name and photograph appeared above an Oxfam campaign advertisement in the national press – 'The day Glenda Jackson helped build an irrigation dam', it read.

She was president of the Toy Libraries Association, which supplied toys to the parents of handicapped children on a loan basis; she supported a home run by former actress Coral Atkins in Berkshire for emotionally disturbed children; and, in 1977, she agreed to make two television commercials for her first employer, Boots the Chemists, on the sole understanding that her entire fee of £60,000 should be donated to her favourite charities.

All this is a little known facet of Glenda's character because most of it went unpublicized. She worked tirelessly on behalf of the National Abortion Campaign and lost few opportunities actively to carry the flag of the abortionists. 'I really don't see how anyone has the right to make a woman have a child against her will,' she argued. 'It should be possible for her to go and have an abortion on the National Health Service without being made to feel criminal or sub-human.' One Sunday, at a benefit performance (*Glenda Jackson and Friends*) for the NAC at a London theatre, she raised more than £3,000. She spoke any time, anywhere, about her feelings on abortion. 'I think this Society for the Protection of the Unborn Child is the biggest load of rubbish,' she fumed. 'They are monstrous, all these middle-aged ladies well past child-bearing age, and all those bloody men, all drooling over babies. Babies grow up; these people are not willing to look after them when they're sixteen and start throwing bricks through windows, are they?'

She nursed a deep-seated belief that most of the social problems which beset our society are totally unnecessary: 'They can and *should* be eradicated.'

Soon after completing work on *The Tempter* she joined the executive of the National Association of Voluntary Hostels, an organization which found accommodation for 10,000 homeless people each year. If she believed in a cause, she would fight for it, whether it was organizing benefits for various women's rights movements or mounting the public rostrum to rally help for Shelter, providing gifts to small theatres going through hard times or protesting on behalf of persecuted Czechoslovak authors and actors. While appearing in London in *Collaborators* she knocked on the door of the Indonesian Embassy as part of a protest deputation to plead for political prisoners held in that country without trial: 'Do you realize Britain gives £11 million to Indonesia every year?'

At other times, she endeavoured to support groups which aimed to improve the position of women within the legal system. 'Equal pay and equal opportunity are derisory at the moment,' she complained. Those who knew her, and even her detractors, watched with amazement as she launched into her work on behalf of 'beleaguered women'. In 1974 she spoke at the adoption meeting of Dr Una Kroll who was standing in Sutton and Cheam for the Women's Rights Campaign. She once said that if she ever became prime minister the first item on her agenda would be the introduction of a housewives' allowance from the state: 'Running a home and raising a family is an extremely difficult job. I'd go as far as saying there should be a standard rate for it.'

Glenda works for causes that can produce changes in the statute book, but declines to support any kind of indulgent fringe. She cannot abide women who want to call themselves Ms and never have the door opened for them. She insists that the women's liberation movement lacks subtlety: 'I'm against militancy, but I think the same ends could be secured in a better society.' Yet it is no coincidence that the two women from history whom she most admires are the women's suffrage pioneer Mrs Pankhurst and the socialist writer and worker Beatrice Webb.

The intensity and complexity of her involvement in good works directly paralleled her growing discontent with acting as a way of life. 'If I could never act again, I wouldn't care,' she confided to her friends. 'This nagging drive to work as an actress regardless of the part or where one has to go or whether the play is good, bad or indifferent – that dreadful yawning void which only acting can fill for you – that's *gone*. Whether it is simply because this drive fades as one grows older, or because I've been fortunate and worked as much as I've wanted for the past ten years, I don't know. But I do know that the drive is gone. In fact, I don't think I'll be acting ten years from now.'

She was committed to contracts, certainly, for two years ahead. Her agent's order book included a stage and film version of Jean Genet's celebrated fantasy play *The Maids*, the former production directed adroitly by Minos

Volanakis at the Greenwich Theatre, on Glenda's home patch. The combination of Glenda Jackson and Susannah York as the maids, and Vivien Merchant as their mistress, would have guaranteed a long, money-making West End season if they had chosen to put it on there. What attracted such stars to an area like Greenwich, besides the blessed relief of a limited run (completely sold out), was the chance to act in something substantial, superior and proven. Glenda, additionally, had nursed a strong attraction to Genet's lurid characters for many years and, in particular, had long been fascinated by the maid Solange: the majority of characters she portrayed continued to fall into two categories, the regal and the obsessed, and as Solange she was back once again among the obsessed.

Although the play is about the nature of illusion and the manner in which we all play the roles expected of us – servants are obsequious when serving, but arrogant when acting the part of masters – it is also about the primitive and violent instincts that take over when the social structure disintegrates. Glenda and Miss York, dressed up and impersonating their hated employer, alternating in the roles of mistress and servant, prowled over the sheep-skin rug floor, mocked and abused each other mercilessly, grovelled at each other's feet and lashed each other with hailstorms of insults. The production left most critics feeling that only the play's surface had been scratched, while Milton Shulman in the London *Evening Standard* felt that the playing of Misses Jackson and York should have been more dishevelled, more earthy and more abandoned – 'but English actresses always tuck away a little of themselves behind an impregnable shell of gentility'. Glenda's director friend, Charles Marowitz, writing for *Plays and Players* magazine, concluded his assessment of her performance with the perceptive observation, 'Jackson gets only limited mileage out of what has now become the J-Effect, *viz* great bursts of emotional effusion unexpectedly cut short by flat, catatonic delivery.'

The previous year, Glenda had been approached by the London-based independent American film producer, Robert Enders, in the hope that she might be interested in one of his projects, a twisty little ghost story called *Voices*. She was not. (Gayle Hunnicutt eventually starred in the movie with David Hemmings.) But Enders maintained contact and when he learned that Glenda was doing a stage version of *The Maids*, and that she was interested in the project being adapted to film, he jumped at the chance of being involved. 'I instantly called up my wife Estelle – who was in the bath – and told her to go to the bookstore and buy a copy of *The Maids*,' said Enders. 'I knew quite a lot about Genet's other works, but I wasn't familiar with this one.' He developed a screenplay with director Christopher Miles, who had won much success with *The Virgin and the Gypsy*. 'I knew we would never please everyone with whatever interpretation we chose,' Enders said, 'but there was one thing I was confident everyone would respond to – excellent performances. And I knew we had those.'

Enders particularly admired Glenda for her determination to give preference to work she found stimulating and rewarding rather than accepting every big-money role offered. And he respected her for staying with the values she understood, which included not altering her suburban life-style. The respect was mutual. Glenda was aware that Enders had once made himself very unpopular with major studios by admitting that critical success was more important to him than box-office receipts. Producer and actress understood each other perfectly, and in 1975 they formed their own film production company, Bowden Films, to work on what Enders described as 'intimate' films. They sealed their partnership with *The Maids*, the filming beginning in April at Elstree's EMI Studios, just outside London, including a few days' location shooting in Paris – in all, a speedy two-week schedule and a modest $250,000 budget – with Susannah York and Vivien Merchant joining Glenda from the Greenwich stage production.

Christopher Miles, older brother of actress Sarah Miles, decided to dispense with the stage production's all-white setting and return to Genet's original conception of 'rich baroque furniture with flowers in abundance'. A new set was accordingly designed at Elstree which could take a tracking camera to any part of the set as long takes were essential on such a tight shooting schedule. This caused problems for all three actresses, but for Glenda in particular.

'She found it difficult to change some stage business as the entire shape of the set had been completely redesigned,' said Miles. 'She was especially concerned about the ending, where I wanted the french windows opened for the death scene of Susannah York, where she orders Glenda to pour her the poisoned tea. The reason for opening the windows, I have to admit, was for a strong cinematographic ending to the film in which Glenda delivered her final speech on the balcony of the apartment. On the lines: "And nothing of them remains, except, floating around Madame's corpse, the delicate per-fume of those saintly maidens, which they were in secret. We are beautiful, drunk with joy and free!" the window had to remain open and wind to blow through the apartment and extinguish the flickering candles around Susan-nah's bed. At first, Glenda wasn't much taken with the idea and, on a tight schedule, even the slightest disagreement seems like an eternity. The crew shrank back into the darkness behind the lights, and even the cameraman, Douglas Slocombe, seemed to be edging away and deserting me. I didn't know what to do.'

But Susannah York, sensing danger, came to the rescue and defused a situation which possessed all the explosive potential of another *Bequest to the Nation*. Glenda's heels were now firmly dug in; and then: 'Go on, Glen,' Susannah York cajoled. 'Leave it open. You know he's right!' The uncom-fortable impasse suddenly gave way, everyone laughed, and, right or wrong, the french windows were left open.

Geraldine Addison predicted that Glenda would direct one day because 'she knows exactly what's needed – she learns everybody else's parts as well as her own'. She was good at prompting people. 'She's a workaholic and hates going on holiday,' explained Miss Addison. 'She knows the part so completely that she goes over it with the director, and the other actors, trying to get what she feels is right. So when she does it, it's how she feels it *should* be. She's a perfectionist. It gets on her nerves if people aren't ready, or doing stupid things, or playing around. When she's working, she feels that the director, in particular, should know *exactly* what he wants. Unprofessionalism in a person is something she abhors. Her favourite word, when she gets angry, is "shit". It's her release. She gets involved in every aspect of a film's acting life and direction, reads the script totally at night, and arrives in the morning with definite ideas for the day's shooting, to which the director says yes, fine, or no, whatever. She likes to sit in her dressing room between takes and read. She reads an awful lot – almost anything that's been printed. She loves the props department. They call her "Brenda", and she likes that. She doesn't like everyone being flowery and smarmy. She likes mild gossip. She's very strong-willed, and, if she thinks something should be done *her* way, the heels go in. But she *is* strong, that's why I think she'll direct one day.'

Glenda justified her often fearsome approach to her work, and her equally formidable behaviour on the set, by stating that *she* never expected allowances to be made for *her*. 'I wouldn't say I have a very high opinion of myself,' she once exploded, 'but I would say that I have a very high opinion of how difficult it is to act well, and I therefore *don't* tolerate fools gladly. I can't be bothered to waste time on people's temperamental nerves and fears. We all experience that; if people can't cope with it, they shouldn't be in this business.'

If she detected that she had been let down, that her reputation as an actress or self-esteem as a person had been jeopardized, she found it difficult to forgive the erring party. She nursed grievances and, in such instances, possessed a long memory. 'I'm the world's worst bearer of grudges,' she admitted in an unguarded moment. 'I'm sure I'll be bearing grudges and paying off old scores on my death-bed.'

Her terse, forthright speech is peppered with the sort of sharply punctuated inflections which make the most ordinary statements alive with energy and potential drama. Perhaps that kind of withering directness was an essential antidote to the fraudulence of the times. Britain's Conservative Prime Minister, Edward Heath, experienced a sample of Glenda's candour soon after the actress had completed work on *The Maids*. He invited her to 10 Downing Street, where she proceeded to admire a Renoir, then worth £40,000, which had been loaned by an American supporter for the duration of Ted Heath's office.

'The painting's too shiny to be genuine,' Glenda informed her host, who endeavoured to maintain a dignified cool.

'It looks that way because it's been cleaned,' said Ted Heath.

'A bit of an awesome responsibility, isn't it, having to look after a £40,000 painting belonging to a friend?'

'Well – it is insured, you know.'

'But you could hardly replace a Renoir!'

That ended the conversation rather sharply. Glenda was good at bringing conversations to an abrupt, premature conclusion. If she was arrogant, and few doubted it, then it was often in an inverted way. She disliked compliments, for instance, and when in danger of receiving them she slid quickly into 'you' or 'one' and away from 'I'. She also felt that life as the 'pursuit of happiness' was absurd, the 'manic pursuit of pleasure' demeaning. 'The point about life is that it's there,' she said. 'At least if you're feeling it, you're alive. The alternative is death, isn't it?'

14
Time-Bomb

An emotional time-bomb was already ticking in the shadows. It was only a matter of months before Glenda's personal affairs would be torn apart in the ensuing explosion and scattered upon an unsuspecting world. The situation was irreversible and she was more than conscious that, where her public image was concerned, she was living on borrowed time. But work momentarily deflected her mind from all thoughts of impending tragedy . . . .

The lights of the London skyline across Hyde Park were beginning to come on in the pale dusk. 'Beautiful, isn't it?' said Glenda, relaxed on a bed in the Royal Garden Hotel, Knightsbridge, a completed *Times* crossword at her side. Then she said in that familiar dry way of hers, 'It is quite a complicated movie. Quite.'

All that day Glenda and Austrian co-star Helmut Berger had been filming a scene in the restaurant on the top floor of the Royal Garden. Black-out curtains were hung in front of the windows because the scene in *The Romantic Englishwoman* was supposed to take place at night. Glenda, as Elizabeth Fielding, wife of successful author Michael Caine, was being taken out for the evening by Berger, the young man she had met on holiday in Baden-Baden – a handsome but rather sordid figure who lives by his wits and the money of rich women and who is the catalyst in the relationship between Glenda and Caine. As might be expected with Joseph Losey directing, the film moved on many levels, hovering between fantasy, melodrama and reality and exploring, above all, numerous sub-strata of human relationships.

The sardonic comedy-drama, filmed entirely on location in Surrey, the South of France and Baden-Baden, Germany, and based on Thomas Wiseman's novel of the same name, was well cast – Caine revelling in scornful lines and stoic expressions, Glenda briskly efficient as his discontented wife, and Berger with just the right edge of glacial glamour for survival as a gigolo – though the film itself confused the critics. Many felt that when Glenda translated her husband's jealous fantasies into reality and ran off with the wastrel, it was asking the audience to believe too much. But Glenda never doubted the vigour of the direction under Joseph Losey, whose work – especially *The Go-Between* – she had long admired, and it was mainly to work with the Harvard-educated director that she agreed to make the film. As for Losey, his admiration for Glenda may well have been of comparable fervour in the early days of shooting, but by the final 'Cut!' he would join many another director in declaring, 'Never again . . . .'

Glenda was Losey's first and only choice for the title role; her name alone went some way to financing the movie: she was bankable. Yet he soon discovered an aspect of her which he found completely mystifying – her apparent reluctance to plumb the depths of her personality. Michael Caine drew attention to it one day quite unintentionally.

'She can do anything in the world,' Caine informed the director, 'anything she's asked to.'

'I think that's probably true,' said Losey, 'bearing in mind the limitations that beset all of us: who we are, what we look like, how we behave personally. But I'd just add to your statement – "if she wants to".'

Losey's leading ladies over the years included Elizabeth Taylor, Jeanne Moreau, Sarah Miles, Monica Vitti, Mia Farrow, Romy Schneider, Julie Christie and Jane Fonda; but Glenda was 'without question the best technical actress I ever knew – and I've worked with hundreds'. He explained, 'There was nothing she could not manage, technically, and almost at a moment's notice, which was pretty remarkable. But I think there was, and maybe still is, some profound reluctance to *use* herself totally, and that for me was a limitation and a difficulty, because I have no reluctance to use myself totally. There was always about her, as an actress and as a person, a kind of reserve which wasn't always easy to penetrate. There's a big difference between being reserved and being a private person, and being reserved in Glenda's case meant not allowing herself to go beyond a certain point. As a director I like to talk with actors, and actors generally like to talk with me; and once in a while Glenda would say she didn't want to do this or that or wasn't clear about a certain point. But by and large she wasn't an actress who wanted to talk very much, and I just felt that there were times when, if she could only have gone deeper into herself to get beyond her own reserves within herself, she might have produced something that would have been a little better.'

Michael Caine described Glenda as 'the best film actress I ever worked with', but he also agreed with Losey that there was a certain reluctance, conscious or subconscious, to expose herself beyond a certain point, an impregnable barrier beyond which, for a director, and always for a co-star, it was not possible to proceed. 'She's like Jane Fonda,' said Caine, 'except that in Jane I can see the vulnerability and femininity – whereas in Glenda I can still see the femininity, but not the vulnerability. But I know it's there, somewhere.'

A revealing facet of her personality is that she is not a weeper. Unlike the majority of folk in showbusiness, who are prone to tears at the slightest provocation, Glenda finds it virtually impossible to release her feelings in that way. 'Is that a virtue or not?' she asked. Clearly, she is reluctant to reveal any chinks in her armour. While Losey and Caine tried unsuccessfully to strike a vein of frailty and helplessness, there were some who felt certain they had detected its presence ... and even she was compelled to confess on one occasion, 'I'm infinitely more vulnerable than any of my characters.' Her friend Gerry Fisher, director of photography on *The Romantic Englishwoman*, concluded, 'Glenda's strong-willed, sure ... but also vulnerable.'

'As you look at Glenda's private life,' said Oliver Reed, 'you begin to notice a certain vulnerability. This vulnerability lies within the domain of her sexuality – and, remember, a woman's vulnerability is only hiding her sexuality. It's a hat she wears with different faces.'

Glenda's disinclination to show even the slightest weakness was perceived by Vladek Sheybal a few years after they had worked together on *Women in Love*. He approached her with a film script, confident that the principal role would provide Glenda with the ideal vehicle for her talents. Having read the script, she phoned Sheybal and invited him over to Blackheath. 'She didn't want to play the part, but she wanted to have someone there to witness the fact that she was turning it down,' recalled Sheybal. 'So her secretary was sitting there, and Glenda was in a defensive position. She was afraid, you see, that through our friendship, by something nice that I might say about her, I might pierce through her armour and she would then have to say, "Okay, I'm willing to do it." She preferred not to reveal any weakness. She wanted to be very much in control – to be the very opposite of vulnerable.'

It is this compulsion in Glenda to remain 'in control' at all times, even when to be out of control may produce a better performance, that most bothered Joseph Losey.

'I approached Glenda in the first place because I thought she would be perfect for the part, as indeed she was – in her way,' said Losey. 'There were perhaps other ways of doing it, just as there were perhaps other ways of writing it. But it always came down to my original statement that she didn't use herself deeply enough. An actress has to be very careful not to make herself invulnerable to the point where her performances are less than they could be, and Glenda never exposed herself at all. If she was saving herself, I wonder who or what it was for. It could merely be a form of self-protection; but, again, if you fall on the side of too much protection, then you fall short of being great.

'An actress has to be prepared to take risks that involve her exploring her innermost private self, otherwise she will never be as near as hell pre-eminent in her craft. Greta Garbo was reserved enough, God knows, but when she was acting she was totally vulnerable. I knew Garbo, though I never actually worked with her, and I saw how she *allowed* herself to be vulnerable in a way that Glenda could not. Vanessa Redgrave is the same: she permits herself to show a vulnerability that verges on the self-destructive; she takes risks with her innermost private self. To be professional can often mean to be mechanical, and while I wouldn't want to suggest that Glenda is just a machine, she does possess the sort of mechanical equipment that can be used in place of emotion.'

While Losey never doubted for one moment Glenda's innate professionalism – or Caine's, for that matter – he was desperately concerned about the more 'relaxed' attitude of Helmut Berger, a protégé of Italian director Luchino Visconti, who nurtured the actor's career and used him to good effect in several films, among them *The Damned*, in which Berger played the neurotic heir to a steel fortune. Berger, the son of an affluent Salzburg hotelier-restaurateur, took an instant dislike to the daughter of the Hoylake brickie – though in choosing Glenda as the butt of his contempt he made a serious tactical error, for she gave as good as she got. Never before had she worked with anybody quite like him, nor he her. Blond, wiry and boyishly handsome, Berger, off-screen, was a hell-raiser of some repute and, two years after his feuds with Glenda, very nearly died of a drug overdose.

He brought Glenda to boiling-point, as well as the director. 'I liked Helmut Berger to begin with, but, on many counts, I didn't realize what a handful he was going to be,' said Losey. 'He was charming, and, in many cases, very effective and right, but he was unprofessional. Glenda, being the sort of person she was, couldn't let his behaviour pass without comment. She said some unpleasant things to him a couple of times; it was highly deserved. He just wasn't bothering to match up to Glenda's style of professionalism. She didn't want to waste time, and, when Berger became difficult, she invariably retreated to her dressing room. He said some very rude things about her, to which I paid no attention.'

Glenda's basic principles were simple, but well defined. 'I'm easy to work with,' she maintained, 'providing I'm dealing with professionals. I'm only difficult if the other people don't know their jobs or are behaving badly.'

With the exception of stand-in Geraldine Addison and director of photography Gerry Fisher, nobody associated with the production – or at least no one discernible – was ever given the opportunity to get to know Glenda personally. Next to Gerry Fisher, her closest relationship was with Michael Caine, though even this was on a professional rather than a personal level. 'There was a mutual respect,' Losey remarked. 'They got on well together in a work situation – talking to each other before the scene, at the scene, during the scene – but then they always went off to their respective dressing rooms. This was Glenda's way. Although this sort of detached behaviour is not unusual in the film business, it's far from standard, and it's certainly rare when it happens *all* the time as it did with Glenda. On the occasions when I directed Elizabeth Taylor, her dressing room was always full of people, of actors, and me, and others, although sometimes she'd kick everybody out; but Glenda preferred her own company. I don't think even the crew were very much aware of her; they just passed each other like ships in the night – with the exception of Gerry Fisher. He probably got closer to her than anybody else on the crew or in the cast or me. She seems to go for cameramen. Maybe she relates more directly to the man who is responsible for the camera and the lighting ...?'

Glenda is not renowned for making apologies, but the nature of her esteem for Fisher was such that he was one of the few people for whom she ever publicly ate humble pie. On location in Baden-Baden the actress and the cinematographer embarked on a heated discussion one evening that embraced two categorical statements.

'Apollonaris Water *is* a British company,' said Fisher, 'and our British system of colour television *is* German.'

'Rubbish!' howled Glenda.

The next morning she strode up to Fisher's breakfast table and announced in a bellowing voice that was obviously intended for more than one pair of ears: 'It's not often I have to apologize to anyone, and certainly never twice. You were right on both counts!'

Fisher later reflected, 'There was pure bright pleasure in her eyes. Had you not known her, though, you might have thought the "pleasure" was in fact malice, her eyes glittered so.'

On more than one occasion during location shooting her eyes expressed emotions that somehow epitomized the very opposite of pleasure. Few people on the set escaped her scrutiny. 'Any lack of concentration on the part of anybody else, any unnecessary details, any kind of chat that would destroy concentration – all those things, whether they came from the crew, from actors or anybody, would screw her up,' said Losey. 'There were many such occasions. We had one scene where there were three children, and they were a little hard to manoeuvre, and I had to change the set-up several times and also cut the scene considerably, and she got rather impatient about that. She didn't hide how she felt. A lot of people, of course, couldn't stand her, and she behaved extremely badly on occasion with folk who, as far as their status on the set was concerned, were her social inferiors. We almost didn't get the film going because of that kind of difference on one occasion. People were afraid of her, because once in a while she would make a crack – and the cracks could be very nasty. Nobody wanted to be the target of that sort of onslaught, so most people made sure they didn't place themselves in that position. I'm sure Michael Caine would have been quite up to it if she ever turned on him, but she never did; he had an immense respect for her and certainly wasn't afraid of her. Helmut Berger wasn't afraid of her either, but only because he didn't care. The atmosphere on the set could sometimes change from warm and open to closed when she came on, though on these occasions that was usually out of respect rather than fear. All the same, it made me extra careful never to provoke any kind of situation on the set where somebody could become a target of Glenda's tongue.'

By this time Glenda's private life was in turmoil, her relationship with Roy in shreds and already beginning to take a toll on her emotional stability. Few knew that her marriage was firmly set on a course of destruction, and Glenda certainly took care that the situation stayed that way; but her personality was inevitably affected by the disintegration of her marriage and she seemed more than usually frosty. All the same, the actress with the sharp-shooter tongue later considered Joseph Losey and declared, 'He's very intriguing.' She reflected on Michael Caine for a moment and concluded, 'He's lovely – he said he'd like to do a comedy with me and I think that would be lovely because he has the most marked sense of humour.' In fact it was Glenda who ran off with all the best reviews. A typical accolade from the *Sunday Express* read: 'Glenda Jackson's performance is flawless. She seems miscast until you realize that Elizabeth is not someone we are being invited to weep for.' Glenda, the non-weeper, could appreciate that.

Romance with 'the Prince of Darkness'

By Christmas 1974 the Hodges' marriage was floundering. Even during better times theirs had been a precarious relationship, characterized by heated arguments. These were two strong-willed, stubborn personalities, but it was Glenda who almost always won the day. During their feuds Roy would tell his battling wife to 'push off', and then it would occur to him that the house and its contents were all hers. The sense of spousal inferiority this imposed on Roy was incalculate, draining him of huge reserves of self-respect.

'We don't agree about anything, *anything*,' he complained to friends.

'The last four years of our marriage have been *horrible*,' Glenda retorted.

The nature of their now scant regard for each other came to a head when one of Roy's projects hit bad times. Having abandoned his art gallery business, the lure of the boards eventually proved too potent for him and he formed his own theatrical company, called On Stage. His efforts as producer–director were for love, not money. While Glenda was rejecting scripts by the cartload, Roy was employing young actors and actresses, many of whom were desperate for work. At first, he said, it was a case of 'no salaries, just expenses – and that includes me'. His first production was a performance of *Romeo and Juliet* at the Old Hoxton Music Hall, a run-down show-palace in London's East End. The problem was that the company of eight performers was not taking in much money, and soon the group hit real financial problems, with Roy's kitty down to the last £100 and no permanent base.

Roy applied in vain for a grant from the state-subsidized Arts Council. He thought it might help his cause if he announced his future plans: he hoped to persuade bare-foot pop singer Sandie Shaw to play Ophelia for £8 a night, and he wanted her to be a Saint Joan in his next production. Although Shaw's *Saint Joan* eventually materialized, the money was running out. As a last resort he approached Glenda and asked her to subsidize his theatrical aspirations. She told him where to get off. 'She wouldn't come near the company with a barge-pole,' said a bitter Roy Hodges. 'She's not interested in what I do.'

Later, in 1975, Glenda disclosed: 'If our marriage had been wonderful, I wouldn't have voluntarily left Europe for fourteen weeks.' In fact, by agreeing to play the title role in a new Royal Shakespeare Company production of *Hedda Gabler*, directed by thirty-five-year-old RSC supremo Trevor Nunn, she hoped to relieve the tension in her fractured marriage – especially as the Ibsen play would take her to Australia, Canada and the United States. By associating herself with the classic Norwegian drama she was, as it turned out, merely banging the final nail in the coffin.

Rehearsals began in earnest in London on New Year's Day, and almost immediately there came into Glenda's life a man who would convince her that there could be more to a relationship than was being offered by Roy. On first sight her liaison with the stage lighting designer, Andy Phillips, was not an obvious one. Small, paunchy, plain, crop-haired, argumentative and possessing what has been described as a 'coarse vitality', the former actor was a good lighting man; and, before the spring was out, he was to receive a Tony nomination for the Broadway production of *Equus*. But the more the relationship deepened, the more it became apparent that the couple had much more in common than anybody could have imagined. They complemented each other supremely. Colleagues in the theatre world who considered Glenda emasculating, perceived that Andy Phillips, then separated from his wife and living alone, was the only man in the *Hedda Gabler* company intrepid enough to make a pass at her. 'They were absolutely two of a kind,' said cast member Patrick Stewart.

'I wasn't very much surprised when Glenda's next choice after Roy was a very masculine, virile, simple electrician from the Royal Court – a workman,' said Vladek Sheybal. 'While Roy was very masculine inwardly, on the outside this wasn't immediately apparent. But it seems he was not manly or masculine enough for her, physically, and so she chose an electrician.'

With her private life crumbling around her, Glenda was more than grateful to plunge into rehearsals for what was undoubtedly one of the most difficult roles in the modern repertoire. It was more than eight years since she last trod the boards with the RSC, scene of her earliest stage triumphs. She was conscious that she was being observed and evaluated in a cast that comprised Patrick Stewart, Jennie Linden, Timothy West, Constance Chapman, Pam St Clement and Peter Eyre. Besides which, the RSC was according her one of the highest salaries it had ever paid to an actor. She was on her mettle from the beginning.

Was it simply poetic irony that the predominant feature of both Glenda's and Hedda's marriages was boredom? Or was Glenda, at this particular point in her life, drawn to the part like a moth to a beacon? Given the enigmatic personalities of both women, the Glenda/Hedda partnership becomes even more intriguing: people did not know how to relate to either of them; and neither would settle in a dull marriage. So was Hedda related to Glenda? George Bernard Shaw, who thought he knew Ibsen's heroine, called her 'a bully in reaction from her own cowardice'. Some critics of the day likened Hedda to 'a horrid miscarriage of the imagination'. Another critic declared, 'She is not related to anyone we know.' Was this Glenda? She certainly nursed a great deal of sympathy for the character and she recognized elements in Hedda because she knew she had them in herself. 'I have her bossiness,' she observed. 'Her belief that she knows better for other people what's best for them – that I have very strongly.'

Patrick Stewart, who played Hedda's one-time lover, the writer Eilet Lovborg, had not previously worked with Glenda, though he had always regarded her professional accomplishments with great respect. He found her performances 'impressive and fascinating', and yet he was always puzzled by her work, confused by the extent to which she could simultaneously intrigue, attract and repel. He was a fellow Northerner, and for a season he lived and acted in Liverpool, all of which helped him to understand some of the 'odd' things about Glenda, though even that did not completely prepare him for what was to follow.

He could remember very clearly the first time he saw her off-stage. It was the first day of rehearsals for *Hedda*. They were both emerging from Covent Garden underground station and he followed her down the street towards an old church hall which was being used for the rehearsals; he was tremend-ously excited at the prospect of the production, particularly because of the opportunity of working with Glenda . . . and the *shape* of her, he said, was un-mistakable. 'She was striding towards the rehearsal room,' recalled Stewart, 'and everything about the way she was moving was determined and pur-poseful; but her head was *so* low down. It could have been, on the one hand, a human version of a charging bull, or it could have been somebody who was going somewhere they didn't want to go to. All this was very marked in her physical appearance as she strode ahead of me, and the bull-like lowered head became, in effect, a characteristic of all those rehearsals: because one often felt with Glenda that it was like being in a bull-ring and not on a rehearsal floor.'

All the excitement that Stewart felt at the prospect of working with Glenda quickly disappeared. Timothy West and Jennie Linden had worked with Glenda on previous occasions and arrived at the rehearsals emotionally prepared. Patrick Stewart could not have known, as indeed could no other member of the cast, that Glenda's bone-chilling behaviour was partly attributable to the breakdown of her relationship with Roy. It was a down-in-the-mouth leading lady who attended rehearsals, described by one cast member as 'miserable affairs'. It was an equally glum leading man who was compelled to play opposite her. 'There was never anything about her that you could actually pin down and positively object to,' said Stewart. 'You could never say, "This has gone far enough; now you stop this," because every-thing that she did, and the way she did it, was always directed towards the work. It was never towards the satisfaction of any ego in her, it was never for a vicarious satisfaction, it was never arbitrarily vicious. But, my God, it was challenging and threatening to everyone around her in such a way that I could see, what I felt in myself, other actors just dying a little bit every time it happened. Now, rehearsals are about flowering, developing, expanding, being liberated: that's what we try to do when we rehearse. In this particular production, unfortunately, the effect Glenda had on us was the exact opposite – we withered, wilted. It varied from person to person. I saw it in one person at almost desperate level. I know that, in rehearsals, I was often grossly inhibited by her, and I would see others just switch off.'

It was the bizarre dichotomy between Glenda's very 'ordinariness' on the one hand and her 'awesome demeanour' on the other that bewildered and misled the cast during the early days of rehearsals. They found her smoking endless packets of cigarettes and almost always tensed for action, like a stretched catapult. 'For Godsake!' she yelled on one occasion after a delay caused by the precise positioning of a tiny stool. '*Come on!*' There was an emotionally charged quality about her, and yet this was allied, strangely, to a contradictory element: a sense of boredom, *ennui*.

It was not simply that, in her presence, other members of the cast were perplexed and stupefied; they actually felt themselves being thrown off balance. 'It wasn't as if she had that kind of unsettling conventional presence that you expect from a star,' Stewart reflected. 'It was something much more graspable than that because, in a curious way, she didn't have a conventional star quality about her. What she had that made her different and unusual and distinct, both as a person and as a performer, was a sort of heightened "ordinariness" – but intensified to such an extent that it became extra-ordinary.'

Glenda gave a whole new meaning to emasculation – few who incurred her disfavour escaped the numbing sensation. Even Trevor Nunn, the director, was not spared the experience. 'You could never tell whether she liked him or not,' said Stewart, 'but from the first day of rehearsals she would never miss an opportunity to undermine him, to humiliate him, often in public. I saw it happen in a restaurant once, and it was just awful. But he always refused to be baited; he didn't rise to the challenge of her attacks. What Trevor had to a huge degree was patience and, because he admired her enormously – and perhaps because he was even a bit attracted to her, too – I certainly was, in some bizarre way, from time to time – I think he somehow learned to cope with it. But I don't think I would have tolerated it as long as he did if I'd been the director. What she did, you see, was a direct challenge to his position as director. It was right on the nose, and she didn't even blink as she did it. She had a way with irony which was fairly lacerating, and it was done mostly through direct challenge to a person's authority, talent, skill, knowledge, intelligence. But she could never actually get Trevor down, though I used to see him kind of reel under the blow. It was really like watching some punch-drunk boxer who couldn't go on any more – but he always bounced back. It was extraordinary. We thought he'd never get up again. ... I mean, this was no way to rehearse.

'And yet, curiously, she was never actually insolent or impertinent, because she never quite abandoned the conventional forms of politeness and courtesy – almost, but not quite – so that you could never accuse her of being rude or impudent. Trevor might have had excuse enough, but I knew that if I, as a fellow actor, accused her of rudeness, she would have said, "But I'm only doing what's best for the play. I'm just trying to make things better, that's all, chuck!" "Chuck" was a form of address we all got to know; God, how I got to hate that sound! She patronized in an ironic way whoever was around her, and she had a way of suggesting that you were not up to your job. She'd say, "In fact, you just can't do it, can you, chuck?" That's just dreadful, having to work with somebody who is constantly suggesting that you're not up to it. The other thing was that she always seemed to know more about one's own part than one did oneself. I never knew whether that was just instinct or more to do with homework, but she did have a terrific flair for understanding roles.'

This 'understanding' reached its most offensive extreme when Glenda began to impose, by sheer force of will, her interpretation of Eilet Lovborg on to Stewart's own interpretation. It was rather like a tennis player in a mixed doubles tournament telling her male team-mate to hit the ball *her* way. 'Throughout the rehearsal period I had to fight against giving Glenda's version of Lovborg, though I lost the battle, because she just saw to it that she got what she wanted. She wasn't prepared to accept something that didn't fit in with her conception of how the play, and all the parts in it, should go; and fitting things in with her plans became one of the problems in rehearsals. To my shame, I opened by giving Glenda's version of my role, though the interpretation shifted in time until it became closer to my own ideas about the part.'

He observed, 'Those rehearsals were an absolute misery. They brought great unhappiness to myself, and great unhappiness to the others around me. I used to come to rehearsals just planning how I could defend myself against Glenda, whereas I should have been worrying about how I'd do the day's work. I don't mean I arrived with clever retorts, because I would never have attempted to take her on on that basis. That would have been just suicidal. No, I arrived wondering how I could cope with the day and come out of it feeling that I'd taken a step forward in preparing the role. Certainly the impression that I got from her was that my role was so hopelessly miscast that it was almost impossible for her to do the play. I felt desperately undermined.'

When Stewart mentioned to Glenda that he felt uncomfortable about the way his role was developing, she dug her heels in, put her hands on her hips, and exploded, 'What do you *mean*? You were there, you had as much rehearsal time as I had. You've got lines to say, you've got thoughts about them, haven't you? You've got a tongue in your head – you speak up for yourself.'

He mused, 'It would be so difficult to pin her down about her abuse of her power in rehearsal. But there was no generosity, no sympathy for anyone else.

It was all so "serious". I can't remember laughing at all during the rehearsals and, I mean, rehearsals can be great fun.'

Glenda, in many ways, could be a Jekyll and Hyde because, in a professional capacity, she displayed two very different personalities. There was the salty, tetchy Glenda Jackson of the rehearsal period, and there was the transformed, unselfish, mild-mannered Glenda Jackson of the performance – the Glenda Jackson the public saw, the Glenda Jackson her colleagues delighted in appearing with. Those who worked with her regarded the metamorphosis as something of a phenomenon. Her Mr Hyde was not for public consumption, and she herself certainly did not give a damn what her colleagues thought about her behaviour during rehearsals because, to Glenda, it was merely a means to an end.

If her energy and determination to obtain results caused anxiety among her colleagues, well – 'Tough luck, chuck.' Trevor Nunn was not talking idly when he declared, 'Of all the actors I've worked with, Glenda had a capacity for work that was phenomenal. There was immense power of concentration, a great deal of attack, thrust, determination. She searched hard. It was quite ruthless.' Nobody knows more than this particular director the precise nature of this particular actress's ruthlessness.

But when Hyde became Jekyll, when by some mysterious process she opens herself to the role she plays and is possessed by it, when the catapult suddenly lets go for a few precious hours during the performance ... well, then you begin to glimpse the whole point of Glenda Jackson. It is magic. Fellow actors who hate her guts during the rehearsal period become themselves transformed, loving her, sometimes worshipping her in performance, when all their offstage instincts are demanding that they should be detesting her. It is this intangible *something* that divides the great talent from the merely average talent. So complete is the change that there is not even a hair's breadth between the actress she is and the role she plays. They become indivisible.

This fact alone is a curiosity for which Patrick Stewart was patently unprepared. 'The actual performance was a revelation,' he said. 'Glenda's contact with the rest of the cast, her generosity, her relaxation, her inventiveness, her niceness was absolutely overwhelming in performance. It was as if, when it came to the performance, all of her strongest personality traits were reversed. She was one of the most, if not *the* most, exciting person to be on stage with, and for all the best reasons: because she worked with you, not against you. You weren't in opposition. All that other shit was abandoned when you were on stage with her, and it was terrific.'

Following a week's preview in February 1975 at the Richmond Theatre, Surrey, Glenda and the rest of the cast flew to Australia for the first leg of the *Hedda Gabler* tour, opening in Melbourne, followed by Sydney. As Stewart was not eager to spend time with Glenda during the day when the company was not working and as he disliked seeing her for the first time when they met on stage, he used to make a point of visiting her dressing room each evening half an hour before curtain up. 'I was never ever refused entrance or told to go away,' he said. 'I'd pull up a chair and chat to Glenda for ten or fifteen minutes. In the play we were a couple who had a "history", you see, so when we came face to face on stage, at least there was something to build on for that evening. Those fifteen minutes, every evening, were the most delightful, enchanting and pleasant minutes of the whole tour. It was my impression that if just the two of you were alone in a room, with no work in hand, just conversation, she could be enchanting. We would only talk about what we'd done during the day; as we were on tour, there were always museums and things we'd been to. Occasionally, we'd talk about the work, and that was fine, too. It wasn't until a stage assistant came to check something that that side of Glenda's personality was all packed away and she suddenly changed and that competitive quality would come back again. After a while I began to detect a certain consistency in her behaviour: whenever there were three or more people around, she would once again revert to this awful creature.'

It was this 'awful creature' whom Andy Phillips won over by his own particular brand of awfulness. From the beginning he was a fair match for her. The cynics among Glenda's acquaintance would have it, in fact, that she fell for him hook, line and sinker, because he would never tolerate her customary line in portentous self-assertiveness, those blood-chilling verbal barbs that could reduce strong men to so much emotional rubble. He told her in no uncertain terms where to get off whenever she adopted that sort of behaviour in his company. He was consistently rude to her. Few men in her experience had ever dared to come on so strong, or challenge and brow-beat her with such fearless relish. All this was such a novelty for Glenda that she found Andy quite fascinating and, subsequently, totally irresistible.

The romance went into top gear on the plane flying to Australia. Glenda travelled first class, while the remainder of the company travelled tourist, but she later walked back to see her colleagues in the 'cattle trucks' – and stayed for hours. One of the reasons she slummed it for so long was because Andy was sitting across the aisle from her, and Andy, the worse for drink, had been totally ignoring her. She was puzzled and tantalized by his seemingly cool behaviour ... and then he turned on her.

'It'll *never* work, you know,' he said. 'Your performance as Hedda Gabler is utterly *hopeless*. It's all *wrong*.'

Other members of the Royal Shakespeare Company listened with unbelieving ears. Nobody, let alone a stage technician, had ever spoken to Glenda Jackson in that manner and lived to tell the tale. But this was different; this was a different Glenda Jackson – something had come over her, and that something was a man who beguiled her like a latter-day Rasputin. 'It took us a while to cotton on where this conversation was going, but Andy was taking her apart,' Patrick Stewart remembered. 'I mean, people don't do that sort of thing to any actor – but to *Glenda Jackson*? It was unthinkable. He was telling her why she could never play the part and what was wrong with it. He was articulate with her on this subject for a good hour, and she just sat there, taking it all like a lamb.'

When Glenda and Andy became lovers, the rest of the touring company found the relationship 'curious' and 'fascinating'. They were also delighted that the couple spent so much time in each other's company. The mutual insults continued. It was as a consequence of these disparaging remarks that Glenda nicknamed her lover the Prince of Darkness – because of the gloominess of his lighting set-ups. His nicknames for her are unprintable. 'It wasn't a very happy time for her, privately or professionally,' commented *Hedda*'s Judge Brack, Timothy West, 'and she had to cope with the extraordinary degree of adulation that was reserved in Australia, and later in the USA, for very important film stars – an attitude she found rather tiresome.'

Certainly, the rather primitive working conditions in Sydney were incompatible with the adulation Glenda was receiving as a visiting superstar. The Elizabethan Theatre, in which the production was playing, had been put up for sale and prepared for demolition before it was switched back into service for *Hedda Gabler* – but not before the carpets in the auditorium and some of the more fundamental comforts had been ripped out. Now the old, once beautiful, echoing Victorian theatre had a huge section missing from its roof. Through this aperture the enormous Australian cockroaches, which abounded in New South Wales in the hot summer months, flew in during matinées and showed a peculiar fascination for Glenda's Hedda wig. 'She never faltered once in our long second act duologue as these fearsome three-inch insects buzzed round her head as she poured tea,' recalled Timothy West. 'From my viewpoint the scene was like something out of a Charles Addams cartoon. The audience gasped.'

On the North American tour, Glenda became public property in whatever corner of God's earth her feet touched. In Los Angeles and Washington the invitations to parties and receptions flew through the air in greater profusion than midsummer midges. But she still regarded social gatherings with contempt. 'She would accept invitations and not turn up,' said Patrick Stewart. 'It was so infuriating. It was left to Timmy West or myself to explain to these people, who didn't want to see us, why Glenda wasn't there. Or, if she did turn up, she would be wearing some horrible old clothes, looking like a used rag. I always used to think it was just too contrived to be impressive.'

Her appearances at the Huntington Hartford Theater in Los Angeles and the National Theater in Washington, DC, were preceded by frantic, heady press conferences. She handled these whirlwinds with such aplomb and cut through platitudes and inanities with such disarming precision, that the interviewers occasionally felt a little short of response but never short-changed. When a representative from the *Los Angeles Times* talked to Glenda at the theatre, she found the English actress, sporting blue jeans and a T-shirt, sitting in a rather tatty dressing room, cleaning out make-up jars with some scraps of cotton wool. 'Her hands were busy the entire time she talked,' the reporter observed, 'giving an insight into the nervous tension pent up in that slim body.'

Glenda intimated that she wanted to play a couple of the Shakespeare ladies, the rest of Chekhov, a few more Ibsen, and the odd Shaw. The only stage play she would willingly do again was *Three Sisters*. In films, she disclosed that she would like to work with the directors François Truffaut, John Cassavetes and Jack Gold, and act with Robert Redford, Paul Newman, Jack Nicholson and Marlon Brando ('he's the best'). She also disclosed two fantasy ambitions: to make first a musical, then a Western.

'Glenda has her heart set on doing a modern musical after these classical flings,' her business partner, Bob Enders, informed Hollywood producer George Barrie.

'Can she sing and dance?' inquired Barrie. 'It sure helps.'

Barrie later announced that he wanted Glenda to do a musical with Barbra Streisand's first husband, Elliott Gould. While in Los Angeles, Glenda signed a multi-picture contract with Fabergé's Brut Productions, of which George Barrie was president; *A Touch of Class* was his first production for the company. The deal included a screen version of *Hedda Gabler*. She told Barrie how some directors twisted roles to fit their fantasies about women. 'Silly buggers!' she fumed.

She fumed with even greater fervour when she read the reviews of *Hedda*, most of which annihilated her. She tried to adopt a sense of proportion about the critical bloodbath by telling people, 'I've had more bad notices than Lipton's has tea bags.' But colleagues and friends asserted that she was incensed and hurt by the critics' lack of appreciation of her efforts. 'The world has not been waiting for, nor is it long likely to cherish, Glenda Jackson's bizarre offering: a comic Hedda Gabler,' complained *Time* magazine in an assessment that said it all. 'She has apparently decided that Noël Coward is really the author of the play. Her performance will certainly rank high in the annals of dramatic travesty. She trivializes every major scene in the play.' The *Los Angeles Times*, while fascinated by Glenda's portrayal, commented: 'We might almost be in a situation comedy about an absent-minded professor and his long-suffering wife. Oh, George, *not* again! When, one wonders as the curtain zips down, does the tragedy start?' The Prince of Darkness was not ignored either: 'The lighting by Andy Phillips is ominous ....'

Her effect on the London critics two months later in July would be little better: 'There is an underlying coarseness in Glenda Jackson's Hedda Gabler which contradicts what I take to be the essential fact of the character's temperament,' claimed *Plays and Players* magazine. 'What is missing almost entirely is the commitment to a higher style of life.' And 'Miss Jackson's approach is to play the character on a gradually rising wave of nausea,' said *The Times*. While Herbert Kretzmer wrote in the *Daily Express*: 'Glenda Jackson brings an inexplicable lack of conviction to the celebrated role, diminishing its rage to a kind of small-town petulance that left me considerably underwhelmed. The role never catches fire, and her eventual suicide seems almost irrelevant.' By comparison, Andy must suddenly have seemed like a sentimental, honey-mouthed old softie.

16
Separation and Divorce

Before she returned to England, Glenda flew to Toronto for the closing performances of *Hedda*'s transatlantic tour – and close on her heels came Roy. A friend in the company had tipped him off that something was wrong. 'I didn't realize it was *this* serious,' said Roy on arrival. 'As usual the husband is the last person to know when a marriage is over.'

He very quickly discovered for himself what was going on between Glenda and Andy Phillips, and was mortified, but, to begin with, at least, he played it cool. When they first met he asked Andy what he wanted to drink – and, before answering, Roy recalled that his wife's lover laughed, and so did Glenda.

'Whisky,' said Andy.

'Help yourself,' Roy replied.

'I already have,' Andy responded with a double-edged look.

Roy turned to Glenda in the uneasy silence that suddenly engulfed the room. 'It's over, isn't it?' he asked her.

'Yes.'

'Well, that's that then.'

'After meeting Andy I felt reborn,' she informed a considerably chastened husband.

Roy explained that he suddenly felt 'quite superfluous'. 'It's not a nice feeling,' he said. 'I suppose the trouble is I'm too old. Past it.'

He was forty-eight; Glenda, thirty-nine. Andy was her senior by one year. Glenda said she had always been one of those people who thought you had to live with your mistakes – but that was how she *used* to think. She had taken stock of her life and decided things could not go on as they were. She had matured. 'This trip abroad has made me grow up,' she declared, 'and it's come as something of a shock.'

Roy stormed out and caught the next plane back to London. Glenda followed him a few days later and affirmed that Andy *was* the new man in her life. She told him they must discuss their future, and that of their son, Daniel, now six. Over red wine and cigarettes, they talked for two hours about what had gone wrong and what should be done. 'It was disgustingly civilized,' said Roy. 'We didn't rant or rave or throw fits. There was no point in that. We just tried to work out the most sensible thing to do.'

At one point Glenda told Roy that he was getting work only because he was her husband. 'I think that's rather cruel,' he said.

Before the evening was out they embarked on what Glenda described as 'the worst part of it' – explaining to Daniel that it was all over between his parents. They told him that his daddy would be working and would not be home as before, but that he would see him from time to time.

While they talked about their future, a £10,000 red Mercedes sports saloon, which had been delivered the previous day, sat outside the Blackheath home. Glenda's old Triumph Herald had been disposed of, and the gleaming new Mercedes seemed to symbolize, coincidentally, Glenda's determination to start a new life.

The very next day Roy informed the press that it was all over between Glenda and him: 'When we married she was unknown, but I don't blame all her success for this development in our relationship – though it may have made life a bit more difficult. So we've decided to call it a day. She arrived from Toronto yesterday and is now starting to make arrangements for the separation. I was confronted by the situation in Toronto, and that was it. I'll be moving out of the house here after she tells me what arrangements have been made later today.'

Within hours of the announcement, the news had been flashed across the world in big bold headlines: GLENDA AND HUSBAND SPLIT AFTER 17 YEARS . . . GLENDA TELLS HUSBAND OF 'OTHER MAN' . . . GLENDA'S NEW MAN GOES INTO HIDING . . . GLENDA FACES DIVORCE. A few colleagues and acquaintances had already perceived that a crisis was brewing, but as far as the public and the fans were concerned the impending marital rift had been one of showbusiness's best kept secrets. It caused a stir.

Glenda and Daniel immediately left for Cheshire – 'for a few days' peace and quiet'. The reality of the situation was that she wanted to tell her mother about Andy. Her father met them as they stepped off the train at Liverpool; then it was off to her parents' home in Hoylake. 'I want to put Mum and Dad completely in the picture about my marriage and new romance,' said Glenda. 'Mum already knew Andy and she was quite pleased. Anything which makes me happy makes her happy too.'

The break-up seemed a familiar story, something that was almost expected to happen in showbusiness relationships. Yet the marriage was really one that failed to work on its own terms. 'We are all fallible human beings and both Roy and I realize there is no point in going on,' Glenda explained. 'I mean, the last four or five years of our marriage have been bloody awful. It hasn't been a marriage at all.' She talked about the series of disagreements they had had over minor things, and that it was always 'the small things' that caused a split. 'We didn't part previously because I was too scared to make the break and because we had Daniel to consider. It has been dreadful living a sham, and when I was away on tour for three months I suddenly realized there was no longer any point in carrying on with a marriage that was dead.'

During the first few days of the separation the most frequent accusation levelled against her was that she had shifted the 'power balance' in the marriage. 'It makes me bloody mad that people should be criticizing and condemning me without even knowing what went on for all these years,' Glenda stated. 'They want to term me an unstable Hollywood type, which is far from what I am. No one knows what I had to go through. I'm not saying there weren't happy, glad, warm moments, but in general my marriage was hell. I finally found out that I'm not the marrying kind or the type who can be expected to live her life exclusively for someone else.'

She told people that there was no reason any more – not that there ever was one – for any woman to support 'a fragile male ego' at the expense of her own happiness and 'ego fulfilment'. 'Marriage inevitably comes to that,' she said, 'since all men who marry have some need of psychological reinforcement. If they didn't, why on earth would they marry in the first place?' She added, 'I haven't made the transition into playgirl yet, and doubtless never will, but I've left behind one frustrated schizophrenic housewife.'

On the day that he announced their marriage was over, Roy packed a couple of suitcases and moved out of the Blackheath house and went to stay with a close friend, actress Anne Berry, at her flat just two miles away in Catford, south-east London. After they had both been in touch with their respective lawyers to sort out the divorce proceedings, Glenda pointed out that she would try to remain good friends with Roy. 'What is the point of being enemies? I think people just grow at different rates.'

Roy was not in such a magnanimous mood: 'I'd quite like never to see her again, but because of Daniel we have to keep in touch. With all the things we have done to each other, why should we be friends? One tends to say what a waste after nearly eighteen years of marriage, but what's the point of pretending?'

The July opening in London of *Hedda Gabler*, at the Aldwych Theatre, generated renewed interest in Glenda's affair with Andy Phillips who, throughout the general rumpus of the initial separation, had deliberately maintained a low profile. When he was discovered drinking white wine in the Opera Tavern, close to the Aldwych Theatre, after morning rehearsals for *Hedda*, he felt obliged to comment, 'Nothing's changed. We're still very close, if that is the word. After all, I am lighting Glenda this afternoon.'

But Glenda was not quite so constrained. 'I love Andy dearly,' she asserted. 'I feel reborn.'

'Now that it's over,' said Roy, 'I'll prove I can get work on my own – not just because I'm Glenda Jackson's husband.'

He was still struggling, in fact, with his On Stage touring drama company. His financially modest productions – 'affairs on a shoestring', as they were dubbed – spanned the entire range of theatrical enterprise, from *Macbeth* to *The Wizard of Oz* and Noël Coward's *This Happy Breed*. Life without Glenda certainly got no easier. Meanwhile, he had moved into a £14,000 apartment on the Isle of Dogs, three miles across the Thames as the crow flies from Blackheath, where he had prepared a special room for Daniel.

In November, when the Hodges had reached a stage of near non-communication, Roy sued Glenda for divorce in an uncontested action, alleging that the marriage had irretrievably broken down because of his wife's adultery – although Glenda continued to insist that her relationship with Andy Phillips was not the cause of the marriage break-up. Roy secured his divorce the following January in a three-minute hearing in which Andy was named as co-respondent. Glenda and Roy were granted joint custody of Daniel, and Glenda agreed to pay the cost of the action. They did not part friends, though force of circumstances eventually drew Roy increasingly towards Glenda. He candidly admitted that he missed all the glamour, the jet-setting and the money that went with being the consort of a reigning movie queen. He now had to live in a tiny apartment while his ex-wife went on living high. Did he not get a decent financial settlement? 'Only if you think two per cent of the gross is decent,' he complained.

Money, once again, compelled Roy to think of Glenda. Although Southwark Council had assigned his On Stage company a year's lease on the 300-seat Duchy Hall Theatre at London Bridge, the enterprise continued to be crippled by exorbitant running costs. Faced with the realization that the Arts Council were never going to pay a £2,000 grant, he had one last resort open to him. 'I'll ask Glenda for a loan,' he said, apparently oblivious of the humiliation. 'I'd rather not, but it could be the only alternative.'

Glenda was suddenly enjoying her new-found liberation in the role of divorcee. Friends were struck by a marked change in her spirits. 'She is a much more outgoing person now, happier,' said Bob Enders. 'She'll always be shy – she once said, "Anyone born poor in Liverpool, as I was, will always be uptight" – but lately she's beginning to light up. For the first time since I've known her she's becoming interested in pretty and expensive clothes, in good food and wines. She even enjoys parties if they aren't too big.'

But there were not many parties, since she had committed herself to tackling the role of Hedda Gabler for a movie at Elstree Studios by day and on the London stage at night. The cast for the film, called simply *Hedda*, was identical to the theatre version, with Trevor Nunn making his directorial début in the cinema. As Bob Enders was producing the project on behalf of their own Bowden Films and that of Brut Productions, it placed Glenda in a unique position as far as her relationship with the rest of the cast was concerned. 'She was, in a sense, employing us,' noted Patrick Stewart. 'The two of them, Glenda and Bob, were a nightmare. You can appreciate that if she had power on the rehearsal floor for the stage production, then on the film-studio floor her power was terrific. And poor Trevor! He was the

award-winning artistic director of the Royal Shakespeare Company, but in
the film studio he was an absolute beginner – and Glenda knew it. She
roasted him about film-making; and even when he was right, she would roast
him. He was really an outsider as far as the machinations and politics of
film-making were concerned. It was only the courtesy and gentlemanly conduct of Douglas Slocombe, the cinematographer, that saved Trevor. I was
probably the closest to Trevor, having known him the longest, and I found it
appallingly hurtful to see what was being done to him when we were making
the film.'

There were some among her colleagues, though, who wondered if Glenda
was being misunderstood. 'I have since realized that Glenda put this film into
train more as an added incentive to the rest of us in the stage production than
for any possible personal advancement,' said Timothy West. 'It worries me
now that we weren't nice to her about the difficulty that she was undoubtedly
having in getting the project off the ground – as I say, largely for *our* benefit.'

Glenda's next project was to portray Sarah Bernhardt, the outstanding
French tragedienne of the late nineteenth century, in a film entitled *The
Incredible Sarah* (1976). Bernhardt was anything but dull – even with a
wooden leg in later age – and conquered a world of admirers, among them
the Prince of Wales (the future Edward VII) and Napoleon III. Victor Hugo
knelt before her. Théophile Gautier sang her praises. Ellen Terry, Burne-
Jones and Max Beerbohm, C. B. Cochran, Colette and Clemenceau: the list
of Sarah's worshippers was as glittering as it was endless. And now Glenda
was to pay her homage. 'There was one reason why we chose Glenda for the
role,' said the American director Richard Fleischer. 'Sarah was the greatest
actress of her day and Glenda Jackson is the greatest today.'

The day after Glenda won her second Oscar, for *A Touch of Class*, she was
invited to lunch at Claridge's by Helen Strauss, for thirty years a respected
literary agent and the newly appointed head of production for *Reader's
Digest*'s film division. When the producer inquired if she would be interested
in playing Bernhardt on the screen, Glenda said yes immediately. She told
Miss Strauss, 'The idea of acting an actress fascinates me because it's something I've never done before. It will make me re-examine acting.' Seven
scripts and several million dollars later, they were ready to roll the cameras at
Pinewood Studios just outside London.

Throughout the filming Glenda protested that Bernhardt, who bathed
daily in champagne, slept in a white satin-lined coffin and kept wild animals
as household pets, was 'quite different from me emotionally', and yet there
were inescapable similarities between the two actresses. Both had been
called eccentric, both possessed an extraordinary energy that drove them like
demons, and both went through unhappy marriages. When Glenda talked of
Bernhardt's marriage she was, in effect, talking about her own. 'There is
some weakness in some people that requires them to constantly fail,' she

observed. 'I think Sarah Bernhardt's husband would have been a failure no matter who he married. What increased his tragedy was that he married such a flamboyant person, a publicly marked success, which must have made his own failure seem even greater.'

Glenda joked to members of the crew that it was no mean achievement to remain monogamous, unconceited or even sane when you were in her 'privileged' position: 'Food, sex, little daggers to stab people in the back with are all handed you on a silver platter.' But her constant work during the last twelve months, plus the emotional strain of the separation and divorce, was beginning to tell. 'I'm so tired,' she protested. 'I don't know why I'm so exhausted. I'm up at six, but I try to get to sleep by ten-thirty. You'd think seven and a half hours would be enough.'

She continued to grumble about having to get up 'almost in the middle of the night to go to work', but otherwise she seemed to be enjoying herself. Fleischer was one of those rare directors in whom and for whom she had complete confidence and respect; she was constantly mindful of a track-record that included *20,000 Leagues Under the Sea*, *The Vikings*, *Dr Doolittle*, *Tora! Tora! Tora!* and *10 Rillington Place*. 'The test of a director lies in his knowing what he wants and having the professionalism to get it,' she said. 'Richard scores heavily on both counts and consequently we are having a happy picture.' That, at least, was a relief to all concerned. Her foxy gigolo screen husband, John Castle, was delighted to find that she was 'splendid to work with, easy and generous, totally unaffected and very intelligent'. Simon Williams, who played the father of Sarah's only child, found himself adopting a similar vocabulary to describe her: 'warm, patient, democratic, helpful, discerning and *very* good'.

Douglas Wilmer (as the director of the Paris Odéon, scene of some of Bernhardt's greatest triumphs) was struck by the fact that she was 'friendly, considerate, unselfish, extremely professional – but rather remote'. He added, 'She jibbed at one scene which she felt portrayed Bernhardt in a somewhat unfavourable light. This was a scene in her dressing room when, because of stage fright, she feigned illness on a very important first night – refusing point blank (in violent terms) to appear. The scene was written as a "barney" between the two of us; but she simply did not like the idea of Bernhardt's unprofessional behaviour. Anyway, most of her lines were subsequently delivered by Yvonne Mitchell, who, as her faithful attendant, previously had nothing to say in the scene. Glenda's objection struck me as unfounded as, apparently, Bernhardt was always being difficult in this way.'

Wilmer then discovered another side to Glenda, the side he referred to as 'her generally good comradely behaviour'. This revelation occurred in a scene set in Wilmer's office at the Odéon. 'Glenda, as Sarah, was storming up and down, passing at one point behind me, while I was giving her a dressing down,' he recalled. 'At this point I heard an inexplicable "whooshing" noise coming from behind me. I couldn't make out what it was. Anyway, I "dried" at this point on rehearsal one and again on rehearsal two. When we came to rehearsal three, I asked Dick Fleischer what the peculiar noise was. In her fury, Glenda was slashing at some curtain hangings with her fan as she swished behind me. But she immediately noticed that it was having a dis-concerting effect on me and, without comment, simply cut it out. This was kind and unselfish of her.'

He reflected, 'The most extraordinary thing about Glenda was her refusal to behave in any way that could be considered extraordinary. I never heard her talk about herself or her performances. When she did talk, it was usually about something very ordinary, such as her son Daniel or gardening at weekends in Blackheath. Rather mumsy, sensible family stuff. She seemed to have no interest in discussing her work, either current or past, which I found very refreshing and "real".'

17
Liberation

People close to Glenda were beginning to wonder if, following her divorce, she really *had* been 'reborn'. She repeated the phrase so often that those who knew her best were convinced that, at the very least, a new side to her personality had emerged. 'She became friendlier and much more relaxed,' said Geraldine Addison, who had worked with Glenda on every film except *The Music Lovers*. 'She settled into a more philosophical way of working. She no longer left the set between takes as she used to. She now tended to sit around and chat to people, or sit on the floor and tell stories. She is a very good story-teller. I used to hate it when I was required on the set and had to miss the end of a story.'

'She was witty, too,' added Simon Williams.

Oliver Reed noted : 'You don't realize how boring society can be when, like Glenda, you live in a high-speed world of rich people, handsome men, fast motor cars, expensive hotels, Caribbean locations, high-flying jets and first-class seats.... I mean, she would *have* to have a sense of humour about all that, wouldn't she?'

Despite all the horror stories about Glenda's frosty behaviour towards some of her colleagues, she herself has always maintained that she takes her work and her responsibilities seriously, but never herself. It is a proposition which draws gales of laughter from many a director and leading man, but Glenda insists that she flounders with anyone who has no sense of humour. 'Anybody who can make me laugh has a great gift,' she says, apparently unconscious of the irony. And she adds, 'If you can't share a giggle, it's hard going.'

When she appeared on BBC Radio 4's *Any Questions* show she was asked what rule she would most like to break. She answered by confessing that she had always longed to rush into the Reading Room of the British Museum and shout 'Fire !' at the top of her voice. That is her kind of humour.

'She has a marvellous sense of humour – a very funny lady,' asserts make-up expert Barbara Daly. 'I was riveted by her particular brand of fun. Mark you, this was her day off; she was posing for some magazine pictures. Maybe when she's filming she is more intense and withdrawn. I've experienced this with actors. You have dinner with them and they're one person, and you meet them on the set the next morning and they're somebody else. I wonder if Glenda's like that?'

At any rate, she was conducting herself like a woman released into the world after years of incarceration. She behaved like a liberated eagle: still lethal, still possessing claws, but buoyant once again in a new environment. For years she had painted a picture of her 'blissful' marriage to the media that was patently false; and her unhappiness and frustration had undoubtedly been expressed in some of her more reprehensible behaviour at work. Divorce had freed her from both the non-fulfilment of domesticity and the 'public relations' sham that stemmed from it: 'For years I was cooped up in my house, doing all the housewifely things I'd been taught should make any woman happy. I'll still be looking after Daniel, but now that he's growing up I'll be able to have a private life of my own. I don't mean I'm going to go out and get myself a bloody lover – I'm not that hot on committing myself. My divorce has left me a bit disillusioned with men.' But not, it would seem, with Andy.

While her life has always been conducted along simple, unostentatious lines, and while she has never been given to displaying her considerable earning power or wearing the latest fashions, she was at last beginning to hint that she wanted to change things – at least slightly. 'I'd like to soften my image a bit, make myself more *human* to men,' she said. 'Most men think I have the personality of Elizabeth I. At times I do, but I'm basically an ordinary woman.'

Yet while she was reflecting on the possible advantages of a 'softer' image, she was still inclined to be one of those people who could talk articulately to another for hours and never unbend for one moment. With Glenda there was always a tendency for her to divide the world into two distinct sections: them and us. 'Us' included everyone within her own profession, as well as close friends from without; 'them' embraced any stratum of society which sought to pry too deeply into her private life, and the press interviewer was the bogeyman. Unlike Bernhardt, who was the delight of Edwardian gossip columnists and couldn't have cared less if her love life was the talk of the town, Glenda cared deeply: 'When my marriage broke up I certainly wasn't too happy seeing my private life splashed all over the papers.'

'She answered questions with an impatience that made one feel like an under-educated child,' said the writer Anthea Disney who had gone to interview her for a woman's magazine. 'Putting one at ease wasn't her forte. In fact, she politely made it clear that I was a nosy pest.'

Another magazine interviewer, Minty Clinch, discovered that talking to Glenda tended to concentrate the mind wonderfully. 'Her answers came staccato like a stream of tracer bullets across the room,' she said. 'Brisk, professional, straight, and without warmth. It was like interviewing a computer that knew exactly what it wanted to print out and didn't mean to waste one megasecond in the process.'

Glenda maintained that she was puzzled by the fact that she struck members of the press, and others, as 'frosty' and 'formidable': 'Some people are absolutely terrified of me, which I find amazing. They say, and they are *quivering* as they speak, "I've been trying for ages to pluck up courage to say hello." I can never fathom why it takes so much bravery; honestly, I am truly baffled by it.'

One woman who definitely was *not* intimidated by Glenda's imposing presence was Vanessa Redgrave, probably because she herself also dispensed quite a lethal brand of threatening 'face language'. During the final days of filming for *The Incredible Sarah*, Vanessa was also at work on a production at Pinewood and telephoned Glenda one morning to lobby support for some socialist cause, if not perhaps her own Workers' Revolutionary Party. She discoursed at length, while Glenda remained preoccupied with her make-up and hair. Glenda then hung up without committing herself one way or the other.

Simon Williams, her screen lover, walked into the room during the latter part of the conversation.

'You surprise me,' he said. 'I thought your politics were, at the very least, left of centre.'

'Yes, perhaps,' Glenda replied sleepily, 'but not before my early morning bacon butty, for goodness sake!'

Glenda has always been a socialist and sees no reason to change her views, 'although I think the endless bickering in the Labour Party is disgraceful'. She is a true socialist in the old-fashioned patriotic sense and has little time for the Marxist and Trotskyist ideologies pursued by some of her acting colleagues on both sides of the Atlantic. Once, when she was guest-of-honour at a Hollywood luncheon hosted jointly by the Los Angeles Film Critics Association and Columbia Pictures, she was questioned about her fellow British performer Vanessa Redgrave. She responded by saying that although she admired Redgrave as an actress, she saw 'something obscene' in Redgrave's residing in a posh London area while campaigning for world revolution: 'If she lived in Palestine or Jerusalem, that would be something different.'

In the early 1980s Glenda demonstrated her rejection of Vanessa Redgrave's extreme Left section of the British actors' union, Equity, by becoming a firm supporter of the union's *moderate* Left, known as Centre Forward. And yet in the early days her beliefs were completely misunderstood, and consequently she was often bracketed with Jane Fonda and the Redgraves, Vanessa and Corin. 'For a while after all those film and television awards came in I was the flavour of the month,' she said, 'and newspapers kept ringing up for quick four-word quotes on how I'd end the war in Vietnam and things like that. As I never believed anyone would print what I said, I always gave out the quotes and that's how people decided I was a "revolutionary"; but for practical work I don't come near Vanessa or Jane, who follow their causes through to some kind of action. Politically, I'm not as active as I should be if I followed my beliefs through, but I vote and I shall vote socialist till the day I die.'

Her views on the upper classes border on rage. It was this rage, 'that over-riding sense of injustice', which motivated many choices she made in her work. She recalled sitting behind two elderly ladies watching one of the early post-war Anna Neagle and Michael Wilding romances. 'It was the one where Anna is a maid and Michael was the son of the stately home and she had refused his offer of marriage. And I remember one old dear explaining to the other, "Of course, she's quite right, you see, she's not a lady." With absolute acceptance. The class thing was ingrained.'

Since her political views were well known – she was always 'the token Lefty' on radio's *Any Questions* and other forums of debate – it came as no surprise when she was approached by a member of the Bristol Labour Party to stand for Parliament in what was a safe Tory constituency. She found the suggestion both amusing and terrifying. Years later she would still be tempted to 'have a crack' at parliamentary politics, but she feared she might be too old: 'I'd do it tomorrow, but I don't have the education. Nor do I think that acting is a good preparation, despite Reagan's election. I must say I'd have suspicions if some actress came along to my front door saying, "Please let me represent you." I'd be extremely jaundiced about it all.'

At the elections which reinstated Margaret Thatcher for her second term as Tory prime minister, Glenda lent her support to Hemel Hempstead's Labour candidate Paul Boateng and to near-by Watford's Labour man Ian Wilson. 'I am a product of the welfare state and owe a lot to socialism,' she said as she signed autographs and chatted to shoppers. 'I was born a socialist and will die a socialist, so why not come here and persuade others it's the best way?'

Most members of Glenda's profession felt that it was better to keep their views on politics, or anything controversial, very quiet. The theory was: Why risk alienating your audience? But this particular actress did not subscribe to such a view. 'I don't see why an actor should not also try to be a complete human being,' she said. 'I've never felt that I should trim my views on *Any Questions* or anywhere else in public in order to play safe.' To underline the point, she was a committed member of the Arts for Labour group, whose aim was to help the Labour Party communicate in a more articulate and 'popular' way. 'Although she's really made it big in showbusiness, she's always kept a very clear idea of who she is and the world she lives in,' said actor David Yip, star of TV's *The Chinese Detective* and a fellow A for L member. 'We're not like the Workers' Revolutionary Party, which puts people's backs up. Glenda's great. She speaks on our behalf at Arts for Labour meetings, writes articles and generally tells people why she's a socialist.'

A newsman once tried to prick the probity of Glenda's brand of socialism.

'Do your riches give you a conscience about the relatively poor?' he asked, carefully setting up the trap.

'No,' she answered crisply, 'I don't feel guilty because most of what I earn anyway goes to the bloody Inland Revenue.'

She was reconciled to paying the Inland Revenue all she owed, but if they started getting really greedy then 'I won't work just for the tax money'. Her money went first to her agent, then to an accountant, and from him to the taxman. It was finally allocated to Glenda if and when she needed it. She believed totally in an egalitarian society and thought it was 'a privilege' to pay tax. 'It's a very easy way of putting your money where your mouth is,' she maintained, 'so I'm quite happy for the government to take two-thirds of everything I earn.'

Whenever any of this was in danger of sounding incredibly noble, Glenda would remind people, as she would reiterate throughout her career, that she never became an actress in the first place to make money: 'I can only do things that I like. Acting is difficult enough when you're doing something you believe in, but it must be bloody impossible if you're doing it just for the money.' And though she has been accused of venality for her acceptance of trivial, meaningless parts, she continued to insist that 'anything I've done in the last ten years I've really wanted to do; I haven't done anything just for the money'.

During most of her married life all the bills associated with her personal and professional life were paid by Roy, who also handled a great bulk of the business problems; if she wanted anything, she just asked for it. Following the divorce she managed her money quite well, though more by accident than design. Unlike her Hollywood peers, Glenda was not manic when it came to her business affairs. 'A good businesswoman?' asked Bob Enders. 'Well, not by corporation or legal standards I suppose. We formed our Bowden company on a handshake, the details worked out later by my lawyer and her business manager, Peter Crouch, who is probably closer to Glenda than anyone in the world other than her son Daniel. Glenda and George Barrie, of Brut Productions, have similar ideas about business protocol – nil. His office is wherever he happens to be sitting or standing, in his private plane, the Polo Lounge, automobile, or the men's room. Glenda's like that.'

When Glenda became only the second British actress to win two Hollywood Oscars, it was automatically assumed by many people that this would mean that Peter Crouch would be able to negotiate more money for his award-winning client's services. But no! It *would* have been the case ten years earlier, when agents talked in telephone numbers if one of their actors won an Oscar. But in the mid-1970s, when the industry had radically altered, it was not likely to make a great difference in terms of front money – the salary an actor got paid for a film. Stars tended to work for smaller salaries, plus a percentage of the profits. That way investors were more likely to recoup their money. Yet Glenda's second Oscar did help achieve other benefits during negotiations. For instance, no commitment until the final screenplay was prepared, and enhanced billing if there was a co-star. And subjects which might have been considered dicey by investors were more likely to get off the ground once it was known that Glenda's name was a part of the action. 'The Oscar also made Glenda's position stronger,' said Peter Crouch, 'so that she could do the work she wanted to do rather than have to do.'

While Glenda was filming *The Incredible Sarah*, Bob Enders boasted to America's showbusiness newspaper *Variety* that England fielded two highly 'financible' film talents in the current international market, Glenda Jackson and Michael Caine. On the bankability angle, Enders claimed that in some territories, parts of Europe and elsewhere, Glenda was even more potent than superstar Barbra Streisand. He said that Ray Stark offered her $1,500,000 to re-team with George Segal in *Black Bird*, but that Glenda refused it because she did not like the script. Enders's business partner, it was now patently clear, did *not* act just for the money; when it came to money, in fact, and the fees she accepted, she was something of an oddity in a profession whose credo, among the movie superstars, was one of 'screw the bastards for every penny you can get.' In matters concerning her worth to a film, her mind simply did not work like that. 'I'm really ludicrously over-paid, bearing in mind that just doing the work is enough,' she stated, sending her agent into apoplexy. 'There's a great deal of jam on the bread.'

The whole question of Glenda's fees and the sort of money she was prepared to accept for certain projects dear to her heart was an intriguing one. By American standards, her price was always right – that is, cheap. When she was playing the Christine Keeler–Jackie Kennedy character with the Theatre of Cruelty, she was being paid £12 a week. She went up to £100 a week for *The Marat/Sade* on Broadway, and for the whole job in *Women in Love* it was £5,000 (Elizabeth Taylor had done better than that in a single day).

Her value rocketed to nearly £30,000 for *Sunday, Bloody Sunday*, close to the top in England at that time, though still petty cash by Hollywood standards. The fees would rise to at least £100,000 for every film, and as she was making on average two films a year, that was enough to put a lot of noughts in her bank balance; but the Americans, anyway, regarded those sort of fees as peanuts: when Elizabeth Taylor won her $1 million fee for *Cleopatra* she was also getting $50,000 a week for overtime, plus $3,000 a week living allowance, plus a big percentage of the picture's gross earnings. Before the project was aborted, Glenda was to star in a film of the West End and Broadway play, *Rose*, with Bob Enders directing, for a fee of £75,000 and twenty-five per cent of the action; had the movie got off the ground, and had it succeeded at the box office, it would have amounted to a very nice deal indeed.

By and large, Glenda was not in the business of movie-making to concoct 'very nice deals' – not financial ones, at least. She was one of the few British actresses who could command a million dollars a movie, but although at her box-office peak she could have got it – and was offered it more than once – she would never actually *ask* for a million dollars. She complained often enough that million-dollar salaries for film stars were an obscenity: 'It's hard enough in this business to be taken seriously as an actress without showing the world you can be bought by a big salary. Every time an actor says, "This is rubbish but I'll do it for $5 million," he's making it harder for all of us.' Which was not to say that she would not accept Hollywood gold if asked. She would, and did, rolling amused eyes at the youth-obsessed, hysterical antics of the town, and then dashing for home to pay her taxes like a good citizen. But, in her uncharacteristic naivety, she put a financial spanner in the works by allowing the news to leak out that, if she was enthusiastic about a project, she would do it for a ludicrously cut-price rate. Glenda Jackson was the actress you could often find displayed on the film world's bargain counter. 'I remember over-hearing a conversation between two producers when I was filming in Rome,' said Vladek Sheybal. 'It went like this: "Glenda Jackson? You can have her for pennies. If she likes the part, she'll do it for practically nothing." I'm afraid she established this reputation that she could be bought for very little money, on the cheap.'

The Hollywood film moguls were genuinely perplexed by Glenda's extra-ordinary reticence where her own fees were concerned. They continued to dismiss her salaries as 'peanuts'. 'Glenda Jackson could command the earth and get it,' said one studio boss, 'but she never makes any outrageous de-mands. She's heaven to work with in comparison to some other female stars I could name. Some of them insert every conceivable clause into their con-tracts. They will dictate all the odds – from the size of their dressing rooms right down to the colour of the telephone in their chauffeur-driven studio-sponsored limousines. Oh, if only there were more actresses around like Glenda Jackson ....'

When Glenda went to New York for the first time during the winter of 1965-6, she was warned about how cold the American city was at that time of the year. She subsequently came across a sheepskin coat in a shop window for £65 and thought, 'That would be just the thing.' She had the money, but could not bring herself to buy it. She paced up and down the street, trying to make up her mind about whether or not to purchase the garment. 'I finally did – but I felt so guilty,' she said.

A feeling of guilt plagues her to this day whenever she spends money on anything other than the bare essentials: 'It's a curious fact, but when you've been so long without money you find it difficult to spend.' For years her family drank out of Sainsbury's glasses because she would not buy more expensive ones. It was not until as late in her career as 1979, when she was filming in Austria, that she ventured into a china shop. 'I bought eighteen glasses *and* a teaset and they were hideously expensive,' she said. 'But, because I was paying in Austrian money, which seemed like Monopoly money, I managed to avoid the guilty feeling.'

If, just a few years ago, she paid more than £20 for a pair of shoes, she thought that it was 'a wicked, monstrous extravagance – it isn't really, because you can't buy shoes for much less, but I remember when you could go to Dolcis and buy a pair for £3.' But her expenditure was not always governed by straightforward rationale. She would cheerfully spend £250 for one of her favourite Jean Muir slinky jersey dresses – though the world would almost always see her in more workaday Marks & Spencer clothes.

She got rid of her red Mercedes because it was drinking up petrol, and she later sold a high-powered BMW because, she thought, 'This is too much.' Glenda preferred simply to get on with her work rather than think about fame and fortune. She had no regrets at ignoring Hollywood and a Gucci life-style; and there would be no exclusive private school for Daniel: he was destined for Kidbrooke, the local comprehensive. Until recently she still pushed a trolley round her local supermarket and complained about the prices. 'Of *course* I notice it when things go up week by week,' she insisted. 'Fortunately I have very simple tastes. It's meat and potatoes in our house. When I'm on my own I'll just have an egg on toast.'

Her home in Blackheath was once burgled and it proved a humiliating experience: the thieves were professionals and they left without taking a *thing*. 'The embarrassment of not having anything worth a proper thief's while!' she told one of the police officers who had called to investigate. 'I know it's no palace, but what an insult.'

'We think they thought you had lots of money stashed away,' said the policeman. 'That's why they swept all the books off the shelves: they were looking for a secret wall-safe.' He thought for a moment. 'Er – you *have* got a safe somewhere, haven't you?'

'What would I want a safe for?'

'There are a lot of people,' he answered, 'who have safes to keep money they haven't declared for tax.'

Glenda was so shocked by this that the police became embarrassed. Then one said, 'But you have valuable paintings, haven't you? I hear one is worth at least £40,000.'

The mistress of the non-burgled house was greatly incensed by this time, and fumed, 'I'd be very grateful if it could be put around that the highest sum I have ever paid for any picture on my walls is £50.'

There is also another side to Glenda when it comes to money which is far from materialistic. 'There is a really lovable side to her,' affirmed Vladek Sheybal. 'I'm sure if I was in trouble and I telephoned her in the middle of the night, Glenda would arrange quietly and efficiently to get me out of trouble. I am sure of it.'

When filming was completed on *The Incredible Sarah* Glenda threw a magnificent at London's celebrated Café Royal. 'It was an enormous "do",' said Geraldine Addison. 'She took over an entire suite. There was a disco in one room, a band in another, and hot food in another. It was really amazing.' One of the revellers, a plate of shepherd's pie in one hand and a glass of ale in the other, staggered up to Glenda in the early hours and asked if she thought she would win an Oscar nomination for playing Bernhardt in the film. She replied, 'Why? Did Sarah ever win one?'

There were no nominations. The film, and Glenda's performance, was almost universally panned. 'Jackson chews the scenery in a flamboyant performance, but someone should have chewed up the script instead,' suggested one American critic. And: 'The movie evinces only the skimpiest interest in recreating any plausible vision of how the real Bernhardt looked or performed. Her style is 1970s, not 1870s,' wrote Alexander Walker in the London *Evening Standard*.

Glenda was in the dog-house again.

Part Five

A Star in Collision

A woman is always a fickle, unstable thing.

Virgil,
Aeneid, Book IV, 30–19 BC

18

Heading for the Rocks?

When Glenda reached the last page of Muriel Spark's novella *The Abbess of Crewe* she immediately phoned Bob Enders and Peter Crouch. 'I've just finished the book,' she said, 'and I think it's one of the funniest novels I've ever read – all these ladies having a great Watergate in a convent. I'll do it.'

Enders was delighted. 'The Nixonian Sister Alexandra might have been made in heaven for you,' he enthused.

In January 1976 Glenda flew to Philadelphia for location shooting on the resulting movie, *Nasty Habits*, a co-production with Brut and her own Bowden company. She was in effect making her first film in the United States, but only 'in effect', because the bulk of the picture was shot in and around All Saints' Pastoral Centre, an abbey built at London Colney within easy commuting distance of London. Her contact with Philadelphia merely consisted of a week's filming in the streets, at the airport, in the busy Wanamaker's department store, and at Liberty Hall. Then it was back to the winter chill of the Gothic abbey, its mellow stonework, blue stained glass and heavy oak woodwork providing a made-to-measure studio, complete with sets and backlot, offices, prop-rooms, wardrobe and dressing-rooms.

The idea of Glenda playing a nun in the mould of Richard Nixon seems absurd at first; and yet, despite drawing a mixed response from the critics, the film succeeded on its own terms. The black comedy is set in an unconventional Philadelphia convent where the Machiavellian mother superior is given to bugging the premises with hidden microphones, closed-circuit television and carefully concealed tape-recorders. The parallels with the Watergate affair are unmistakable, especially when the deposed but unrepentant Glenda Jackson bids farewell to a batch of reporters by saying, 'Well, you won't have Sister Alexandra to kick around any more.'

While Glenda felt invigorated by being part of a cast which represented the first movie in recent years with women playing all the key roles – Melina Mercouri, Geraldine Page, Sandy Dennis, Anne Jackson, Edith Evans, Anne Meara and Susan Penhaligon – she was not greatly enamoured of the film's title. 'It sounds like a cheap sex thing at the moment,' she complained unsuccessfully to Bob Enders.

In May, when filming was completed, Glenda reneged on a lifetime's dislike of birthday parties. She felt that her fortieth birthday required some sort of public celebration, so threw the first and only birthday party of her life, a huge affair attended by Andy and all her showbusiness cronies. 'It seems quite wonderful to finally be forty,' she told her guests, 'although I suppose all it really means is that I've had the sense to look both ways before crossing the street for thirty-nine years.'

Several times during the evening Glenda and Andy Phillips disentangled themselves from the merrymaking to 'talk shop'. In partnership with Bob Enders the couple had formed a new, unsubsidized, co-operative theatre company called Bullfinch Productions to stage short West End seasons. And now, all through the night, they discussed their first season at the Old Vic, opening with the Jacobean play by John Webster, *The White Devil.* They already knew that the twenty-strong company would be led by Jonathan Pryce, Jack Shepherd, Frances de la Tour, James Villiers, John Kane, Madge Ryan, Miriam Margolyes, Patrick Magee and, of course, Glenda herself, and that they would perform mainly difficult and essentially uncommercial plays. As the wine went to her head, Glenda's enthusiasm for the venture grew by the minute. She and Andy agreed that the top salary should be only £250 a week and the lowest £75, which was somewhat above the subsidized companies; but they wondered if the £30,000 budget for *The White Devil* would be sufficient. It was, just, though plans to stage Webster's *The Duchess of Malfi*, and a Restoration comedy in the autumn with American film and Shakespearean actors Stacy Keach and Irene Worth among the stars, would not materialize through lack of funds.

The production opened in July 1976 to mixed notices, and played initially at slightly under break-even point, but business picked up slowly as the summer tourist season gained momentum. *Nasty Habits* director Michael Lindsay-Hogg was again at the helm in a mainly downbeat production conceived in modern clothing with a set which resembled a vast hotel lobby made of tortoise-shell; Andy was in charge of the lighting.

Webster was a contemporary of Shakespeare, and *The White Devil* is one of those revenge tragedies in which so many people are deceived, plotted against and brutally slain that the curtain comes down on a stage littered with corpses, while sections of the contemporary audience can only giggle at the exaggerated mayhem they have witnessed. More than one critic argued that Lindsay-Hogg's direction stifled the fiery grandeur of Glenda's murdering adulterous Vittoria Corombona, while Jack Tinker in the *Daily Mail* complained that although she managed to suggest that Vittoria's adultery and complicity in her husband's murder might have stemmed from 'an intellectual loathing of women's bondage', it went 'no deeper than discarding the use of a bra she plainly does not need'. On the other hand, Herbert Kretzmer in the *Daily Express* noted that she 'suffered magnificently and should draw in sympathetic crowds'. *Plays and Players* reviewer David Zane Mairowitz lamented the fact that Glenda brought a 'bored arrogance' to the production:

full of her famous cynicism and world-weariness which infects the stage from her very first entrance. Once again Jackson gives the impression she knows the entire plot from the outset, so that we never get Vittoria's freshness or vitality. If any of Webster's characters retain an openness of mind it is his two central women, but here the quality is thoroughly subverted by Jackson's tendency never to *learn* anything while on stage, in the cause of promoting the action.

The eight-week season at an end, Glenda flew to New York for business meetings. Among other things, she discussed with theatre producer Joseph Papp the possibility of starring in the title role of a London production of *Hamlet*. Papp told her that he believed Hamlet was actually born a female but was groomed to develop male interests and attitudes in preparing for the throne. Glenda was intrigued by the theory and was disappointed when the deal fell through.

A few days later Bob Enders called round to her hotel room in a highly agitated mood and handed her a copy of the *New York Times*, already opened and well-thumbed at a page bearing the headline 'It's Time to Hold Glenda Jackson Accountable'. Underneath was a long diatribe by Vincent Canby accusing Glenda, among other things, of allowing her film career to go up in smoke by associating herself with such movies as *Mary, Queen of Scots*, *Bequest to the Nation*, *The Tempter* and *The Incredible Sarah*. He said there came a time when actors who had reached a certain status, as Glenda had now, must share the blame when a film dive-bombed. It was no good making excuses for her any more; it was no longer sufficient to say, for instance, 'Glenda Jackson did the best she could with the idiotic material and abysmal direction, though no one could have saved the picture.'

Glenda blinked with fury when she read Canby's conclusion: 'It's time to hold Miss Jackson accountable. She isn't having a run of bad luck. She's accepting roles in junk movies that can't even be rationalized for meeting some peculiar popular taste. The movies are duds. Something is happening to her touch. Is it dire financial need, greed, a woeful lack of judgement? Unless she pulls herself together, a serious career could be heading for the rocks.'

Glenda's immediate inclination was to dash round to the newspaper's offices on West 43rd Street and violate Canby's head with a rolled-up copy of the *New York Times*. Instead, she poured herself a stiff drink and ploughed through the personal attack to the bitter end:

I've never really been bored by any of her performances, even in something as silly as *The Tempter*, but her strength is beginning to look strained. Or perhaps we're starting to lose patience. I, for one, am tired of toting a lot of high expectations to a Jackson film only to wind up having to make excuses for her. She, her agent, her best friend, her hairdresser, someone should suggest that she slow down, read a script before signing a commitment, and make bloody sure that she can trust the talent around her. Otherwise curtains.

Glenda exploded, and Enders ducked as her whisky glass went flying. 'I accept full responsibility for everything I've done,' she raved, 'but if an actress never worked until she found something she thought was wonderful, then she'd probably never work at all. The only way to get better in this business is to work.'

Enders nodded.

'It's no good sitting at home waiting for the great script to arrive, is it?' she continued. 'As we all know, it hardly ever does. And ability atrophies through lack of exercise.' She reminded Enders that ninety per cent of the stuff she was offered was 'rubbish'. It always had been, even after winning her Oscars. 'And the strange thing is the worse the script I'm sent, the more money I'm usually offered – you know that. But if I've done things that weren't good, it certainly wasn't for the money, was it?'

Enders, of all people, knew this to be true. It was this fact alone which, when allied to accusations of financial greed, so infuriated her.

Before returning to Blackheath Glenda embarked on a New York shopping mission, to purchase a Captain America doll for Daniel, who was now nearing his eighth birthday. When his mother was away on business, or engaged on a film, there was always a pool of people to attend to his needs: the home-help, his Aunty Lynne, his paternal and maternal grandparents, as well as his father. But none of this altered the fact that the role of combining motherhood with acting was one that preyed heavily on Glenda's conscience. Ibsen noted at the time of writing *Hedda Gabler*, 'Women aren't all created to be mothers. They all have a leaning towards sensuality, but are afraid of the scandal.'

On the plane back to London she admitted to Bob Enders, 'You just have to accept and learn to live with the guilt one feels by being a working mother. That one is expected to be at home and not go to work, certainly not expected to work in anything that brings in large rewards. Not allowed to do anything that could be called a career.' She did not think that Daniel had been much affected by either her separation from Roy or her work. She explained to her business partner that her ambition for her son was to make him totally independent: 'I think children should move on from what their parents have done. Hopefully he will discount everything that I or his father have done.' She then added: 'You can't actually stop being alive for fear it destroys your child.'

As a mother, she felt that her biggest responsibility to Daniel was to ensure that he grew up with the ability to love other people – 'which, of course, carries with it all the other nightmares, middle-of-the-night fears, of just how hurt he is going to be as a result. Being a parent is a bloody dangerous job.' But one area Glenda and Roy still agreed on was the sincere hope that their son would never show aspirations to be an actor. 'No bloody fear!' the actress sighed as she sipped a glass of in-flight orange juice.

Neither the 'glamour' of his mother's profession, nor the big name it spawned, seemed to touch her son. This was illustrated soon after her return from the States, when Daniel came home from school and said to his mother, 'You are famous, aren't you?'

'What do you mean?' asked Glenda.

'You are *famous*, aren't you?' he repeated.

'I'm comparatively well known, but why do you ask?'

'Because a boy at school said you weren't famous and I said you were.'

'Well, what am I famous for?'

'Oh, *I* don't know.'

That greatly appealed to the world's Number One anti-fuss, anti-glamour movie star. 'The camera doesn't give a bugger for ego, only what you've got to sell,' was how she looked at it. Bob Enders knew more than most Glenda's simple approach to film-making. He explained: 'The things that interest most actresses when starting a picture – who is designing the clothes, who the cameraman will be, who is to do her hair and make-up – interest Glenda not at all. I remember on *The Maids* we brought in a fine make-up chap with a reputation on two continents for his expertise. On meeting Glenda for the first time he said, "Miss Jackson, what 'look' do you wish to project?" She answered, "Unspotted. Just cover up the blotches."' Glenda's acne plagued her still.

There were times when Glenda's tendency towards self-deprecation verged on the affected, the contrived. When she teamed up with Walter Matthau and someone suggested that they had a new Tracy–Hepburn partnership on their hands, the remark went over like a lead balloon. 'It's not that sort of film,' she said matter-of-factly, 'and we're not that sort of talent.' When a friend complimented her on being a great success story, she rejoined icily, 'What does it mean? It means I get well paid, I have a certain amount of power over what I do, but is it really, is it *really* success?' When she was complimented, she would admit later, 'To be honest, I've never received a single compliment that wasn't delivered in a tone of total surprise. So on the few occasions when someone has said, "You look marvellous," they've said it with such shock that it's meant nothing.'

Glenda is not, of course, the simple 'together' person she likes to convey to the world. 'I noticed that she had a way of constantly down-grading herself,' remembered Joseph Losey. 'Maybe it was just a mannerism, or maybe she was using it as a form of self-protection – but who will ever know?'

19
Men

The rumours were born when Andy Phillips failed to turn up to a backstage party to celebrate the opening of *The White Devil* at the Old Vic. Glenda embraced this guest and that, but the man who had just lit her new stage show so brilliantly was nowhere to be seen. The talk all evening, over the Chablis and toasted sardine canapés, was that the sixteen-month romance was over. The first-night carousers could think of little else.

They had argued. There was nothing unusual in that; there were frequent rows. But this time it was serious enough for her lover to declare 'Enough's enough!' The day after he walked out of Glenda's house in Blackheath he was in Paris to light a production of *Equus*, and he was still in indignant mood. 'Glenda?' he blustered. 'She'd make a fantastic wife – but she's a rotten landlady.'

A close friend explained, 'Andy had felt increasingly like a lodger ever since he moved in with Glenda.'

There had been a plan during the summer for them to buy another house where she and Andy could make a fresh start, but that fell through at the eleventh hour. The last straw in their relationship seemed to come when Glenda flew to New York and it was arranged that Roy should move back temporarily to look after Daniel. Andy was less than happy about *that* particular idea.

By Christmas the actress and the lighting man had resolved their differences and were together again, by which time Glenda tried to dismiss the whole débâcle. 'I have a suspicion that there is a section of people who would be delighted if our relationship all turned out to be a disaster,' she said tartly. 'Well, I just go bowling along with Andrew and lucky I am to be so doing. We're still happily together – but we aren't getting married. I have no interest in that at all.' Unlike Andy. And it was about this particular subject that so many of their lovers' tiffs occurred. It was a major bone of contention between them. 'I would love to marry her,' he disclosed, 'but she is a tough lady to persuade.'

Glenda had few illusions about the sort of wife she would have made for Andy. 'I know I must be difficult to live with,' she said, 'because I brood if things don't go right. I wish I could explode more. It would do

38
In John Mortimer's stage comedy *Collaborators* (Duchess Theatre, London, 1973), a love triangle involving a barrister-playwright (John Wood, *right*), his wife Katherine (Glenda), and a film producer (Joss Ackland).

39
Right Glenda and Susannah York as the servants in Genet's *The Maids*, produced in 1974 both for the cinema and for London's prestigious Greenwich Theatre.

40
Below Glenda camouflages a crooked, slightly overgrown tooth during filming by wearing a special dental cap – identifiable in the picture to the immediate left of the upper central incisors.

41
With Andy Phillips. Their romance blossomed in 1975 during the RSC's Australian and North American tour of *Hedda Gabler*.

43
Romance of a different kind – as Elizabeth Fielding, seduced by Helmut Berger's second-rate gigolo, in Joseph Losey's *The Romantic Englishwoman* (1975). Off-screen, the Jackson-Berger relationship was rather less romantic.

42
In the title role of *Hedda* (1975), Trevor Nunn's screen version of his touring RSC stage production of Ibsen's play.

44, 45
As the actress Sarah Bernhardt: (*above*) Glenda portrays Bernhardt portraying Zanetto in *The Troubadour*, and (*right*) as Bernhardt enacting the Maid of Orleans in *Saint Joan*.

46
In her award-winning impersonation of the eccentric English poet Stevie Smith in *Stevie* (Vaudeville Theatre, London, 1977), which was transferred to the cinema screen a year later, with Mona Washbourne repeating the role of the poet's aunt.

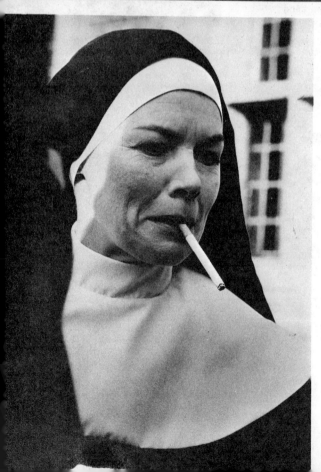

Nat Cohen presents for EMI Film Distributors Ltd

GLENDA JACKSON
CLAUDIO CASSINELLI
LISA HARROW
in
THE
TEMPTER
AA

Story by DAMIANO DAMIANI
Screenplay by DAMIANO DAMIANI · FABRIZIO ONOFRI · AUDREY NOHRA
Music by ENNIO MORRICONE
Produced by ANIS NOHRA British Producer MARTIN C. SCHUTE

Directed by DAMIANO DAMIANI

An Anglo-Italian co-production Lifeguard Productions Ltd.
Euro International Films S.P.A. Prints by Technicolor
Distributed by EMI Film Distributors Ltd.

EMI

47, 48
Vows of poverty, chastity and obedience in a new cinematic light: (*above*) as the sadistic, sex-starved Sister Geraldine in the Italian-made film *The Tempter* (1974), and (*left*) a between scenes taste of nicotine while portraying Sister Alexandra, the Machiavellian mother superior in *Nasty Habits* (1976).

49, 50
Togetherness ... with a brace of American movie actors renowed for their penchant for wry comedy: (*left*) with Walter Matthau in *House Calls* (1978); and (*above right*) with George Segal in *Lost and Found* (1979).

51
As Rose, the Midlands schoolteacher in the stage comedy *Rose*, which was an unparalleled success in London at the Duke of York's Theatre in 1980 and an unqualified Broadway flop a year later at the Cort Theater – seen here with Diana Davies, as Sally, rehearsing the West End production.

52, 53

Soaking up the sun in the South of France for the International Film Festival at Cannes. (*Above*) At the festival in 1976 with (*left to right*) Brut Productions' George Barrie (executive producer of *Nasty Habits*, *Hedda*, *A Touch of Class* and *The Class of Miss MacMichael*), Faye Dunaway, and *Romantic Englishwoman* co-star Helmut Berger. (*Below*) French actress Michelle Morgan presents Glenda with an award for Distinguished Service to the Cinema at 1983's festival.

54
Above A triumph at the Cannes Film Festival in 1982: Glenda as a dowdy First World War housewife and Ann-Margret as the soldier's repressed spinster cousin in the film adaptation of Rebecca West's semi-autobiographical novel, *The Return of the Soldier* (1983).

55
As the tough, shrewd TV documentary director Sophie, with Kenneth Colley, in the low-budget made-for-TV film, *Giro City* (1982).

56
Glenda with her father, bricklayer Harry ('Micky') Jackson: 'a wonderful banjo player'.

57
Glenda's mother, Joan Jackson: 'There was always a lo of the actress in our Glenda May, you know.'

58
The Glenda Jackson Theatre, situated in Birkenhead's busy Borough Road and named in the actress's honour, was officially opened by Glenda in 1983.

me good. But when I do lose my temper it's awful, and I carry it around with me for days because I'm so appalled at what I've done.'

She confided to friends that, although her relationship with Andy was basically a happy one, she had come to the conclusion the hard way that there was no 'right man' for her when it came to marriage. 'I think it must be incredibly hard to make a second marriage work because you inevitably carry so much of the past with you into it,' she confessed. 'You can't chop off a first marriage and pretend it never occurred. I simply don't understand the attitude of women you read about who have had five or six husbands. I remember someone saying to me once, "I can never understand why actors smile at each other when they're supposed to be in love, because love is the most miserable experience," and there's a great deal of truth in that . . . for some of the time. But I think I am actually far happier when I'm in love – though I *don't* want to enter into a marital state again. It's far, far too easy to get married. I think marriage should be made very, very hard and divorce easier.'

As far as Andy was concerned, pronouncements such as these fell on completely deaf ears.

As so often in her career, Glenda next embarked on a project which, in certain respects, almost exactly mirrored the state of her personal life at that time. In March, she starred as the eccentric English poet Stevie Smith in a new West End play by Hugh Whitemore called *Stevie*. This is not to suggest that Glenda's life thus far resembled that of the poet who had died just six years previously of a brain tumour. For Stevie Smith looked and sounded like something out of a nursery rhyme – the Old Woman Who Lived in a Shoe was close, except that Miss Smith's shoe was No 1, Avondale Road, Palmers Green, North London, where she lived not with so many children, but her aunt (an efficient lady known affectionately as 'the lion of Hull'), with occasional visits from a mysterious male 'friend'. She was small, frail and spindly, 'a sharp little mouse of a thing with a sly smile', recalled an acquaintance. She was also gauche, shy, excruciatingly personally insecure and lacking in confidence, and afflicted with a girlish giggle. She used her awkwardness almost aggressively, turning her dowdy manner of dress into a trademark of eccentricity.

At fifty, Stevie Smith was still wearing rumpled corduroy pinafores, shapeless cardigans, white collars, ankle socks and sandals, and had an endearing way of dropping in unexpectedly for tea. She penned such cryptic, succinct verse as 'This English woman is so refined, / She has no bosom and no behind', and the poem whose metaphoric title has become a common British expression: 'Not Waving But Drowning'. And, at some point, she experienced a mild foretaste of sexual 'bliss', in the middle of which her fiancé, Freddie, solicitously inquired, 'Are you enjoying it, dear?' Whatever her answer, she certainly declined marriage, and for much the same reasons as Glenda.

'Will you marry me?' asked Freddie.

'No, thank you,' Stevie replied. 'I'm a friendship girl, not the marrying kind.'

'If you changed, it could work. . . .'

'No, thank you.'

Andy, who was responsible for lighting the Bullfinch group's second production, persevered during the play's previews in out-of-town Richmond, Brighton and Bath. But Glenda remained firm: 'No, thank you.'

She identified wholly with Stevie, who, by the time of her death, was one of Britain's most admired poets – awarded the Queen's Medal in 1969 – as well as a novelist, broadcaster and social celebrity. The manner in which they conducted their personal lives had much in common: they rejected lovers and suitors, fashionability and the trappings of fame, and dedicated themselves to their particular crafts. Stevie looked after her aunt, Glenda cared for her son. They both lived in unfashionable suburbia.

By a quirk of fate, Glenda met the poet soon after joining the Royal Shakespeare Company in 1964. 'Evenings of jazz and poetry were very fashionable then,' she recalled. 'I'd never heard of Stevie Smith and there was this extraordinary woman with an enormous grin standing dead straight in front of me. And I mean *straight* – there wasn't a protective curve in her body. She was tiny and had a long skirt with ankle socks and sandals, and a little girl haircut with a straight fringe, and an immensely penetrating gaze. Then she romped on to the stage and straight into "Not Waving But Drowning" and I thought, "There's something amazing about you, lady." I never saw her again.'

When it was announced that Glenda was to play Stevie the proposal was greeted with hostility by Stevie Smith's friends, who feared that the actress would depict the poetess as a 'dotty', disparaging caricature. Their apprehension was mollified when they saw the play at the Vaudeville Theatre. 'Stevie would love *Stevie*,' they said almost in unison, adding, 'But she'd have made some acid comment on it just in case someone thought she was being sentimental.' Equal praise went to the redoubtable Mona Washbourne as the aunt and to Peter Eyre as the all-purpose male in Stevie's life – Freddie, narrator, literary friend. The critics were delighted – 'A lovely evening,' noted the *Sunday Express*; 'A remarkable play,' agreed *Plays and Players* – while they were ecstatic in their plaudits for Glenda. After years of theatre disasters, and more than her fair share of junk reviews for junk films, she was once again the flavour of the month in the West End. Yet no accolade meant more to Glenda than when Stevie Smith's executor, James MacGibbon, published an anthology of her poems for Penguin and dedicated the book to Hugh Whitemore and herself. 'To see my name on the fly-leaf of a book – now that really *was* a thrill,' she said.

The subsequent movie version of *Stevie* (1978), with Mona Washbourne again repeating her award-winning role, but this time with Alec McCowen as Stevie's suitor and Trevor Howard as her literary agent, was one of the cinema's surprise successes – following a bumpy launch – proving that there was still an audience for the 'little' type of film; Bob Enders, making his directorial début, brought the film in for half a million dollars. Laurels flew in all directions for cast and film alike, Glenda receiving Actress of the Year awards from the Variety Club of Great Britain, the Montreal Film Festival, New York's National Board of Review of Motion Pictures, and the New York Film Critics Circle – a lot of additional pieces of silver for Mrs Joan Jackson to clean at the awards' ultimate Hoylake destination.

Even the dreaded Vincent Canby, who had speculated that Glenda's film career was heading for the rocks, dispatched such a rave review in the *New York Times* that the result was *Stevie*-mania, a phenomenon that baffled Glenda. 'You explain it to *me*,' she told everybody who congratulated her. 'Somebody up there – I can only presume it was Miss Smith herself – encouraged Vincent Canby to go and see it and write that notice.' Bob Enders had assured everybody that while Palmers Green and poetry was hardly the stuff of which blockbusters were made, there *was* an audience for 'both Camus and Harold Robbins'. The critics seemed to agree.

The movie was one of those rarities: a 'fun' project for the entire cast and crew, where personality clashes – and not least those involving Glenda – were kept resolutely in the background. 'I loved Glenda because she was so down-to-earth and called a spade a spade,' said Mona Washbourne. 'I never stopped admiring her superb professionalism,' added Alec McCowen. Ace cinematographer Freddie Young, who collected Hollywood Oscars for *Lawrence of Arabia*, *Doctor Zhivago* and *Ryan's Daughter*, said he agreed with McCowen. 'She never fluffed a line of dialogue, and always moved to the correct positions so that the camera operator was never thrown into confusion by a faulty move or gesture. It was truly remarkable; the film crew thought she was marvellous.'

A Glenda Jackson who was universally loved on the film set was a remarkable phenomenon indeed. Whatever was happening to her? When someone on the set expressed surprise at her anti-marriage philosophy, she took him by the arm and insisted, 'I'm not cutting men out of my life altogether, you know – I hope I'm not past that kind of challenge.'

It should perhaps not go unnoticed that Glenda regarded men not so much as love objects but as entities to challenge and be challenged by. Her relationships with men, in fact, were invariably imbued with a certain level of contempt. 'Men,' she insisted, 'demand far too much from women. They expect us to be far more patient, understanding and undemanding than anyone has any right to expect of a person. Is it so amazing that I don't find men very likeable when you have to spend so much time pandering to their egos? Personally, I think with most men there's one heck of a lot of outlay for a very small return.'

A glint would register in Glenda's eyes whenever she recalled the men she had physically punched out of her life. 'Oh, yes, I've struck men and I've no regrets at all about it,' she said. 'I don't think I like men really. When I've hit them, it's usually happened in situations where it was the last resort. I have to be driven some way, though, before I land a blow; and usually the men have hit back after recovering from the shock. That's when I got beat. Though I'm not very keen on men, I've always had them around me and have been pretty fortunate. They always have to succeed, however, which makes things difficult for them and then they become very boring. In a way I'm wary of them, disillusioned. But I can tell you with complete honesty that I find the unadulterated company of women tedious beyond belief.'

Nevertheless, a certain predilection for the company of her own sex was evident during the tour of *Hedda Gabler* in Australia and the United States. 'She gathered around herself, and bound to her, a group of women who became known as "Glenda's groupies",' recalled Patrick Stewart. 'It was weird, *really* weird, and they actually wore T-shirts with her name emblazoned across the front. This went on for about five weeks. A private jet was put at her disposal by Fabergé, and all the girls went with her. There was never any suggestion that the fellas – Timmy West, Peter Eyre, me, the understudy Oz Clark, an odd assortment of blokes – should be invited. Men never figured in Glenda's mind in this respect, because, after a while, she simply cut herself off from all the men in the company.'

Her dealings with actors tended to be conducted along the lines of 'work with 'em and leave 'em'. Such a sentiment was even more pronounced when it came to her leading men. Once, during a season of a play with the RSC at Stratford, it was observed that she and her leading man were never seen engaging in conversation for the entire rehearsal period. 'She was never in the Green Room having a cup of tea and chatting with him,' said one member of the cast. 'But with your leading man you *need* to get to know that person.'

It made little difference. Whether it was in the theatre or in films, she preferred not to like her leading men. 'I find I work better if I dislike them,' she said. 'It makes me more objective.' She later admitted, 'I really don't find actors attractive, or the most interesting company.' None of her leading men had attracted her sexually; and yet, 'I'd be turned on by Brando, but then he's about the best actor in the world and it would just be admiration for that alone.'

While it was true that Glenda had managed to arouse many of her male co-stars, it was usually their temper that had exploded rather than their sexuality. But there have been some exceptions; Oliver Reed continued to find her 'a very sexy bird', and, under certain circumstances, so did actor Patrick Stewart. On the *Hedda Gabler* tour he was astounded to see her using her gender in restaurants to beguile waiters. 'She was incredibly charming to them, but charming in a kind of provoking way,' said Stewart. 'By that, I mean sexually provoking. She used to flirt, that's what she did, and flirting wasn't something that she did very much. It was odd. And yet at times I also used to find her *so* sexually attractive – when she was being nice. When she was nice, she was absolutely irresistible. I particularly remember one evening in Australia, when there were just the three of us – Glenda, Trevor Nunn and myself – sitting on a balcony; and it was just the two fellows and her, and the whole conversation drifted into a kind of sexually "dangerous" area, and I could see how all that worked for her on the screen.'

None of this altered the fact that many men felt threatened by her. Yet this was undoubtedly because she was so obviously a man's woman, not a boy's fantasy female. And if most men preferred to remain boys into their dotage, well, that was hardly her fault. Having said that, it can only be repeated that men were often frightened of the actress with the caustic tongue.

On the subject of Andy and the question of marriage, she was still undecided. Nevertheless, she had something significant to say on the like-lihood of a more permanent relationship: 'For marriage the best man is the man within oneself. Most women need to develop their own "masculine" qualities of independence, pride, courage and open sexuality.'

20

Matthau and Segal

The wounds were healing, if not actually healed. Glenda and Roy had made a pact: for the sake of Daniel, now eight, they would meet on common ground in an attempt to make his life less burdensome. 'The most important thing is not to use the child as a football between the two partners,' she said. 'All you can do is hope that you get it right, but I don't think you can guarantee anything. For me, the hardest thing would be if, in some serious situation with Dan, I couldn't ring up his father and say, "There's something going wrong here."'

So when Glenda flew to the United States in July 1977 to make her first Hollywood movie, *House Calls*, with Walter Matthau, Dan went along and so did Roy. (Andy Phillips had a stage play to keep him busy in London.) While Glenda stayed at the Beverly Hills Hotel, Roy and Dan lived in a rented beach house in Malibu – Roy in the role of 'nanny'. 'At the moment I have the best of both worlds,' Glenda confided privately. 'Roy and I are now the best of friends, touch wood, and I've also got a very good relationship with Andy. But I just don't want to go through the whole marriage thing again – even to Andy. There's too much risk involved, and I simply don't want to be lumbered with it. You can avoid a dangerous piece of road, maybe, but you can't avoid those hideous pitfalls of other people.'

There were few pitfalls where Walter Matthau was concerned. Indeed, the opportunity to work with the actor with the crumpled, mortician's smile and the voice pick-axed out of the streets of Brooklyn was the only reason Glenda agreed to make the romantic comedy in the first place – that, plus the fact that the filming schedule happened to coincide with Daniel's school holidays. As with all Matthau's fellow performers, Glenda was soon doting on him, even though he frequently acted her off the set and into the streets. It made no difference. 'I'd take him home and put him on my mantelpiece any day,' she told visitors to the studio.

The critics mostly loved the partnership, described by one reviewer as 'dynamite on a short fuse'. Another noted that it was 'more like a slugging match between two punchy old pros who hadn't heard of the Queensberry rules'. A third had some words of wisdom to offer Glenda: 'While the Matthau character continues to be a comically stylized creation, the Jackson one begins to act as if she's in Strindberg. "Don't analyse it – play it." That should have been the advice.'

The film, for all that, was tailor-made for the two stars. It centres on the on again, off again romantic involvement between Matthau, a recently widowed surgeon who wants to be a latter-day Casanova to compensate for thirty-one years of marital fidelity, and Glenda, a divorcee who refuses to share him with other women now that she is rid of a philandering husband. Observers on the set likened the teaming of Jackson and Matthau to the pairing of Hepburn and Tracy in those comedies of the 1940s. But Glenda simply gave such comparisons the old cold shoulder. 'It's absurd to think we could be like them,' she said dismissively. 'There's no virtue in repetition.'

Matthau thought otherwise when asked if the world was about to see the emergence of another screen team. 'Me and Glenda Jackson? Gee, I hope so! It would be terrific to work with her again and again. She is just so good, an absolute dreamboat.' According to producer–director Mel Frank, Matthau indicated that he would have been prepared to make another film with Glenda without even reading the script. Yet not so Glenda. 'A partnership, like a marriage, will only continue if it's got good foundations,' she observed. 'I don't see any virtue in working with anyone, however magical the rapport on screen, if what you're working on is rubbish.'

She frankly confused Hollywood ... and, in turn, she was confused by it. On the first day of shooting, the moviemakers did not know whether to peck her cheek or curtsy. It seemed impossible for the inhabitants of the film capital to disentangle the real-life Glenda Jackson from her screen image as Elizabeth I and Lady Hamilton, which, for a town accustomed to the ephemeral world of make-believe, was rather odd. Even her leading man was initially thrown off balance. 'The first time I saw Glenda I thought she was one of the electricians,' said Matthau. 'The next time I saw her I thought she was the Queen. She has that effect.'

Glenda was dumbfounded. 'They expected me to be amazingly brilliant,' she informed a friend. 'Then they got used to me.' But *she* never quite accustomed herself to the obligatory ritual star treatment accorded her by Universal Pictures: 'On the set I had what they call a travelling home, which was a damn sight grander than my actual home in Blackheath.'

Away from the artificial climate of a studio which bent over backwards in its efforts to pander to her, she found it even more difficult to relate to life in Los Angeles itself. 'One has to have a reason for coming here,' she told columnist Rex Reed. 'If you have a job here, it's like a passport or a visa, and you can always get out. But I should think to be stuck here all the time you'd go mad.' The essentially seductive climate of Los Angeles frightened her, or at least made her feel extremely uncomfortable, while it was quite out of the question that she would ever be even remotely tempted to join the growing British colony there.

So, although she just padded around her hotel digs during the week, at weekends she and Daniel could be found sniffing around the broken-down Santa Monica pier. 'Ah, now, I can relate to Santa Monica! It reminds me of British seaside places – the crowded beaches and the smell of coconut forever in the air. It must be all the suntan oil they use.'

But there was no smell of suntanned bodies when she returned to England in October and went straight into location shooting in London's East End for her next film, *The Class of Miss MacMichael* (1978), with Oliver Reed and black American actress Rosalind Cash. Written and produced by Judd Bernard, who had produced *Negatives* a decade earlier, the low-budget, tight-schedule, pitch-black comedy did little to enhance anybody's reputation, despite the fact that it was a film which Glenda had wanted to make for eight years. In it she played a dedicated, if unorthodox, schoolmistress who battles gamely against her slum surroundings, her delinquent pupils and her tyrannical headmaster (Oliver Reed in his third movie with Glenda). The result, shot in a disused (and now demolished) Victorian school in Bethnal Green, was a thorough, misguided mess, more resembling an updated version of the St Trinian's films of the 1950s than *The Blackboard Jungle* or the cosmetic *To Sir, With Love*.

Glenda, in the title role, came in for a great deal of stick from the critics, one of whom accused her of being 'neither sufficiently gullible nor sufficiently likeable for the part'. The consolation prize came when the Variety Club of Great Britain awarded her the trophy for the Best Film Actress of the Year; and not just for one movie, but for three: *House Calls, Stevie* and *The Class of Miss MacMichael* ... more silver for mother to clean.

Oliver Reed, years later, was still angry about the conditions under which the film was made. 'They cheap-skated it,' he thundered. 'Even in the most complicated scenes there was no time for rehearsals. It was just "turn on the lights and fucking shoot it".' How did Glenda get on with the pupils? 'I don't know. I just saw her working, and I then went to my room and she went to hers. We didn't socialize, ever. She certainly never went to the film unit's communal lunches; but on the set she kept slapping everybody on the back, saying, "We're making an art film." Otherwise she kept herself to herself.'

The film's Canadian director, Silvio Narizzano, whose earlier London-based movie was the engagingly bright *Georgy Girl*, at least had something nice to say about his star when everybody else seemed to be using her for target practice. 'Glenda,' he told people, 'is the only British actress who can compare with Simone Signoret and Jeanne Moreau. All of them are more, rather than less, attractive to men as they become older.'

Glenda was forty-one. Now, eighteen months into society's concept of middle age, she had acquired the kind of striking and absolutely original good looks which she did not possess twenty years earlier, and, professionally at least, she had a firm sense of what to do with them. But, just a matter of months from her forty-second birthday, Glenda knew, as Monroe and Loren knew, that there was a limited lifespan for movie actresses whose reputations have been constructed, in one form or another, on a charismatic sexuality; she knew that when the face-lines show and the figure sags, as hers was now doing, you have to draw on other talents if you are lucky enough to have them. Those other talents, fortunately, she has in abundance: classical stage actresses of repute can draw on such expertise in their advancing years much as others can fall back on a company pension.

Her absence of personal vanity, nevertheless, appeared so total it could almost be a pose. For instance, 'I haven't got any make-up at all. Nothing. If I do have to be photographed they usually find me some that a model has left behind. I don't think make-up ever improves my face, anyway.' And yet, when the actress tried to generate the kind of beauty required by a particular character, that bony, raw, disproportioned face could become utterly transformed.

This did not alter the fact that when many people met her for the first time, they *were* disappointed by what they saw. They would invariably cover this up by saying, 'Oh, you're much smaller than I expected.' They meant plainer. The classic example of this occurred in Hollywood when a movie mogul met Glenda in the studio lift on a day when the actress thought that, for her, she was looking not too bad. But she could see the thought running through his head: 'Oh, God! Have we spent all that money for *that?*'

Yet her face, which she frequently described as 'bloody awful', was still very much in demand. Brash American comedienne Carol Burnett wanted her for a movie comedy called *Two Girls from Topeka*; London film producer Irving Allen provisionally signed her up, along with Diana Rigg, Vanessa Redgrave and her idol Bette Davis, for *The Family Arsenal*, about four women who steal the takings from several drug pushers and manage to get away with it; Columbia approached her to play in a film about a British journalist whose American boyfriend turned out to be a mass-murderer; and the BBC talked of starring her in an eight-part television series based on the scandalous Margot Asquith, wife of the twentieth-century British Prime Minister Herbert Asquith. In the event, Glenda's services were not called upon, since most of the projects never proceeded further than the drawing-board.

None of this was a tragedy. Glenda, as always, had plenty of other irons glowing quite nicely in the embers. Ever since *A Touch of Class* became an international hit six years earlier, bringing her a second Oscar, Mel Frank had been trying in vain to re-team Glenda with George Segal. She had turned down *The Duchess and the Dirtwater Fox* and *The Black Bird*, though Segal, in both cases, remained in the films. But now, in *Lost and Found*, Frank at last succeeded in bringing them together again. 'They both work so much,' said an exhausted Frank, 'it took me three years to find them both free at the same time.'

While not a sequel to *A Touch of Class*, the new film was written in a similar vein. Glenda portrays a newly-divorced English secretary who bumps into Segal's equally recently-widowed American college professor in the French Alps, where they are both endeavouring to get over their respective heart-aches. Romance leads to marriage and the eventual realization that they are incompatible. 'I wanted to do *Lost and Found* because I was keen to work with the same team again,' said Glenda, 'and because I thought it had an interest of its own in its attempt to deal with an extremely painful subject in a way that was funny.' The outcome was merely more old-fashioned nonsense posing as hip comedy.

Glenda was accompanied by Andy Phillips when she boarded a plane for Canada at the beginning of March to begin location shooting in the snowy Rockies for the 'French Alps' ski sequences; other scenes were to be filmed in and around Toronto (posing as New England). It was no secret that Glenda hated the cold – 'It didn't put me in the best of moods' – and the Canadian chill at that time was worse than usual. Equally, she hated to be away from Daniel – Roy and sister Lynne were looking after him – and this film commitment would keep her out of England for fourteen weeks. She phoned the nine-year-old lad every day, boring him to distraction with details of the cold. 'Acting's difficult enough as it is without having extra problems to contend with like being half frozen,' she objected. She also complained of chilblains; but then earning £100,000 a film could be tough all round.

As with the Jackson–Matthau partnership in *House Calls*, the pundits were again noting that the complementary personalities of Jackson and Segal seemed to spark off a magic reminiscent, this time, of the long-ago part-nership of Myrna Loy and William Powell. But anyone who mentioned Jackson and Segal in the same breath as Hepburn and Tracy (and they did, oh they *did*!), got a blast from Glenda. 'It *really* makes me cross, it's so ludicrous!' she would explode. 'It's a monstrous impertinence and an insult. It shows a lack of imagination.'

When I asked Segal if *he* felt insulted, he smiled broadly. 'No,' he said, 'I take it as a compliment. I know Glenda admires Katharine Hepburn and for me it's a great tribute to be compared with Tracy. They had an organic thing going for them, but I think we have the professional capacity to fall into a relationship at a moment's notice.'

'Everybody keeps telling me about this magic, but personally I have never seen it,' Glenda rejoined. 'I don't see this added dimension we're supposed to have. I'm only prepared to accept it's there because so many people have told me about it.'

But behind the scenes their relationship was not as cordial as before. They stayed in different hotels, Segal with his wife and children, Glenda secretively with Andy, to whom no one on the set ever referred. The writer Anthea Disney was there and observed that the two stars arrived for each day's filming in different cars, that they had separate trailers, separate lunches, separate dinners. 'None of this was particularly extraordinary for the world of movie-making,' said Miss Disney, 'but when the two refused to have their photograph taken together off-set you realized that, out of the context of the film, they were simply uncomfortable with each other.'

According to Segal, when he met Glenda again after *A Touch of Class*, at first 'it was a little strained'. However, working with her once more was 'like being with a very old slipper and suddenly it becomes easy to slip it on and find each other's rhythms again'. He reflected, 'We *work* together and if there is any magic, that's where it happens, in front of the camera, in front of the watching eye. We do have a basic respect for each other.' When told that Segal regarded working with her again as akin to slipping into an old slipper, Glenda uttered a very fast expletive. Segal laughed out loud when informed of the outburst. 'Ah, well,' he said, 'it's good to know Glenda hasn't changed overnight.'

Mel Frank was compelled to agree. He also discovered that in script discussions there was nothing to choose between her bite and her bark. About his two luminaries he then became unusually lyrical: 'George is absolutely a big-city man, the archetypal American. Glenda, on the other hand, seems to be a big contradiction. She's a slightly more rough-hewn looking person, with a kind of indestructible elegance of thought, manner and of speech. So when these two get together, it's like putting a bunch of ingredients in a crucible you know is going to produce a wonderful new product. I'd love to do a picture with them every four or five years.' Those years would disappear in the mists of time, the hoped for third film from the stable of Frank–Jackson–Segal never materializing; but then perhaps the public's lacklustre response to *Lost and Found* contributed in no small way. As Glenda was forced to conclude, 'It proved that repetition doesn't always work, because *Lost and Found* wasn't a success either critically or financially.'

There were also those who wondered whether Glenda's changing appearance, and the fact that she had never really been a funny girl, might not have entered the equation at some point. Her old friend Vladek Sheybal reflected, 'Glenda, you know, was the kind of actress who could look stunningly beautiful one moment, but quite plain and ugly the next. She had a period, while making *House Calls* and *Lost and Found*, when she started to look very plain indeed. Maybe it had something to do with the wigs she wore. But then I don't think she's a good comedy actress: I think she merely achieved her "humour" by being detached and cool – and very English.'

Despite what people were saying about her talent (or otherwise) as a comedienne, Glenda would pursue the genre in two further movies before finally abandoning it. She was never one to surrender easily: it was challenge, after all, which was the essence of her credo, professionally as well as personally. If her current work in the cinema seemed to be in the doldrums, the year 1978 would at least produce a brace of pleasant surprises. She received an honorary D.Litt. from Liverpool University at the midsummer congregation, and, in the Queen's Birthday Honours, was named a Commander of the British Empire. When she received the honour from the Queen at Buckingham Palace, she was playing Cleopatra in the Royal Shakespeare Company's production of *Antony and Cleopatra* at Stratford. She said after the investiture, 'I've got a performance tonight and so I won't be drinking today. But I've got two bottles of champagne which I shall no doubt crack tomorrow.' She did, and the drink did not do her much good. She got drunk quickly, what she called 'morose drunk', on three drinks – even though she once admitted on BBC radio's *Any Questions* that she came from a family of 'dyed-in-the-wool alcoholics'. She concluded, 'I don't like drink very much.'

Her season at Stratford-upon-Avon should have been a time of rejoicing, for audiences as much as for Glenda Jackson, CBE, but somehow it was not. From the moment it was announced that she would play Cleopatra in a production by Peter Brook, the whole venture became the year's most eagerly awaited theatrical event. But the outcome became merely an exercise in matching expectations against performance, eliciting a generally muted response from the critics for a production which never totally succeeded in taking fire. With Glenda *and* Brook making their return to the company, much was expected – perhaps too much. There was world interest in the event. At the dress rehearsal, to which photographers were bidden, there were some fifty cameramen laden with hardware occupying the first two rows of the stalls, with Lord Snowdon crowded into a corner. Playing Antony was Alan Howard, the new lion of the English stage. In other parts, the RSC was fielding very much an 'A' team, with Patrick Stewart as Enobarbus, Jonathan Pryce as Octavius Caesar, Paul Brooke as Lepidus, and Marjorie Bland as Octavia. The concoction comprised the very best ingredients, but it all somehow fell flat. Years later the question of what went wrong was still being debated.

More than a decade earlier, Brook told Glenda, 'If anyone asks you to do Cleopatra, say no.' A year prior to the new production he told her, 'I think you're old enough to do it now.' It seemed that, at last, she looked the right age.

Glenda was thrilled to be teamed once again with a man she regarded as the greatest director with whom she would ever be associated. 'He makes work so incredibly difficult and therefore interesting,' she enthused before rehearsals got under way. 'It's like going into a punishment park.' But the actress who disliked company life intensely, especially the pointless politicking, found that the combination of Brook and the RSC was not what it had been when she appeared in *The Marat/Sade* all those years before. The intensity of commitment from the company, and the total involvement in what Brook was doing, had gone. 'People are just too involved in other productions or their own off-stage lives to give Brook the kind of absolute dedication he needs and expects,' she complained during rehearsals.

Of those rehearsals – and, more particularly, of Glenda's relationship with Brook – cast-member Patrick Stewart recalled: 'She worked with Brook in a way she never worked with Trevor Nunn on *Hedda Gabler*. She didn't challenge him the way she challenged Trevor. She *listened* to Peter; she never listened to Trevor. She teased Peter, and that was something she did not normally do to people. There was a kind of "niceness" about her, and they did work together very well; in the first three weeks of rehearsals the atmosphere was terrific – some of the best rehearsal time I've ever had. In those early weeks there were only six of us, Glenda, Alan Howard, Jonathan Pryce, Marjorie Bland, Paola Dionisotti and myself, and the mood was gentle, subdued, cooperative, friendly, everything that an actor in a rehearsal could desire. Yet there was still something about her relationship with Brook that mystified and beguiled us. One had heard so much about Peter's relationship with Glenda, how confusing and difficult it was, and that it was based on a lot of things that had nothing to do with the theatre. It was fascinating to watch.'

One instance of the 'confusing and difficult' Jackson/Brook relationship occurred towards the end of the rehearsal period. In front of the assembled company, Brook delivered some crushing 'notes' to Glenda, outlining in graphic detail where and how she was going wrong in her portrayal of the seductive Serpent of the Nile. The other actors froze. Nobody, apart from Andy, had ever talked to Glenda in that manner. But this was Peter Brook. He just went for her, for ten or fifteen minutes, in what amounted to a long, careful, detailed, calculated destruction of the work that she had done in the production so far. And then he stopped, and paused. Nobody spoke. The silence was almost painful. Glenda never took her unblinking eyes off Brook; and then she opened her mouth.

'Oh, my *God*, Peter!' she exclaimed, her voice gorged with a crucifying sarcasm. 'You're *not* going to burst into *tears*, are you?'

Brook, for once in his life, was speechless.

'It was fantastic, absolutely fantastic,' reflected Stewart. 'But, yes, that was very much the nature of their relationship. She worked for him bloody hard, and it was just unfortunate that it was in a production where her efforts weren't going to be that fruitful.'

Audiences and critics were largely perplexed by a play which for once had nothing to do with cosmetics, camp wigs or the faked splendours of ancient Rome and Egypt: a semi-circle of frosted glass, resembling a blow-up of a bus shelter, was compelled to pass for the magnificence of Cleopatra's court and the luxury of Caesar's chambers. Glenda's Chelsea-set gowns would have looked well at a cocktail party, but even the full regalia in which she died was simple and scarcely Egyptian. Yet while one notable theatre critic loved the pared down simplicity of the proceedings, most agreed that *Antony and Cleopatra* was tamed and diminished with the glory and grandeur gone.

Glenda, her arms free-wheeling into frieze-like poses, was a quicksilver Cleopatra, switching her voice and demeanour faster than an eye could blink: all majesty one moment, all woman the next. This was a modern crop-haired, kaftaned, tough lady who put the boot into servants, messengers and even Antony with equal ferocity. It was very much in the customary 'aggressive' Glenda Jackson idiom, prompting Gregory Jensen of the *Los Angeles Times* to conclude that she was hardly one of nature's Cleopatras. 'Despite her cheekbones and tigerish grace,' he said, 'she never looks a voluptuous, seductive temptress.' But then grace, tigerish or otherwise, was hardly the description one would normally bestow on Glenda's particular way of walking, as Jack Tinker of London's *Daily Mail* subsequently acknowledged. 'She might even succeed in disproving Kenneth Tynan's theory that no English actors can play this part,' he noted, 'were it not for her walk, which unfortunately has the suburban waddle of a housewife rushing to the supermarket before it closes.' Glenda, being Glenda, had probably done just that prior to the performance.

21
Changing Pattern

Glenda entered 1979 innocently enough – little realizing the tremendous changes that were about to affect her life. The two comedy films she would make that year, for instance, would be her last in the 'funny' idiom. There was also the fact that the momentum and regularity of her film career had begun to waver quite perceptibly. Until then her association with the cinema produced an average of two films a year, but soon this pattern would be broken. Along with her age, times were changing, and the sort of roles in which producers once envisaged her no longer suited either her looks or her personality. So the situation was this: she would not appear before the camera in 1980; it would then be two films again in 1981, but just a film apiece in 1982, 1983 and 1984.

She speculated at the time, 'I would like to think I'm better now than when I first began, but I don't know how much the sublime confidence, rooted as it was in absolute ignorance in my first performances, would counterbalance the now painful knowledge that it's a damn sight harder than you ever think it's going to be. The one thing it seems to me that I have consistently learned is how amazingly easy it is to be bad and how inordinately difficult it is to be good.' And then: 'I need to be stretched, but I find it harder and harder to find something that extends me. There doesn't seem to be any major movement towards choosing subjects in which women are the dramatic engine as opposed to just adjuncts. The women are there all right, but they're not in the centre of the screen. Or, if they are, they're clichés. Look at *Dallas*.'

The fact remained that her film career was not what it had been. It was in the doldrums. Precisely the same thing happened to the fortunes of her idol, Bette Davis, at precisely the same age. When the American actress's screen career faltered in the 1950s, she refused to be beaten; she even resorted to advertising her availability for roles in the trade press, and a decade later she emerged triumphant – but it *was* a decade. By then she was in her mid-fifties. If the same pattern emerges in Glenda's career, the 1990s will be the years to watch. 'You know something?' she confessed to an old confidant. 'I'm sick to death of looking at myself and worrying about my hair and my clothes. And one's got to look the facts in the face. A woman's face grows too old for films much sooner than a man's. And in the theatre there's a big lack of interesting parts for an actress to play between the ages of forty and sixty. It's very sad.'

In February 1979 she flew to Florida, where, at the West Coast 'Sunshine City' of St Petersburg, in Pinellas county, she had a film to make for Robert Altman, the director who had won a justified, if controversial, reputation for his satirical eye for American ways of life, exemplified in movies such as *M*A*S*H* and *Nashville*. His latest picture, *Health*, for which Glenda was at his disposal, was very much in the same mould. The zany romp centres on the crazy goings-on at a national health convention at an opulent hotel in Florida. Rivals for the presidency of the convention are the cigar-puffing Glenda, who seems to think she is running for the presidency of the United States, and the supposedly eighty-three-year-old, ever young Lauren Bacall. James Garner and Carol Burnett join in the satirical tomfoolery.

Contributing both to Glenda's acceptance of the role and to her endurance of the Florida sun – 'I found I liked heat as little as I liked cold' – was the opportunity to be steered by a man whose films she greatly admired. 'There aren't many directors for whom I would work without seeing a script,' she told people on her arrival, who could not have known that there were also many directors for whom she would not work even if she saw a script. Filming took place in a hotel which, she said, 'looked as if the architect's mother had been frightened by a confectioner; it was bright pink with a trim of white frosting.' And, because it was a health-food conference, people in the film were dressed as carrots, avocados and tossed salads. 'The whole thing was quite hysterical.'

During the course of the film's production she was asked what she herself did to stay healthy. 'I overdose on coffee and cigarettes,' she answered, straight faced. 'And between nervous shaking from the caffeine and coughing from the nicotine, I'll have as thorough a work-out as if I'd jogged for seventeen blocks.' When the mirth was over she eventually admitted, 'Actually, I'm basically a lazy person. I've always had to work, so maybe the laziness does not show to outsiders. But it is there, and so I tend to do much more than is necessary in order to prove to myself that it isn't taking hold. I'm really guilt-ridden. Yet I'm not lazy to the point of being able to sit in a room if it's untidy. If I'm answering letters, the desk is absolutely littered with envelopes and pieces of paper and a great muddle, but if I want to sit down in the living room and do nothing more energetic than read a book or knit or watch the telly, that room has to be tidy. It would irritate me if the floor were littered with newspapers and the ashtrays were filled to overflowing ... but they never are because my neurosis is untidiness.'

However, her commitment to the movie could do little to save its eventual release from virtual extinction. Despite the high-powered cast, not to mention the enormous reputation and following of Glenda and Altman, 20th Century-Fox practically abandoned *Health* after its production. Such things happen. Glenda remained philosophical: 'You win some, you lose some.'

Before returning to Blackheath, Glenda passed through California, where the Los Angeles Film Critics' Association hosted a luncheon in her honour at Jimmy's. Here she informed the merry throng that 99.9 per cent of everything offered to her for film production was 'rubbish'. She said she planned to continue her bipartite existence in both films and theatre. 'But I'm not all that interested in doing a commercial stage play for more than a three-month run,' she added, noting that this made things difficult because most producers wanted her to give a longer commitment. Asked about the increased opportunities in films for women, she acknowledged there had been more words written for women, but described herself as 'astounded' that more screenwriters had not taken note of the political changes her own sex had undergone in the past few years. This particular theme was an old hobby-horse.

Hollywood *per se* still exerted no lure for her. 'There is a very clearly defined pecking order here,' she reminded her hosts. 'It would be very difficult to be a star over here and keep total control of everything in your life. You're not treated as a thing any more, but as a balance sheet. You're either in the red or in the black. And if you're in the red, you're very quickly moved on to a new balance sheet. . . .' Instant applause.

Next day she gave a number of press interviews in her Los Angeles hotel room. Pouring tea at high noon, and wearing a pair of faded blue jeans, a striped blouse and a gold stud in each ear, she told Samantha Dean of the *Boston Globe Magazine* that all Hollywood signified to her was a sign on a hill. The journalist then pressed her further.

'Do you think you, as an actress, would have developed in Hollywood?' she asked.

'I don't think any actor does,' said Glenda. 'You have to be extremely fortunate. I think the development of most actors – most people – occurs when they're actually struggling to reach something. And there is a time when that struggle carries you on, on its own created energy. And then, unless you're extremely lucky and get a lot of demanding and different parts, there comes a marking time process. And then something else comes into play – perhaps it's just the amount of time that you've lived – and you move into another energy drive.'

'And that's where you are now?'

'I've been there for a bit in the sense of marking time and I think I'm about ready to move into another area. Whether it will carry me further, I don't know. I don't mean further in terms of money or glory or whatever, I mean further in terms of development as an actress.'

'Have you defined that area yet?'

'Not really. I don't think you can define it until you get there – until you actually find yourself in a situation where you need that added energy.'

'You don't make career-plotting moves then?'

'No, I never have, and I don't know how you would, although I know people do. But I feel if I made those kinds of decisions, they would invariably be the wrong ones.'

'Do you make those kinds of decisions as far as your life is concerned?'

'No, I'm very haphazard there. I'm not a planner in that sense. But then I'm also not a person who changes things very easily. I mean the order that I find myself in is the one I'm happy to stay in.'

'That sounds fairly passive – and out of character with the type of destiny-controlling women you portray on screen. It's an interesting dichotomy.'

'I think it's difficult to define what constitutes passivity. But being an actor you're always to an extent in a passive situation, because however practically you go about trying to set up a scene which you think may work best for you, the indefinables don't rest within your actual area of control. An audience's reception of your work is outside your manipulation. And in life, although I don't make life goals, I'm not a fatalist. I think we're always in an area of choice. Most of us are, anyway. What conditions those choices is, I think, extremely difficult to define. No one has ever come up – to my satisfaction – with what constitutes the real formative influence in one's life. Would the opposite of passivity imply absolute freedom? If it would, I don't believe in it. I think if one had that much freedom and resultant power, one would be morally obligated to decline it.'

She admitted to being 'intensely secretive' about every facet of herself and seemed happily resigned to getting no enjoyment out of the things other mortals viewed as necessary release. Having compiled a catalogue of the little luxuries in life that she passionately hated – drinking, eating, holidaying – she would exclaim quite seriously: 'I just like work, I suppose. I know that I do make a great virtue out of work for its own sake.' As indeed she did. But then again, in her own words, she had 'worked very consistently over the last eight years', an admission that many more glamorous actresses would have been happy to match.

In the summer of 1979, while appearing in London at the Aldwych Theatre in Brook's *Antony and Cleopatra*, again opposite Alan Howard, a lifetime's ambition seemed about to come to fruition: to star in a stage musical. Melvin Van Peebles, an American renowned for his infinite capacity for surprise – as director, producer, writer, composer, actor, in films, theatre and television, it was small wonder – had collaborated with Mildred Kayden in the writing of *Becky*, a musical version of *Vanity Fair*, and Glenda was to play the title role. While delighted to be offered the role in the $1.5 million musical, Glenda said she could only play Becky if the show was done in London. Van Peebles agreed. Once she had committed herself to the musical for the better part of a year, her agent, Peter Crouch, explained: 'Glenda has a perfectly reasonable singing voice, but it will mean lessons three times a week for four or five months to get it in trim.' Everybody was ecstatic, not least the show's director:

'It's going to be a gigantic show, like *Evita* or *Sweeney Todd.* You know what that means? It means I'm suddenly, "Hey, Mel, baby," again. I like that.' Alas, it was not like that. *Becky* failed to cross the Atlantic, and Glenda's ambition was unrealized.

But there were other stage vehicles. At about this time a British agent phoned Walter Matthau in Hollywood and inquired whether he would like to fly to London to play in *Uncle Vanya* with Glenda. He replied, 'I'd love to go, but I know I wouldn't be acceptable to English audiences; and they'd be quite right. You have enough great actors of your own over there.' Another dream vanished like so much sand between Glenda's fingers. The actress was always highly superstitious; when she spilt salt, she speedily threw some over her left shoulder, and she was 'deeply neurotic' about crossed knives. Now she began to fret over the ephemeral fortunes of her career. What, she mused, was Fate trying to tell her at this juncture? She became uncharacteristically low, dispirited.

And then the phone rang late one evening at her Blackheath home. It was Matthau. He said, 'I'm doing this film and there's a script in the post, and if you even vaguely like it, would you do it?'

Matthau was pretending he was going to be a lost American alone in Europe and he needed a friendly European face around, all of which Glenda knew was a load of rubbish. You could stick Matthau down in the middle of the jungle and he would come out the other end probably owning the jungle and all it contained. *Hopscotch* (1980), a genial but patchy spy comedy caper, with locations in Munich, Salzburg, London and parts of Georgia in the United States, seemed to appeal to Glenda for reasons which could not be explained by mere logic.

'I think it's quite complimentary, actually,' she remarked later, 'when an actor with as much quality and experience as Walter asks you personally to do a film with him. We'd had such fun making *House Calls*, I just couldn't refuse.'

Glenda's customarily rigid criterion in selecting a role – that it must not be a cipher – was temporarily abandoned in the case of *Hopscotch*. Her character was indeed a cipher in a plot in which ex-CIA agent Matthau is hunted across Europe and America by both the CIA and the KGB for threatening to publish his memoirs. Glenda, as his sleek former mistress, languishes in Salzburg while he is on the run, occasionally relieving the monotony by telephoning our hero. Glenda's role was so small and so undemanding that it was a mystery why she agreed to do it – even for Matthau. Her work on the film entailed only two weeks of her time in Salzburg, though she was accorded equal above-the-title billing with Matthau. Even she herself admitted later, 'It was money for old rope. I played her with my usual mid-Cheshire accent, but I hardly look on it as a major contribution. Still, it gave me two weeks in Austria and I'd never been there before.'

Matthau, in fact, was one of the few men for whom Glenda relin-
quished all her normal prejudices. While preferring not to like her leading
men, her professional love affair with Matthau was absolute. Between
scenes she played Scrabble with him, a game which bored her so much
that she usually refused to play it. In Matthau's company she became a
different woman. 'They were just magic together,' said Geraldine
Addison. 'They had this happy, wonderful rapport, which was like a little
love affair without actually being an affair. I can't explain it; it was very
strange. I mean, I'd never seen her like that with anyone.'

'When they met again for this film, the warmth that she normally contrived to conceal came out,' added executive producer Otto Plaschkes.
'They had this great respect for each other. Walter's sense of humour was
somewhat lugubrious and long-winded, Glenda's was fast and dry acid,
and yet the two matched perfectly. They sparked each other off. The sense
of winding up which was Walter, and the sense of sharpness that was
Glenda, made for a wonderful duet act – and I think they both knew it.
And on the personal level they were extremely happy to be in each other's
company – delighted, in fact.'

For a woman who preferred to be 'objective' about her leading men, it
said reams. Her relationship with Matthau was about as subjective as it
was ever likely to get, and Matthau appreciated the gesture. He rated her
'a number one talent and a terrific lady', adding: 'Glenda is class and
she's fun. I love working with her.'

Matthau, despite being a great technician, in terms of movement,
response, wisecrack and exaggerated alarm, shares with Glenda one vital
flaw in his acting: a final reluctance to reveal himself. It is this gap in
Glenda's dramatic armoury which so disappointed Joseph Losey when he
directed her in *The Romantic Englishwoman*. At the end of the day, both
Glenda and Matthau hold something back; whether each recognizes this
in the other is doubtful, but, in the final analysis, it is the thread which, in
some metaphysical way, unites them – though Glenda is no fool when it
comes to 'guarding' herself against Matthau's phenomenal talent. 'You can
never underestimate him,' she said. 'Not for a minute. He's dangerous to work
with, that man, because you never know what he's going to do.' Glenda knew
all about that; it was an accusation often levelled against *her*.

On her return to London she spoke the narration for *The Foundations of
Life*, a seven-part international documentary film series made in New
Zealand and Australia by the United Nations Children's Fund. She also
lent her services for various other causes associated with the International
Year of the Child. Her own child, meanwhile, was approaching his
eleventh birthday, and in September he would be leaving the local primary
school round the corner to start secondary school. The thought of it made
Glenda more nervous than even Daniel could fully comprehend.

'I never realized until I had a child how much my life would alter because of that enormous responsibility you have to someone else,' she said. 'I once read a marvellous piece about the constant anxiety of being a mother. That anxiety is always there, just below the surface. It may be an utterly erroneous theory but I feel that going from a small school to a bigger and unknown one will be a great trauma for Dan. Certainly for the first year, while he's settling in, I feel I should be there all the time. It may be that he'll tell me, "You're getting awfully boring, hanging around my neck all the time", but it is something I would quite like to do. I just hope that if I give up for a year, no one will come along with something absolutely fascinating that I feel I have to do.'

Part Six

A Star in the Unknown

What is already past is not more fixed than the certainty that what is future will grow out of what has already passed, or is now passing.

G.B.Cheever,
Accidence, 1674

22

Dirk Bogarde and the Dahls

All her life, despite the tough 'I-can-cope' exterior which she presents to the world, Glenda has been a chronic worrier. She is a born pessimist. She has always suffered a terrible dread of not being able to get about, of being paralysed. She is always greatly affected by the weather, grey days inducing grey depressions. She has always suffered from severe stage fright before a theatrical first night, hoping against hope that, en route to the theatre, fire will engulf the building and raze it to the ground. Her fear of flying has been lifelong and enduring. She possesses an over-developed sense of responsibility, which she acquired early in life and which, indeed, is often the case with an eldest child.

'Oh, I'm one of the world's great worriers,' she affirmed in a tone signifying achievement rather than failure. 'I think I spend most of my days worrying about something or other. Anything will do. People. Plans. Schedules. I spend half of my life worrying about arrangements. I'm one of those people who have to be met wherever they go. I have to know where I'm staying and who the people are and all that dreary business. It's so *boring*.'

She recovered her composure and continued, 'I used to worry about not being offered work, then it was worrying about choosing between work which was interesting, and now it's worrying about if there *is* any interesting work at all. No matter what, I'll always find something to worry about – worriers *do*. God! Pessimism is an indulgence none of us can afford. It *is* hard to be a realist for all that. But I try – I *try*....'

She endeavoured, too, to revitalize London's West End. When, in January 1980, she went into rehearsals for *Rose*, a comedy by a virtually unknown playwright, Andrew Davies, the West End commercial theatre was in a state of shell-shock, with darkened stages and wailing impresarios heralding gloom and doom. And then Glenda of Blackheath appeared like a latter-day Joan of Arc leading an army to free besieged Orleans, although a cricket analogy was popular at the time – that she was like an English batsman preparing to face an avalanche of Australian bumpers, padded up and ready in her resolve to restore confidence to London's ailing theatreland. Someone had decided that if Glenda in full sardonic flow could not bring people back into the stalls, then nobody could. Her colleagues shared the conviction. 'I know Glenda doesn't regard her work in the London theatre as in any way paying her dues to the theatre in general,' said Michael Graham Cox, an actor who had worked with her in *Women in Love*. 'However, I have considerable admiration for the way she does help to keep the theatres open by lending her star status, as well as her talent, to stage plays. There are few Oscar-winners who do.'

None of this, needless to say, was Glenda's reading of the situation. 'I don't think that works any more,' she said on the eve of the play's opening at the refurbished Duke of York's Theatre. 'An actor alone can't fill a theatre. The play must be worth going to.' And it was.

Almost without exception the critics were beside themselves, dispensing paeans of praise about both the play and Glenda's performance as a Midlands schoolteacher thwarted at every turn – by the headmistress, who says Rose is too lacking in experience and dignity to be promoted; by her monosyllabic husband, who becomes alarmed when she suggests they spend an evening, you know, *talking*; and by her seductive colleague, Jim Beam, whose romantic overtures consist of, 'I'm married too. Can't take you back. Thought we might do it in the car. It's a Maxi.' *Rose* played to capacity houses throughout its six-month run. After the sparsity of comic bite in *Hopscotch*, Glenda at last had something to get her teeth into. More importantly, she had a *success* on her hands, and she had experienced precious few of those in recent years, either in films or theatre. It was a nice feeling. She even stopped worrying for a few minutes.

The London *Evening News* set the tone for everybody's renewed love affair with the star of the show: 'One day Glenda Jackson will give a bad performance, and on that dire date there will be a total eclipse of the sun, fountains will run blood, and terrible will be the cries of anguish. This extraordinary actress so lights up the stage that once again she is going to dim the brightest adjectives in my armoury.'

A few more love letters: 'Glenda Jackson plays the leading role with superlative skill and a wry sense of detachment,' said the *Daily Express*, while the *Sunday Express* noted: 'Miss Jackson gives a performance that holds one in thrall with every nuance.' Again: 'Glenda Jackson, as Rose, displays an amiable note of cheerful cynicism about everything that happens to her,' observed the London *Evening Standard*. 'She is really funny outlining to an astonished male all the seduction techniques she expects him to try before he has laid a finger on her.' And *Newsweek* magazine wrote: 'Jackson succeeds triumphantly, seeming to embrace every spectator with her gallant sweetness, ironic humour and bedeviled intelligence.'

There were others.

Despite her success it was not a particularly happy actress who embarked on her forty-fifth year. The next decade, or even longer, she surmised, would be bleak years in terms of the roles she could play in the cinema or on stage. But she was not resigned to 'sitting it out'. She talked again about abandoning her craft.

People did not take seriously these periodic statements about her imminent 'retirement' from acting. She had been dispensing the claims for too many years for the pronouncements to have even the remotest ring of conviction. 'I must sound like the biggest whited sepulchre on earth,' she admitted. 'I'm always talking about giving up when I'm in one thing and planning to do another. But there just isn't enough interesting work for women in the theatre. It's not so much I want to give up, but I have to be realistic. You get to a certain age, and the parts aren't there any more. There is no continuous flow of work for actresses. In theatre there's almost a great big full-stop. In the cinema it happens much earlier and quicker: your face just gets too old. I know it will happen to me long before I'm willing to sit at home and just garden or polish the furniture.'

For the moment, her life would continue much as before. After completing her contractual six-month run in *Rose* in September, and with the play's Broadway opening a further six months away, she came close to realizing one of her fantasies when she performed a song-and-dance routine on television's *The Muppet Show*. 'In my dreams I've always seen myself as Ginger Rogers,' Glenda informed the puppets' creators, Frank Oz and Jim Henson. 'I've been offered musicals in the past, but I really can't sing or dance.' Oz and Henson did not believe her, but nevertheless coaxed Glenda – dressed as a pirate – to get moving to the music. She accomplished a sensational hornpipe, though when the routine was completed her legs felt 'like strings of spaghetti'. Her son Daniel had certain reservations about her singing. After seeing a recording, he told his mother: 'You should have been dubbed.' Mum was dumbfounded: 'Charming!' It was not on record what the lad thought of his mother's appearance on *The Morecambe and Wise Show* that Christmas, taped just after the Muppets caper, in which she played a hello-and-good-bye joke with Eric and Ernie. If he blinked, he would have missed her.

And then there was Broadway. Her imminent return to the 'Great White Way' had become the talk of the town. Much had happened to Glenda's career since her first – and only – appearance on the New York stage in 1965 in *The Marat/Sade*. Then she was the unknown actress from England who bedazzled Broadway; she could only go up. In March 1981, when *Rose* opened at the Cort Theater on 138 West 48th Street, the view from the summit was breathtaking, but, inevitably, there was nowhere else to go but down, and to keep the Jackson flag fluttering on the peak was what now most occupied her thoughts.

The terms were right. *Rose* would run for three months only, to accommodate the fact that Glenda would not countenance long absences from twelve-year-old Daniel. She would receive 10 per cent of the weekly box-office receipts, rising to 12½ per cent of the gross after recoupment. The rehearsal period was also a week longer than in London. She was happy. Everything had been arranged to make her stay a comfortable one, right down to ensuring that there was perking coffee and orange juice whenever she wanted it. She had booked into a large suite in a midtown hotel. Close on her heels came Andy Phillips, who had lit the London production and who was now responsible for illuminating the American restaging; they were still close, Glenda and Andy, even though theirs was by now, at best, an erratic liaison. Her private life had become an area where she felt more than usually tongued-tied. 'I have a live-in relationship with Andy in as much as when he's not away working he is with me,' she conceded. A planned marriage was cancelled on at least two occasions; and now work, as nearly always with Glenda, was the passion in her life.

Then the bombshell struck: *Rose*, an unqualified hit in London, was a Broadway flop.

The play set a record for unanimous reviews – all negative and, perhaps more unusual, in general agreement as to why. Critics either half-loved or grudgingly loved Glenda in the title role; they positively flipped with admiration for Jessica Tandy as her widowed mother. Yet none could fathom what either actress was doing in a play such as this ('flimsy', Clive Barnes called it in the *New York Post*; 'a toothpick of a play', wrote T. E. Kalem in *Time* magazine), unless, in Glenda's case, drawn by the power of the part. The *New York Times*'s Frank Rich, while admiring Glenda, and saying what a pleasure it was to see her on the New York stage again, found her performance 'unfailingly self-possessed, even-tempered, good-humoured – even a bit smug', when, in his opinion, she should have been ambivalent and weaker. It was, said *Variety*, 'seriously and perhaps fatally flawed by audience-repelling elements and technical crudities.' Mr Kalem in *Time* endorsed this last criticism and, in particular, the playwright's use of Glenda as a narrator and monologuist directly addressing the audience. Kalem observed: 'This is a drastic "alienation effect" for which Brecht himself would have disowned his disciples.'

No one associated with the production was more floored than the star herself. How could a play which went down so well in London fail so disastrously in New York? *Newsweek* said it in a nutshell: '*Rose* doesn't transplant.' And this was the vehicle that Glenda had chosen, over all others, to make her return to the American stage. The view from the summit was suddenly not quite so breathtaking. If ever Glenda had cause for worry, it was now. One minute she was right up there in the public's esteem, the next she was struggling among the ruins of a professional collapse – even though the critics spared her from many of the personal attacks which, when cornered, they were more than willing to use.

But they could still bare their teeth. 'Miss Jackson can of course handle both the self-assurance and the eventual bewilderment well,' wrote Walter Kerr in the *New York Times*, 'drawing her upper lip tight and wrinkling her nose as though she were still intent on snagging a role in *Watership Down*. But not even she can sustain interest indefinitely in this undefined character with an undefined goal.' *Newsweek*, while sympathizing with Glenda, repeated the basic home truth: 'It's too bad that an actress of Jackson's stature has to cross the Atlantic to reap the embarrassment of chilly reviews and audience indifference toward a work that earned her plaudits in her own country. Some plays simply don't – and shouldn't – travel.'

The show, reminiscent of a punch-drunk fighter, struggled to stay on its feet; but, inevitably, there came the final knock-out blow. It closed in May, a month earlier than its scheduled three-month run due to a drop in business. By now, the weeping was over. But, despite the play's critical annihilation, Glenda was nominated for a Tony award as Best Actress in competition with Elizabeth Taylor, Jane Lapotaire, Linda Ronstadt and Lauren Bacall; it eluded her. She jetted straight back to England the day after the play closed, anxious to see Daniel again – but also with thoughts of Patricia Neal on her mind.

A month before the Broadway opening of *Rose*, Glenda was in Hollywood filming the first half of *The Patricia Neal Story*, a made-for-television movie for CBS. The original plan was to go into production immediately after Glenda finished the stage play, but the film-makers were worried about an imminent directors' strike in Hollywood and so Glenda was asked if she would complete the American scenes before doing the play and work on the scenes in England after it. Now the cameras could roll again a month earlier than anticipated. The film, which marked Glenda's return to television drama for the first time since *Elizabeth R* a decade earlier, was based on the best-selling book *Pat and Roald* by Barry Farrell.

Glenda assumed the role of Miss Neal, the Hollywood actress who, in 1963, was accorded an Oscar for her portrayal in *Hud* of the sensual, laconic housekeeper who is sexually attacked by the drunken Paul Newman. Two years later, at the height of her career, and while three months pregnant, she suffered a series of massive strokes that damaged her nervous system and left her confined to a wheelchair in a state of semi-paralysis with severely impaired speech. The TV film confined itself to this tragedy, chronicling her subsequent period of recuperation in Los Angeles under the deliberately bullying encouragement of her British writer husband, Roald Dahl – originator of the *Tales of the Unexpected* TV series – and later in England at their Buckinghamshire home, 'Gypsy House', culminating in Miss Neal's successful return to acting in the film *The Subject Was Roses*.

The two-hour film, which went through numerous title changes (*Gypsy House*, *Patricia and Roald*, *The Miracle of Love* among them), was originally to have co-starred Glenda's old colleague Alan Bates in the role of Dahl, but the part eventually went to Dirk Bogarde in his first ever TV movie. Dahl was delighted that he was being impersonated by Bogarde; they were old friends. But Glenda had never met Patricia Neal – 'We said hello on the telephone' – nor did she want to meet her until after completing the film, though she had called to ensure the project had the Dahls' approval before taking the part. In portraying the American actress, whose much publicized three-year romance with Gary Cooper ended in her nervous breakdown, Glenda made no attempt to sound American.

'Listen,' she told producer Don Silverman, 'if you want a clone of her, don't come to me. I can't mimic. I can try and find an essence of her, but I can't just *be* her.'

In the event, while avoiding an outright mimesis of the inimitably seductive Neal voice, Glenda captured the style and spirit of the woman with uncanny accuracy. And in the rehabilitation scenes she registered each small advance in astonishing detail, evolving from a helpless creature with cropped hair – bearing some resemblance to Charlotte Corday in *The Marat/Sade* – to a beautiful and assured woman hampered only by barely perceptible traces of her ordeal. Glenda said later, 'What interested me about this – and I think it's important – was that Roald ignored expert opinion to follow his own feelings and to work very hard to bring Pat back to real life. What an individual can do with faith is highly important.'

The behind-the-scenes relationship of Glenda and Bogarde began in Los Angeles on a peculiarly awesome note: each seemed to be equally anxious about the other. 'I expected him to be rather intellectual and aloof, but he wasn't at all,' announced a much relieved Glenda. 'I love him dearly.'

It had been more than a dozen years since Bogarde was last in Hollywood, and over four years since he had confronted a movie camera. In his journal, after his arrival in the film capital, he found himself in particularly reflective, if uncertain mood. The sixty-one-year-old veteran of some sixty-five films was *nervous* at the prospect of meeting Glenda:

I saw her standing in one of the doorways, as I wandered along my corridor. She didn't beckon me, or solicit my favour. She didn't even move. But she was Lorelei; and I, like the bewitched sailors on the Rhine, found myself unable to resist. I am told that she is very dedicated to her work, and doesn't suffer fools gladly.

So here I am. I do hope it doesn't lead to destruction?

No one else on earth but she could have got me back to Los Angeles. Should I tell her? It might please her; and she might smile kindly on me. I do hope so. I have no reason to suppose otherwise, of course, but one is always uncertain; even in limbo.'

The outcome was that the two stars developed a real rapport. 'He's great,' said Glenda. 'She's a wonderful pro,' said Bogarde. A shared trait was that they abhorred bullshit, pretence in others as well as in themselves, and that they spoke their mind sharpshooter-style, straight from the hip. They laughed a lot together. 'Their closeness was wonderful to see,' observed

Geraldine Addison. In all her years in the business, only one other world-class actor, Walter Matthau, had ever come as close to sharing such an intimate understanding with Glenda. Coincidentally, both men were born in the same year, 1920. It is difficult to define exactly what, for Glenda, was the quality which was possessed by Bogarde and Matthau and not by her other leading men – Segal, Finch, Chamberlain, Reed, Garner and Caine among them.

Glenda, as we have seen, was not a woman who cherished any particular affection for those with whom she was expected to share a screen kiss. It was purely business. It never overflowed into pleasure. Her leading men were little more than a necessary evil. Their world was not her world; better not get too involved with their private affairs. Objectivity, that was what mattered. Deep friendship was not cultivated or desired, because it could obtrude on the work. 'Leading men?' one could almost hear her saying. 'Bah!' Her affection for Bogarde and Matthau was extraordinary, then, because it *was* extraordinary. In the company of each man, Glenda came alive, was elevated, transformed to a pitch of exaltation which was probably not even matched in her more personal relationships with Roy and Andy.

With Bogarde and Matthau, she felt their equal, which in itself was a novel situation, bearing in mind her 'superior' behaviour towards her former husband and her lover's overbearing behaviour towards her. The ability to meet Bogarde and Matthau on equal terms, both as artists and as people, was what characterized her attitude towards them above all else. And, because of it, she could relax with them, on and off the set, in a way she could never unwind with all her other leading men. 'Dirk claims to be stupid, but he isn't,' she said. Matthau once also intimated as much to her about himself. It was this disparity between avowed stupidity and actual unforced cleverness and natural wit which struck a chord in Glenda. 'I've often found,' she said crisply, 'that I can talk to someone I'm working with very intently about a scene, then we finish the rehearsal and find we have absolutely nothing to say to each other.' This never happened with Bogarde and Matthau. With them, there was always a great deal to say. With these two men far from her mind, Glenda then added, 'I really don't find actors attractive. Essentially they are much more self-involved and much more neurotic than actresses. They seem to feel there's something sissy about acting and they're obsessed with proving themselves. The good actors are concerned with acting rather than their own egotistical *need* to act.' Bogarde and Matthau, presumably, were neither neurotic nor nursed thoughts about being 'sissy'. Certainly their appeal, for Glenda, was a dominant, all-embracing one which, when they were together, dispatched to oblivion an otherwise prickly, caustic personality. It was a love affair in the truest and most innocent sense.

Ironically, the Dahls' personal love affair took a turn for the worse as the production proceeded. Barry Farrell's original book, and now this film, brought nothing but unhappiness to them. They claimed it intruded into their lives. When executive producer Lawrence Schiller bought the film rights to the book, the initial response from Roald Dahl was one of alarm: 'We said "No" for a long time, but when we were eventually persuaded that it might give help to other patients who had suffered strokes, we agreed.' Bogarde later rang Dahl to assure him that he and Glenda would do everything within their power to honour the two people whose lives they were portraying. This pledge clinched the deal. But by the time the film was ready to be screened, Dahl was reluctant to discuss the project because of the distress it had caused his family. More sadly, their twenty-nine-year marriage had collapsed, bringing to a close one of the great love stories of the era. Less than a year later Pat and Roald were divorced.

From the very beginning, the film had met with the stern disapproval of their eldest daughter, Tessa, who affirmed that none of the family was happy about it. 'We all thought differently about the film. It's so incredibly bizarre to sit down and watch our family life story pressed into a couple of hours. I was eight at the time of my mother's illness, and I think I had forgotten what had happened. When I saw the film with the producer, he watched me like a hawk – waiting for me to burst into tears. I refused to give him that pleasure. I cried later in the hotel.'

But although the film itself caused so much pain to the Dahls, they both expressed nothing but praise for the performances, and Bogarde's friendship with the divorced couple continued. After one of the early private screenings, Glenda and Pat spoke on the telephone. 'She told me she thought my performance was "marvellous",' said Glenda, 'and I was so anxious in case she would be distressed. Then I would have been mortified.'

'Playing Pat Neal was the best thing I'd ever seen Glenda do,' recalled actress friend Jean Marsh. 'It was a wonderful performance, and bloody difficult. What a nerve to do it when Pat Neal is so alive. I would have been tempted to say no. I thought she was terrific, and totally unsparing.'

Had Glenda for the first time in her life *really* revealed herself? Shown the true vulnerability of not just Patricia Neal's nature but her own too? Many agreed with Jean Marsh that her portrayal of the American actress amounted to one of her greatest performances, albeit at times harrowing. As Bogarde commented, 'Of course it's a weepie, but it isn't schmaltzy.' In Hollywood, they nominated her for an Emmy award, on the occasion of which Patricia Neal exclaimed, 'Glenda was beautiful; couldn't have been better.' This had not been an easy film for Glenda, but now the pain of the labour was behind her.

It was intended that she should fly directly to Vienna to start shooting Ken Russell's *The Beethoven Secret*, with a cast line-up that included Anthony Hopkins, Charlotte Rampling and Jodie Foster, but the project was postponed when interim financing from West Germany fell through. An envisaged 'opened up' screen version of *Rose*, with Glenda repeating her stage portrayal alongside Angie Dickinson and Mona Washbourne in featured roles, also came to nothing. Enders–Jackson Bowden Productions were meantime actively engaged on a television film biography called *The Rosalind Franklin Story*, dealing with the British scientist whose research on heredity and nucleic acids (DNA) won three men Nobel Prizes but earned her little credit as she died at the age of thirty-six before the prizes were inaugurated; it was also hoped to team Glenda with Carol Burnett in a musical, and to generate another Jackson–Matthau vehicle: Enders suggested a straight non-musical version of *Sweeney Todd – The Fiend of Fleet Street*, but Matthau said no to playing a Cockney role. None of the schemes materialized. Glenda was in low spirits. She felt abandoned. There were more sleepless nights.

23
Glenda's Last Stand?

Just when Glenda was beginning to wonder whether her name meant anything any more, BBC Television promptly brought her to her senses in September 1981 by beginning a season of eight Glenda Jackson films, starting with *Sunday, Bloody Sunday*. 'I don't want to sound churlish,' she told a friend, 'but aren't I supposed to be dead before the BBC starts putting on a season of my movies? They didn't even tell me they were going to do it.' Her attitude was ambivalent. 'On the one hand I'm flattered but, on the other, I'm wondering if someone up there is saying: "Glenda's had a good run. Now let's give her a nice send off."'

Too many years had been spent as an unemployed actress for Glenda not to be superstitious about the tribute. Yet just to add to her paranoia that this really was 'Glenda's Last Stand', she was also receiving similar treatment in the United States. Unlike the BBC, not only did the Americans inform her in advance, they also sent over a camera crew and prevailed upon Glenda to introduce, with suitable anecdotes, each movie on the Bravo cable network that covered the States via satellite. And yet, at forty-five, she was alive and well.

In October, halfway through the two TV seasons, Glenda joined forces with Julie Christie, Ann-Margret and Alan Bates on location in the East Sussex countryside to begin work on a big-screen version of Rebecca West's semi-autobiographical novel, *The Return of the Soldier*. It pleased her enormously that it was scripted, as *Stevie* had been, by Hugh Whitemore and that the director was Alan Bridges, who had worked with her many years earlier on the television play *Let's Murder Vivaldi*. Their new movie centred on a well-heeled soldier (Bates) who, having returned from the First World War with twenty years shell-shocked from his memory, no longer remembers his wife (Christie), and instead is consumed with longing for an earlier love, an innkeeper's daughter who is now a dowdy housewife (Glenda). The tensions in the story are increased by the feelings of the soldier's cousin (Ann-Margret), a repressed spinster who is also in love with him. It was all very much in Glenda's emotional territory, even if the frumpish exterior was a novel departure.

The main location, the large house to which the soldier returns, was at Firle Place, the ancestral home in East Sussex of the late Henry, 6th Viscount

Gage; the small Edwardian house where Glenda was supposed to live was filmed just outside Nottingham, in a hamlet where the National Coal Board housed their employees in one of the few remaining terraces to have retained their original character. 'I looked at the three of us standing there on the first day,' Glenda recalled of the East Sussex location, 'and I thought to myself, "What are we doing here?" You couldn't have found three more different people. It was a laugh.'

It wasn't really. Not for the producers, Ann Skinner and Simon Relph, whose inaugural independent film production this was. It was also the first occasion Glenda, Julie Christie and Ann-Margret had ever worked together and on a tight-budget movie with a short schedule it was crucial that time was not lost during production by the clash of three unpredictable star temperaments. Initially, laughter proved to be the key to keeping the ladies' varied dispositions on a neutral plain; but eventually there was a sort of unspoken agreement not to disagree. They almost worked at the task of retaining their separate identities. Thus, Glenda drove home each night to Blackheath for the sake of Daniel, while bachelor-girl Julie Christie, who had temporarily abandoned the rural seclusion of her farmhouse in Wales, and Ann-Margret, who had jetted in from Los Angeles with her husband–manager Roger Smith, both found rented accommodation near the location. During the day when not needed, especially at lunchtimes, the three women made a hasty retreat to the privacy of their respective caravans. They kept themselves very much to themselves, not wishing to tempt fate.

At other times, when working together on the set, the quality of their harmonious relationship owed a tremendous amount to the shrewd diplomacy of the amiable Alan Bates. He became their go-between, acting as a buffer to any possible clashes. When Glenda stood up to the director, Bates shook his head in admiration. 'Glenda has enough balls for all of us,' he said. By constantly deflecting their conversations on to neutral subjects, it was not long before the three female stars were chatting about recipes and restaurants, which, certainly as far as Glenda was concerned, was no mean achievement.

Nevertheless, despite a certain similarity in their respective temperaments, there were sufficient differences in their outlook on life, and on each other, to compel the captains of the ship to tread very carefully and to ensure that opportunities for disagreements would not present themselves. Said producer Simon Relph at the time: 'Julie is shy, Glenda has always been a recluse, and Ann-Margret is shyer than shy – the Ann-Margret in her nightclub act is a character she plays. Julie and Ann-Margret get on very well. Glenda and Ann-Margret get on very well. Julie and Glenda get on, but just. Basically they challenge one another. Julie thinks Glenda is more of an actress than she is, and Glenda thinks Julie is more of a star than she is. They admire those qualities in each other, but it's still a bridge to cross.' The passage was not easygoing. Despite the shared laughter, they were each about as relaxed in the others' company as over-stretched violin strings – and always 'on guard'.

The selection of *The Return of the Soldier* for the Cannes Film Festival was an indication of the quality of the completed product. 'I went to Cannes once,' said Glenda. 'It's the same people you see in Los Angeles and New York talking to one another in the hotels. You're escorted through police lines while somebody whispers, "Keep your head down. Don't look." It's very queer.' All the same, she flew in for just one day to help promote *Return* and, dutifully, was photographed aboard a yacht rented for the occasion. But Glenda, who always hated the strident razmatazz of film festivals, made a quick, discreet exit and flew back to London. The film, made on a modest $4 million budget, was an enormous success at Cannes and far beyond. Margaret Hinxman in the *Daily Mail* expressed most people's view when she said that it was doubtful whether the year would see many better films or many finer performances. It was seen both as a showcase and a homage to three outstanding actresses; none was singled out for special mention, all being of equal excellence. This was something new for Glenda; like her or hate her, the critics always managed to say something specific about her particular contribution.

After spending Christmas at Hoylake with her mother, and sisters Gill, Lynne and Elizabeth – her father had died that year – Glenda embarked on 1982 with renewed spirits; the taxing schedule of the previous year had practically drained her of any emotional or physical reserves. In February she made *Giro City*, a low-budget thriller intended both for Channel 4's *Film on Four* slot and theatrical release. It was shot on location in London, Belfast and Wales over six weeks and was accorded rave reviews.

This time Glenda was more her real self, as the director to Jon Finch's reporter on a television programme specializing in exposé-type documentaries. Her assignments include uncovering evidence of local corruption in Wales and interviewing the fugitive head of the IRA – but the difficulties and dangers of getting the stories prove to be less formidable than the problems of getting the too-hot-to-handle material on the air owing to internal censorship. It was an angry film, written and directed by a former TV current affairs man Karl Francis. 'Glenda's support was vital,' he explained. 'She immediately liked the script, but I was in a constant state of uncertainty that she would pull out and we wouldn't get the backing her name could command. But she didn't. She was great.'

So what was the attribute of a film with a budget of less than £½ million that tempted Glenda to do it? 'Well, it certainly wasn't the role,' she said frankly. 'But I found the ideas very interesting. A film that tackles censorship in this way has got to be admired.' The critics shared her admiration, not least for her presence in the proceedings. 'Glenda Jackson comes on strong,' said one reviewer. 'Her gaunt good looks always seem clenched in commitment. But if she is not the usual stuff that stars are made of she proves, in this exciting British movie, that the force of her personality can be very much for the good of a film's truth.' Another drew attention to Glenda's 'sturdy resolution' and 'forthright character'.

Certainly the essential factor of strength, which was central to her disposition, was never better utilized than here. Ann-Margret, talking to me about the two facets of Glenda's personality which she most admired, said the analysis could be adequately compressed to just two words: 'strength' and 'character'. The only chink of vulnerability in that toughness, or at least the only betrayal of strain, was the interminable cluster of cigarette stubs in the ashtrays to which she added at regular intervals. Part of her strength continued to reside in her verbal utterances. You rarely heard her say 'I don't know' or 'I'm not sure', since she fielded questions on most topics, including the Queen, whom she regarded as 'a wonder and a whizz'. Any vulnerability and romanticism she might possess is hidden behind an ironic, self-mocking exterior, in an inherently English way. 'We don't cry a lot outside,' she would explain briskly.

Like many strong women, Glenda hates accusations of 'unfemininity', although she is not sure if the outrage she feels is caused by the 'injustice' of the charge, or by her persistent sensitivity to it. She possesses the inevitable arrogance of many self-fulfilled, talented, ultimately tough personalities. This was supremely illustrated on radio's *Any Questions*, when she was asked what she thought was the best way to start a conversation when introduced to someone on whom she would like to make a good impression. She confessed, in so many words, that she always opted for a course that indicated sublime arrogance: she put the ball in the other person's court and made it perfectly plain that it was *their* job to make a very good impression on *her*. Gestures speak louder than words. Her body, though spare as a boy's, hints at physical power. It is made manifest in performance.

Glenda was always conscious of the tremendous mileage to be derived from nurturing what was in effect an inherent fearsomeness, despite her statements to the contrary. But privately, in the company of close friends, she occasionally relaxed and became as starstruck as the next pop-crazed adolescent who had just seen her idol. 'Oh, she's a great star-lover,' said Geraldine Addison. 'We were filming once at Pinewood when Harry Belafonte walked on the set – and Glenda, the great star, suddenly became like a girl. She just stared at him with wonder in her eyes, muttering, "Oh, *God*, I always thought he was *wonderful*...." On another occasion we were shooting some scenes at Hyde Park for *A Touch of Class* when, across the way, she saw Ben Murphy of the TV series *Alias Smith and Jones*. Her face lit up and she said, "Oh, look ... it's *him*!" He was on his own and Glenda hoped against hope that he would come over and talk to her; she was so disheartened when he didn't.

When she'd heard that I'd worked with Katharine Hepburn, she wanted to know *everything* about her. She was fascinated by the whole "star" thing; she's been like that for as long as I've known her.'

Again: 'I once met Glenda backstage at a rock-'n'-roll concert,' recalled Jean Marsh. 'We were both waiting in the corridor to meet Mick Jagger, and it was obvious that the prospect filled Glenda with an odd combination of excitement and anxiety. I thought, "How hilarious! Here we are, two ever-so-serious actresses, both rather nervous at the idea of meeting this big rock-'n'-roll star." She was with two of her sisters, and it was obvious that she was as starstruck as they were.'

These brief, private aberrations aside, Glenda was 'strong, strong ...'; and strength was certainly the quality which stood her in good stead for her disastrous springtime foray into the West End. From now on, it seemed, she had lost her touch in the choice of stage vehicles. Flop followed flop. A sense of artistic disorientation, a sort of blurring of standard vision, conspired to lead her time and again down theatrical blind-alleys. How else could you account for her role as Hitler's mistress, Eva Braun, in Robert David Mac-Donald's misguided comedy–drama *Summit Conference*, which opened at the Lyric Theatre in April 1982? In it, Glenda and Georgina Hale, as Mussolini's mistress, Clara Petacci, got together over tea in 1941 Berlin to embark on a duel of bitchy wit embracing the Nazi supermyth. Miss Hale was accorded the flashier assignment as a hip-wiggling Latin floozy, whereas Glenda, sporting a Nordic blonde wig and adopting an accent recalling Northern MP Barbara Castle at her most assertive, was wickedly cerebral, cynical and, yes, tough. But the play itself, which steered a confusing course between the two main characters as women and as symbols of the nations they represented, was more intriguing for its hypothesis than its execution as a theatrical narrative, in which the satiric humour too quickly ran out of steam. Critics slated it and audiences, too, quickly ran out of patience and, in time, stayed away. Glenda was unmoved. She thought the play's intentions – 'a savage indictment of Fascism' – were grossly misinterpreted. 'I feel no obligation to do what people have seen me do before,' she told Veronica Groocock and Rita Black in *Woman's World*. 'My only obligation is to do my job to the best of my ability – because people are paying. That's the only bargain I enter into.'

Few seemed to be impressed by the transaction and *Summit Conference* was not permitted to outstay its welcome. So she talked again about giving up acting; she talked for the first time about directing ('I think I'd like to have a go. Not a play, probably, but a film'); and she talked about her essential ordinariness. This was a disturbing time for Glenda. Her type of rough-hewn beauty was no longer fashionable, a fact which brought her little comfort. Such discomfiture was being reflected more and more in her daily conversations: 'If you look around, most of the young actresses – with a few notable exceptions – seem to be throwbacks to the thirties and forties. Suddenly they're all *pretty* with fluting voices again.'

At forty-six, Glenda's life was coasting along on an unnerving wave of indecision and instability. It was as if somewhere deep in her personality there was some sort of built-in obsolescence, prodding her to make decisions which could lead her nowhere in particular, merely detract from her fundamental status as an actress. She had toyed with social work, but social workers always wrote to her and said, 'Please don't do it – stay where you are!' She had had a brush with the Open University, reading social sciences, but failed to keep it up: 'I'll have to say, "Sorry fellas, can I try again another time?"' And, on a personal note, she had contemplated re-marriage – and firmly rejected the idea.

For the first time in the seven years that they had been together, a stage play (*Summit Conference*) in which she had starred had not been lit by Andy Phillips. But then behind the scenes all was not what it had been between them. Over the previous year they had grown increasingly apart, and the relationship which had known its more tempestuous moments became too much even for Glenda's strong-willed constitution. They had parted and Glenda was once again living alone without a man to share her life . . . not, at least, on an intimate level.

Roy still hovered on the edges of her existence, a loving father, whose relationship with Daniel never faltered, an ex-husband whose support in times of strife was always reliably close at hand. Glenda could tell people with candour, 'We seem to get on better now that we're not married than we did when we were. I know that if there was ever a decision that affected Daniel, then Roy would, in my view quite rightly, expect to be consulted about it.' The time was fast approaching, certainly, when Glenda would need a dependable man – any man – to fall back on.

24
A New Tomorrow

Life would go on for Glenda Jackson – but not, it seemed, with a second husband. 'I cannot conceive of a situation where I'd ever put the man first,' she said. 'I like to think there'll be a grand passion in my life again – though I'm not sure I've got the energy for it any more – but the truth is I'd never put any man before acting. If a man asked me to choose between him and my work, I'd probably leave him anyway. Having said all that, I must explain that I never seem to meet anyone any more. I go to the theatre, I do the play, and I go home. It's not the most social existence.'

Her attitude towards men, nevertheless, remained as practical and as dogmatic as at any other time. 'I think one has to acknowledge that men are the other half of women – but, having said that, I don't think one should settle for believing anything is better than nothing. Relationships require a great deal of effort and work, but there comes a point when you have to recognize that if the effort is all there is, if that's simply what's keeping you together, then it's a great mistake to continue.'

She also said, 'I would hate to think that, because I've had a couple of experiences that weren't particularly happy in a sense, I'd say, "Well, I'm never going to bother with that sort of thing again." That would be stupid and silly and essentially dishonest. I think you learn from how you are, and how you are hopefully develops and grows.' Asked if she might suffer a handicap that many successful and famous women experienced – namely, that men were intimidated by her stature – Glenda glowered in surprise. 'I've never been aware of men finding me intimidating,' she replied, not wholly convincingly. 'But that, in a way, weeds them out: if they find me intimidating, then they *certainly* aren't worth the effort!'

Denied the solace of close male company, Glenda submerged herself completely in her work, just as she had always done in times of crisis. She narrated a meandering film documentary called *The Thames*, a picturesque panorama of the river itself – the first woman ever to narrate a National Geographical Society production. Together with such fellow stars as Sheila Hancock, Diana Quick and Miriam Karlin, she began negotiating for the lease of London's Garrick Theatre, which she hoped would eventually be controlled exclusively by women. Her group, the Women's Playhouse Project, claimed that women were denied the powerful, policy-making jobs on theatre boards and managements, and that actresses played insubstantial or stereotyped roles.

She recorded a guest spot on *The Morecambe and Wise Christmas Show* in 1982, and then flew out immediately to Hollywood to discuss the possibility of making her first American television series. If she wanted to recite the telephone directory, said the producer dining her at Beverly Hills' Ginger Man restaurant, CBS would buy it in a flash; it was a wholesome meal, but the anticipated series failed to materialize. She then dashed to the South of France, to the rural backwater of Châteauneuf de Grasse, where Dirk Bogarde had his farmhouse, in an attempt to lure him back to the big screen after five years' absence. Although she succeeded, the movie in which they would have appeared together, *Buried Alive* (an adaptation of the Arnold Bennett novel), failed to materialize for the intended stars and was eventually made two years later with Peter O'Toole.

But other matters were occupying her thoughts just before Christmas: with fellow actors Albert Finney, Diana Rigg, Richard Johnson, Maggie Smith and John Hurt she had joined the board of directors of a new production company, United British Artists. The company's aim was to stage West End productions with limited runs of eight weeks a production. Immediately following the theatre run, the production would be revised and adapted for taping in a television studio or on location. This programme, with backing from the City, would then be distributed worldwide by Lord Grade's Embassy Communications to television, cable and video markets. UBA would also produce independent film projects, of which *Champions*, starring John Hurt, was the first. Glenda was tremendously enthusiastic about the project – not least because her services would be required for only *limited* stage runs – and was acutely conscious of its historical context, for never before had a consortium of British actors come together to control their own future. The obvious precedents in America were United Artists, formed in 1919 by Charlie Chaplin, Mary Pickford and Douglas Fairbanks, and the short-lived First Artists, brought together by Barbra Streisand, Paul Newman, Steve McQueen, Sidney Poitier and Dustin Hoffman.

A probing reporter inquired how many good new scripts UBA had attracted. 'Not a lot,' Glenda answered crisply. 'The problem is that all of us in UBA are "of a certain age", and particularly as far as the women are concerned, it's an age where nobody really reckons us in theatrical terms. If one can spark a few good writers to find our age group interesting, it would be marvellous.'

Glenda was well aware that a spate of stage flops at this point in her life could be disastrous to her career. 'Women,' she explained, 'are seen almost always in terms of the emotional life of the story's dramatic engine, which is invariably a man. We are then slotted in the pigeon-holes – beddable, which usually means wives or mistresses; or non-beddable, which means mothers, grandmothers or aunts.' In her favour was the fact that she had so far been spared the 'non-beddable' roles, though she knew that that could only be a matter of time. Her great fear was that, when it came, her career would assume a low-key profile and perhaps go into decline; but then this is the fear of any movie superstar approaching a fiftieth birthday, male or female.

For all her apparent lack of pretensions, Glenda had avoided the 'non-beddable' roles as far as possible. That was no mere coincidence: her vanity was as keenly pronounced as the next star's. Only when she became an Aunt Alice or a Granny Gabriel would the world be informed that she had at last decided to throw in the towel; from that moment forward she would be a different person. She would be able to relax, resigned to her new status in the scheme of things; but until that auspicious time, a fretful Glenda Jackson was destined to prevail.

The very nature of her pronouncements indicated the instability of her life and the unease she felt. 'This isn't a world I want to inhabit unless I'm fully involved – and now I've decided I really want to go into politics,' she informed anyone who cared to listen. 'I feel I'm at a watershed in my life now. It's something I've been building up to and living with for the past five years. Acting is not completely satisfying, you know. It never has been for me, whatever the rewards. My feelings stem from the inevitable slowing-down process. The local Labour Party asked me once if I'd stand in the elections and I said no. They should ask me again ... I'd say yes right away.'

But when, a few months later, she was offered the chance to stand for Labour in a Welsh seat, she tactfully declined. She was in a constant whirl of indecision, precipitated by the fact that she believed she might be on the verge (yet again) of forsaking stage and screen for the groves of academe. She had applied for a three-year, full-time BA course in humanities at Thames Polytechnic. 'Work is not going to stay interesting forever,' she reiterated, 'and I'm not going to sit at home and polish the furniture. The whole idea is to try something new. I would forget acting altogether. After three years, acting would also probably forget me. I have asked my family what they think and they have said, "Do what you like, our Glenda." They always do.'

Glenda had arranged to star in a production of Brecht's *Mother Courage*, playing a limited season at London's Haymarket Theatre in the spring. Just before going into rehearsal she discovered that the Royal Shakespeare Company currently held the rights and so appealed for permission to stage a commercial production over the next few months. Permission was refused even though, claimed Glenda, the RSC did not intend to produce the play until the end of the following year. She kicked up a tremendous fuss, stating that companies which bought rights and then sat on them were legally within their rights but 'morally culpable'. She fumed, 'They have no right to deny work to actors at a time when three million people are unemployed. Subsidized theatre was not brought about to produce a safety net for those inside and a noose for those outside.' Her angry words fell on deaf ears, and another potential Glenda Jackson stage vehicle was consigned to oblivion.

After flying to the Cannes Film Festival to receive a gold statuette for Distinguished Service to the Cinema – 'a hysterical experience and nothing to do with artistic validity' – Glenda plunged straight into rehearsals for her next (as it turned out) infamous stage disaster. Even her best friends believed she was pitting her wits against what could only be described as the world's worst play. *Great and Small*, by Botho Strauss, known to some as 'the German Pinter', confused and irritated audiences on its pre-London run in Richmond, Leeds, Manchester and Bath, and no less bamboozled all and sundry at its ultimate West End roosting, the Vaudeville Theatre, at the end of August. Taking on the role of Lotte – the play was a surreal account of one woman's frantic attempts to fit in with the world around her – merely confirmed that, in theatrical terms, Glenda was a glutton for punishment.

In Leeds she broke the house records for non-attendance, and in Manchester, where they stormed out amid boos and shouts of 'Rubbish!', one critic described the play as 'a wildly episodic, faintly absurd piece, full of assorted, barely identifiable nutters, parading their stream of consciousness ravings in front of one another'. In Bath the local review called it 'a gloomy ramble among the darkest recesses of the German race', and producer Peter Graham Scott – the man who gave Glenda her earliest TV work – deemed it 'not a play at all, just a piece of self-indulgent psycho-analysis'.

The truth was that nobody but Glenda had a clue what the play was about. Before it reached London she was even disclosing, 'We are emptying theatres wherever we go. Nobody seems to like this play except me – and I love it.' There was the rub. But audiences were most puzzled by unexplained details, such as stagehands who wore yellow safety helmets and wellington boots when they moved the scenery. At a London preview one man shouted his agreement when one of the characters said to Lotte, 'I think there's something wrong with you.'

With *Great and Small*, certainly, Glenda had taken her defiance of the traditional commercial values of showbusiness to a new level. 'I left with the sad feeling that Miss Jackson may grow to know what real loneliness is before the play is gone and forgotten,' predicted Jack Tinker of the *Daily Mail*. But Glenda remained unrepentant: 'If you're going to settle for a play which is utterly conventional, which disturbs no one, which causes one to think not at all, then we're going to watch diminishing theatre diminish even more.' She is probably right – at least in theory. In practice, however, few of her fans were interested in witnessing new theatrical frontiers being charted.

A happier, indeed momentous event occurred in September when, between shows, she journeyed north to the town of her birth. Here, amid the merry jostle and throng of half the population of Birkenhead, she officially opened the playhouse on the main Borough Road that was named in her honour – the Glenda Jackson Theatre. Joan Jackson and all the family was there, and 'our Glenda' took it all in her stride. Opening a new theatre was not something about which to become sentimental, even when it bore your name. Secretly, though, she was touched by the accolade.

Glenda Jackson had changed. One bright, cold morning in Vienna, in October of 1983, when filming commenced on *Sakharov*, the former Boots girl from Cheshire at last succumbed to the inevitable. Thickly bespectacled, with her hair made into a dank grey bunch, and wearing an unflattering baggy cardigan, Glenda joined the ranks of the 'non-beddable'. She was not simply a mother in her latest film, but the mother of two grown-up married children.

This was the breakthrough she had endeavoured to postpone for as long as possible. She knew, and the world knew, that when the moment came for her to leave behind the domain of the 'beddable' she would have entered a decisive new phase in her life. Producers, who were not always the most imaginative of people, would see her in future in terms of 'Glenda the mother figure', and those roles – even Glenda had to admit – were invariably not the most interesting or the most demanding of dramatic challenges. But the decision had been made because, she perceived, there could be little sense in fighting the obvious: at just a few months short of her forty-eighth birthday, she was already well into middle age.

The frothy frolics of *A Touch of Class* were a thing of the past: now it was grey-haired motherhood for the Glenda Jackson whose writhing bare flesh and orgasmic groans had once occupied the movie world's consciousness. And yet, when the moment came for her to apply spirit gum to her grey wig, she did so without ceremony, without flinching, even without rancour. Her mind was made up – the avoidable could no longer be avoided – and so she would venture into this new phase of her life with the minimum of fuss and the maximum of dignity.

Sakharov, the film in which this transformation was effected, featured the veteran American actor Jason Robards in the role of Russia's most famous dissident. Andrei Sakharov, inventor of Russia's H-bomb, youngest member ever elected to the Soviet Academy of Sciences, and winner of the Nobel Peace Prize, was arguably the most celebrated Russian ever to join the human rights campaign. The film chronicles the events that led to Sakharov's growing disenchantment with the Soviet system, his work as a dissident and human rights activist, and his treatment by the Soviet establishment which forced him into exile in industrialized Gorky, stripped of the Stalin Prize and Order of Lenin bestowed on him while he was still a golden hero of the Soviet state.

It was this grim tale which Glenda, as Sakharov's second wife Elena, re-created on location in Vienna (standing in for Moscow), London and numerous Russianesque sites all over the English countryside. As a vehicle for introducing the world to the 'new look' Glenda Jackson, it could not have been bettered – not least because of her political ideology. 'If you are in my position anything you can do as a performer to draw attention to the story, to show what some of your fellow human beings are going through, you should do,' she said. 'The Sakharovs are remarkable people of huge courage; and as for Elena, she's certainly a very brave, staunch woman, very motherly, comforting. If I met her I would want to ask whether she was ever tempted to give up.'

Elena's married children, daughter Tanya (played by Catherine Hall) and son Alyosha (John McAndrew), now live in the United States, and it was due to them – as well as their respective spouses, Efrem Yankelevich and Lisa – that the film's script was so authentic. The 'American' Sakharovs gave the film their fullest support and warmest blessing. Each day Glenda drew inspiration for her portrayal of Elena simply by following the news reports in newspapers and on television, for the movie was in production during co-ordinated efforts worldwide to free Sakharov, a now sick man who had suffered two heart attacks and was being denied the use of hospitals run by the Academy of Sciences. Elena, who voluntarily joined her husband in exile, was always by his side. Glenda fervently hoped that one day, under happier circumstances, her path would cross theirs; in the meantime, *this* was her homage to two people with whose ideals she totally identified: 'If there are no ideals, there can be no hope.'

Although Glenda had now become almost completely reconciled to this new phase in her life, and although in general terms she was more relaxed within herself, her once-reliable vital spirit had lost something of its former impetus. Her celebrated energy was no longer what it was. 'I wanted to do some gardening the other day,' she informed a visitor to Blackheath, 'but I fell asleep on the sofa instead, which was most irritating.' That sort of thing was happening far too often now, she lamented.

The profoundest change and, undoubtedly, the most surprising, was a rapidly diminishing self-assurance. It was not so much that she had lost faith in the particular goods which she had to offer – rather that there was a diminution of nervous energy with which to nourish her craft. A role, for Glenda, had always been a fierce testing of her mettle, a challenge in the medieval sense, a combat, tremulous with personal danger and charged with incalculable hardship. There was in her nature a quiet conviction that applying greasepaint and projecting one's ego for the edification of a waiting public was somehow the most important act of the creative mind. Now the security of mind and the positiveness of approach which had once provided the main thrust to her dramaturgical adventures had all but abandoned her. It was not a fact she was keen to discuss openly – nevertheless: 'I'm less confident now than I've ever been,' she finally admitted. 'In this peculiar craft, confidence is something you spend a lifetime losing. I used to be frightened only one night a week but now I'm frightened of every performance. I mean really frightened.'

For Glenda, however, trepidation did not automatically mean capitulation: it could act as a red rag to a bull. It was largely because of this masochistic tendency that, in the spring of 1984, she continued her one-woman crusade against the august theatre companies and West End conventions. The light of battle danced in her eyes as she went into rehearsals for Eugene O'Neill's epic, five-hour *Strange Interlude*, a play which hovers precariously between a latter-day Greek tragedy and the fraught and frequently farcical domestic intrigues

of American TV soap opera. Veterans of Glenda's last West End campaign, *Great and Small*, started to gird their loins as soon as this latest enterprise embarked on its provincial previews in Croydon and Nottingham prior to the London opening at the Duke of York's. It was all so – well – familiar, with Glenda as a bewildered neurotic in New England going in search of an identity and, in the course of thirty years, becoming entangled in the lives of three men. Along the way there is scandal, concealed parentage, illegitimate birth, overtones of incest and all manner of Freudian psychology at work.

Asked if this latest undertaking might not be seen as just Glenda coming to town to play, after dotty Lotte, yet another mad lady, she replied, 'That may well be the case, though I do think there is a difference between a neurotic and a nutcase. But at the moment I do feel I am pushing a pea up a mountain with my nose. Let's face it, it is a bloody long play.'

On that point there were few dissenters. 'You have to hand it to her,' said Jack Tinker of the *Daily Mail*, 'Glenda Jackson is nothing if not game. She spares herself nix whenever she brings her commanding presence to the West End. And make no mistake, she expects no less from her audience.' In fact, in this new period of changing direction, there seemed to be something almost defiant about her reformed working process. 'Defiant?' Yes, she said, she would not argue with that. Despite her declared diminution of energy, Glenda remained a fighter to the end. She was game.

In retrospect, the most characteristic feature of Glenda's stardom can be seen as her refusal to compromise, her determination to achieve her goals and not settle for less. It was partly for this reason that, since 1970, she had repeatedly vowed to give it up. Her regular pronouncements on the subject of retirement began to acquire an implication all their own, as if acting were a bad habit like smoking, contracted casually, practised guiltily and due for replacement by some more approved alternative. She talked now about joining Voluntary Service Overseas – but admitted that she would have to get an education first: 'There's very little a retired actress can teach a developing country.'

Movie stars of an older generation regularly flayed their studios for perfectly logical professional reasons, more often than not to do with abysmal roles; but modern stars of Glenda's epoch prefer to impute a moral foundation to their rejection of the waste, hypocrisy and egoism of the movies ('one is ludicrously overpaid'). Glenda cannot help making statements like: 'I suppose it is true, this is a trivial profession. I think of all the energy I pour into what may turn out to be a very unimportant film and I feel it should be channelled into something more worthwhile, helping the homeless or the handicapped.' Yet repeatedly to cite the attractions of a socially useful life, while at the same time continuing to scoop up Oscars and sign ever more lucrative contracts, is an odd sort of protest. 'What gives her career its defiantly modern ring is her apparently impenitent desire to publicize how much she dislikes a lot of it,' affirmed London *Evening Standard* film critic Alexander Walker. 'Her rather puritan nature undoubtedly feels the pressures of stardom painfully. Maybe that is what gives her screen personality a certain rasping impatience.'

Approaching fifty, she is acutely conscious that acting is not something you walk away from; it walks away from you: 'A woman's face goes, as far as the camera is concerned, when you are quite young.' Hers had 'gone'? Oh, yes.

'That's her vulnerability coming through,' said Vladek Sheybal. 'She looks at herself on the screen and thinks, "I look awful." I think she's wrong; when I meet her again, I'll tell her so. When she was an unknown repertory actress I told her that she had great star quality, and now I'm telling her not to worry, that she has a very interesting face, and that she could become a character actress quite easily, like Bette Davis. These women are ageless. She could come back to the cinema in her sixties and be a sensation. She could have us all trembling in our seats by the absolute force of her performances.'

'When she goes on about her face, she knows exactly what she's talking about,' added Oliver Reed. 'What she means is that she is getting lazier, and the camera is getting busier, and the film is getting quicker, and that means you don't need as much light – light which has perhaps flattered her. Now, while Glenda has never really concerned herself with how she looks, she *is* now probably concerning herself with the egotistical problem of playing senior, older characters ... and that is something that middle-aged actresses have to try to come to terms with. How do you cope with that?'

Well, in Glenda's case, she talked about politics and social work and polytechnics. It all amounted to the same thing: abandoning acting because it was abandoning her. All in all, life was becoming tougher. 'Who could blame her for wanting to quit?' asked Joseph Losey. 'Acting is a passionate love and deep agony, and passionate love and deep agony are very hard to go through with a bunch of shits, which is what major stars like Glenda Jackson have to deal with. Whether or not she is getting the parts that she thinks she ought to have I don't know, but I can't believe that she will be really happy if and when she walks away from the profession. I refuse to believe it.'

'I think in the future she should be playing horny old aunts,' reflected Oliver Reed. 'But then she talks about retirement, doesn't she ...?'

A few questions I wanted to ask her: 'You might miss the acting world?'

'I might miss the acting.'

'Could you really kill the acting bug in you?'

'Well, I'll leave the door open – though the fear is that even though the work remains plentiful, it may not be interesting enough to justify all the agony.'

'Is it still agony?'

'It's always agony.'

For Glenda Jackson the quest in her professional life is still for the hundred per cent performance. She has not yet achieved it and hopes she never will. 'If the point comes when you think, "Yes, that's absolutely it, the way I originally imagined it, and I've done it and it's terrific", then the only way you can go is down, rather rapidly. That's never been my way. I never regarded it as a glamorous profession; to me the interest was always the difficulty of it. It's very difficult to act well. So I was always concerned that I would have the opportunities to work within the most difficult fields, and I've been given that. I've been very fortunate. Looking back I suppose that I've had more than my fair share of the good stuff, but there's still a chronic lack of good parts for women in the cinema or the theatre. At least I'm in the fortunate position of being able to say that I've usually done the roles I wanted to, and I really don't miss the ones that got away.' She worked hard at being the realist.

Years ago she decided that she would give up acting before it gave her up. When that would be she still did not know, but she was quite certain that one morning she would wake up and decide that there was nothing in the six months stretching ahead that she really wanted to do. And that would be the time to quit. 'So, when the time comes that the work that is offered me is no longer interesting, I will say, "Thanks very much," and wander off and do something else. What exactly, I don't know.' Living on her own without a special man in her life, and with a grown-up son developing a sense of independence, something beyond the home would *have* to occupy her thoughts.

Old age and death do not engage her mind to the point where they cause undue anxiety. On the contrary: 'I can't wait to be old because I think when you're old it's terrific. As long as I've got my health and strength, I'm going to be the most *appalling* old lady. I'm going to boss everyone about, make people stand up for me when I come into a room and generally capitalize on all the hypocrisy that society shows towards the old. And I shall become irritable and tetchy, and I shall make the lives of a lot of people around me quite miserable. Oh, yes, I fancy being a rather rowdy old lady! Old age seems the only really irresponsible time of your life. As the eldest of four daughters I think I have an over-developed sense of responsibility anyway. So I'm looking forward to growing old. I shall go round the world being outrageous. I can't actually see myself putting make-up on my face at the age of sixty, but I can see myself going on a camel train to Samarkand. I certainly don't envisage myself at sixty-five sitting in a chair on a movie set. That would be ludicrous. At that age one should be patting the heads of one's grandchildren.'

While she does not find the idea of death frightening, or indeed morbid, she does acknowledge there are frightening ways of dying. But what strikes her as both morbid and self-indulgent is a preoccupation with death rather than life. Death and what happens after death is – and she presumes will always remain so until we are actually in the ground or in the fire – a mystery about which we can only hypothesize: 'Life is actually now and it seems to me that our energies in that sense should be directed towards that.' As for life after retirement, Glenda admits: 'I don't like graves and cemeteries. One should really donate one's organs to science, after death, I suppose, but what I intend is to be cremated. I don't care where they spread my ashes.' It was nice to have things 'well planned'.

Oliver Reed, who always saw Glenda as few others saw her, spoke for millions when he concluded, 'When all the great ladies of the theatre are dancing round the maypole upstairs with their petticoats showing, Glenda will be resoundingly applauded by the great pundits of the theatre. Once there's a spark there's always a fire, depending on where the wind blows and how much water you put on it. With good movement of air there is always combustion, and Glenda will always be Glenda.'

Ignoring the evidence of box-office returns, certainly as far as her theatre appearances are concerned, she refuses to accept that she is 'a star'. George Segal told me once, 'The trouble with Glenda is that she genuinely does not nurse too high an opinion of herself, genuinely does not believe that she is *that* good, genuinely cannot fathom why people make such a fuss of her. It's got nothing to do with modesty. It's simply that she hasn't come to terms with the fact that she is a unique, solid gold talent in a world where great fame and utter tin-plated mediocrity often go hand in hand.' Because, to Glenda, acting is just a means to an end – to *do*, to *make*, to *utilize* the energy inside her – she scorns all the customary trappings of celebrity and fortune, and the flattery which theatrical acolytes habitually shower upon a luminary's private as well as public life. 'Hate it, hate it, hate it,' she utters vehemently. 'I have few, if any, social graces. I have always felt completely inadequate when I am surrounded by people who are performing when they are off stage.'

A cynic might suggest that Glenda herself goes to considerable lengths to seem ordinary; her detractors, indeed, will argue that she *is* ordinary. In a way, the cynic and the detractor are both correct. Charles Marowitz, the theatre director who, with Peter Brook, gave her her first significant acting break, has said, 'If the fine hard marble of an actress such as Glenda Jackson can be scraped out of the drab clods of a suburban terrain, there is no mystery in art and a superstar is no more remarkable than the girl next door.' If Glenda Jackson *is* the girl next door – and, when we talk of 'ordinary', that is really what we mean – then she must not be confused with the well-scrubbed and disinfected variety most typically (and erroneously) represented by Doris Day and Julie Andrews.

Like her mother, who spent most of her working life scrubbing other people's floors and serving behind bars, Glenda, when encountered at home in Blackheath, south-east London, will probably be attending to some domestic chore, and exhibit the appearance and demeanour of a Cockney washer-woman – or, to place her in the context of her upbringing, a Cheshire washerwoman. She certainly does not care how she looks once the camera is no longer turning or the curtain is down: 'Most mornings I look like something the cat brought in.' She has never had illusions about her looks.

Displaying a sallow complexion with, these days, razor-lopped hair resembling an argument between streaky bacon and a shredding machine, she is built like a stair-rod with a couple of obligatory but hardly detectable curves.

The adjectives in most common currency to describe Glenda's no-nonsense looks are 'plain' and 'gritty'. But, as Ken Russell has commented, 'Sometimes she looks plain ugly, sometimes just plain and then sometimes the most beautiful creature one has ever seen.' Another of her notable directors, Joseph Losey, confided to me, 'I don't think she had or has any sense of what was or is correct for her as far as her personal appearance is concerned: her hair, her wigs, her complexion, her make-up, her clothes. I think she advises herself badly, or is badly advised and takes the bad advice and not the good. That's stupid in an actor, but, on reflection, she's probably right: make-up isn't going to make her look better but worse.'

'The camera,' I suggested, not entirely originally, 'has a sort of love affair with her?'

'She has a strong camera *presence*,' Losey answered, 'but "a love affair" is not the kind of label I would personally suggest.'

Images, images. She does not give a fig about such things. Once, while on a publicity binge for a new West End play, her press agent was waiting anxiously with photographers and big-name Fleet Street journalists in an upstairs bar of a London theatre; Glenda was eventually discovered in the foyer downstairs talking to a pensioner who had just popped in from Marks & Spencer to visit the ladies. While she has scant regard for self-generated, trumpet-blowing publicity and, in a profession renowned for its gargantuan egocentrics, hates talking about herself, she assumes a braver front when it comes to playing parts which some performers might find unsympathetic or distasteful. 'It's important to discount images,' she will tell you. 'If you begin to believe them you begin to think that you have to conform to whatever your image is ... and when you get to the image stage, you might as well pack.'

'I didn't think I was going to like her,' confessed TV's *Upstairs, Downstairs* star Jean Marsh, who met Glenda for the first time in America. 'I always thought there was something severe about her, certainly as far as her public image was concerned. Yet I found her surprisingly "available". There was a sort of sweetness about her. I don't know if she wants that: maybe she wants her image to be one of toughness, I don't know.'

'I don't think she is worried too much about her image,' I proffered.

'But *everybody* is,' Miss Marsh said firmly, 'even the man who sells newspapers on the street corner. Most people "act" more in their private lives than actors do on the stage. So everybody cares about their image. Glenda *cares*.'

Otto Plaschkes, executive producer of Glenda's second film comedy with Walter Matthau, offers the intriguing speculation that what is so unique about the actress is the very fact that she does not have a specific image. 'If she *has* an image,' he says, 'then it's one of razor-sharpness and sublime intelligence and common sense, without any bullshit ... that's exactly what the good lady is.'

For two decades observers have tried to come to terms with the Glenda Jackson mystique, tried to reconcile her worldwide film success with the sort of woman she is. The ordinary suburban mum seems incompatible with the sexually charged character who assails you in films like *Women in Love*, *The Music Lovers*, *Sunday, Bloody Sunday*, *A Touch of Class* and *The Romantic Englishwoman*. Being intelligent, complex, paradoxical, she has largely defied those who have tried to label and thereby diminish her. Most writers, despite liberal expenditure of printer's ink and reams of copy, wide application of pop psychology and diverse speculation, have come away from her company feeling frustrated and cheated.

A newsman once tried to unwrap the enigma. 'Well,' he began, 'what do you think we might talk about?' This received the withering look of what is known as the dead albatross.

Glenda said, 'That's your problem, chuckles.'

'But you're the one with the information.'

'Prepare yourself for a shock,' she replied. 'I haven't got any. Me as myself couldn't stop a tortoise.'

'*Try.*'

'I do try. It's just that when it comes to it I can't think of anything more boring.'

'Than?'

'Well, *me*. Who else are we talking about. God, you're *slow*.'

The newsman liked her immediately, but he got no nearer to solving the mystery. So an impression or two. In my own meetings with her I would invariably find her blunt, down-to-earth, reasoned, a little bit dour. Pleasant, but no-nonsense. No make-up, lank hair, snub nose, flat planes to the face, doughy complexion, widely set eyes. Plain, but with a strength and depth that, when needed, could project a haunting beauty.

She may have made a fool of herself in some of her 1970s performances, but no one could accuse her of settling into an interminable rut. In the past decade she has played comedy and tragedy, classical and commercial parts – Hedda Gabler, Cleopatra, the fluffy roles in *House Calls* and *Hopscotch*. For this particular woman, acting was first an escape-hatch from tedium, but then it became an education more rigorous and rewarding than the university she never attended. Coolly intelligent, widely read, immensely professional, her very range as an actress has sometimes been her undoing in the cinema, for once she can see a beguiling character she is prone to accept a challenge or an interesting idea rather than a completely satisfying script.

But, for all that, she belongs today to one of the most exclusive clubs in motion pictures. There have been only nine other actresses to win more than one Academy Award: Katharine Hepburn (three), Bette Davis, Luise Rainer, Vivien Leigh, Ingrid Bergman, Olivia de Havilland, Helen Hayes, Elizabeth Taylor and Jane Fonda; and when Glenda Jackson's Oscars came her way, they were for films made quite early in her career, in 1970 and 1973. She mocks that time blithely by saying, 'Oh, yes, there was that whole period when I was flavour of the month.' And yet as Charles Marowitz, who knew her well during this period, pointed out, a couple of years after her second Oscar, Glenda may well have possessed the grittiness of Bette Davis and the same independence of spirit one associates with Katharine Hepburn, but she was – and remains – quite conspicuously odd-woman-out in that charmed circle. 'All the other actresses not only personified Hollywood stardom,' observed Marowitz, 'they also exemplified the Hollywood Ethic. Their Oscars crowned a success that was as much life-style as it was career achievement. Not so with Glenda, who, apart from her stage and screen impersonations, is enveloped in an anonymity so pervasive it must daunt even the CIA.'

The same American director then reminded us that during the New York Critics Award ceremony, when Glenda was being honoured for her performance in *Women in Love*, Bette Davis, who was conferring the award – and who happened to be Glenda's lifelong idol and ideal – remarked that she felt a little like Margo Channing, the ageing star of *All About Eve*, handing over her trophy to her ambitious rival. 'Although there is certainly no rivalry between the two actresses,' added Marowitz, 'there is a certain temperamental affinity which is immediately visible when their work is compared. With Bette Davis, one was always aware of a hyperactive inner life ready to explode at any moment. Her best performances were always mounted on her nerve ends. With Glenda, no matter how composed she may appear to be, one senses that same galvanic inner self – a quality that combines contradictory emotions such as anguish, fury, boredom and mania, suggesting that one or all of these may leap out at the slightest provocation. It is this sense of being close to elemental forces that accounts for much of Glenda's fascination; the knowledge that she is capable of manifesting those potent inner states that, in most of us, remain contained or suppressed.'

Her unique achievement, as with her prototype, Bette Davis, four decades earlier, has been to transcend the stereotype of the glamorous film star. She is a paradox made flesh, a star who behaves more like an understudy, a great actress who is not in the least stage-struck, a *grande dame* of stage and screen who personifies a kind of anti-sentimental candour which, in our finest moments, enables us (in Marowitz's words) 'to reject the pap, kitsch and schlock that stultify our daily lives'.

As a girl, back home in the North Country town of Hoylake, Glenda had spent much of her childhood and adolescence attending the local cinemas, avidly watching practically all the films Joan Crawford and Bette Davis ever made. 'Those ladies had incredible style and ability,' she said in 1970. 'They knew their medium and what they could do with it. They had a superb sort of arrogance. When they walked, they ground the poor beneath their heels.' When Joan Crawford was later informed of the homage, she asked blankly, 'Who is Glenda Jackson?' A few million other folk asked the same question when her name was announced in Hollywood as Oscar-winning Best Actress of 1970. But, from that moment on, the inquiry would never again be made. Glenda Jackson had arrived.

At the end of Alderley Road in Hoylake, just a few hundred yards from where Glenda's mother now lives, and just round the corner from where Glenda was raised as a girl, there is the Classic Cinema. It is a modest, compact establishment, very much a neighbourhood picture house. When you approach it at night, its illuminated marquee – 'CLASSIC' in bright yellow letters set against a blue background – beckons you towards it like a moth to a beacon.

'You should see the place when they're showing one of Glenda's films,' said Hilda Bethell, Glenda's friend from the YMCA days. 'It's packed solid. The whole town turns out in force. You couldn't park your car where it's parked now; you wouldn't find a vacant space anywhere. Oh, there's great excitement when one of Glenda's films is showing.'

Appendices

Filmography
Theatre
Television
Honours
Awards

Filmography

1. *This Sporting Life* (1963) Directed by Lindsay Anderson. GJ in bit part. With Richard Harris, Rachel Roberts, Alan Badel, William Hartnell, Colin Blakely, Vanda Godsell, Arthur Lowe. AAN: Richard Harris, Rachel Roberts.

2. *The Marat/Sade* (1966) Directed by Peter Brook. GJ as Charlotte Corday. With Patrick Magee, Ian Richardson, Michael Williams, Robert Lloyd, Freddie Jones, Brenda Kempner, Ruth Baker.

3. *Tell Me Lies* (1968) Directed by Peter Brook. GJ in semi-documentary role. With Peggy Ashcroft, Mark Jones, Kingsley Amis, Stokely Carmichael, Paul Scofield, Robert Lloyd, and members of the original Royal Shakespeare Company production of *US*, of which this is a screen adaptation.

4. *Negatives* (1968) Directed by Peter Medak. GJ as Vivien. With Peter McEnery, Diane Cilento, Maurice Denham, Steven Lewis, Norman Rossington.

5. *Women in Love* (1969) Directed by Ken Russell. GJ as Gudrun Brangwen. With Oliver Reed, Alan Bates, Jennie Linden, Eleanor Bron, Michael Gough, Norma Shebbeare, Alan Webb, Catherine Wilmer, Sarah Nicholls, Sharon Gurney, Christopher Gable. AA: Glenda Jackson. AAN: Larry Kramer (producer–screenwriter), Ken Russell, Billy Williams (director of photography).

6. *The Music Lovers* (1970) Directed by Ken Russell. GJ as Nina Milukova. With Richard Chamberlain, Max Adrian, Christopher Gable, Izabella Telezynska, Kenneth Colley, Sabina Maydelle, Maureen Pryor, Bruce Robinson, Andrew Faulds, John and Dennis Myers, Georgina Parkinson, Alain Dubreuil, Peter White, Maggie Maxwell.

7. *Sunday, Bloody Sunday* (1971) Directed by John Schlesinger. GJ as Alex Greville. With Peter Finch, Murray Head, Peggy Ashcroft, Maurice Denham, Vivian Pickles, Frank Windsor, Thomas Baptiste, Tony Britton, Bessie Love.

AAN: Penelope Gilliatt (screenwriter), John Schlesinger, Glenda Jackson, Peter Finch.

8. *The Boy Friend* (1971) Directed by Ken Russell. GJ in cameo role as 'famous entertainer'. With Twiggy, Christopher Gable, Max Adrian, Tommy Tune, Barbara Windsor, Moyra Fraser, Bryan Pringle, Vladek Sheybal, Antonia Ellis. AAN: Ian Whittaker, Peter Greenwell, Peter Maxwell Davies (all musical directors).

9. *Mary, Queen of Scots* (1971) Directed by Charles Jarrott. GJ as Elizabeth I. With Vanessa Redgrave, Trevor Howard, Patrick McGoohan, Timothy Dalton, Nigel Davenport, Ian Holm, Daniel Massey, Jeremy Bulloch, Beth Harris, Frances White, Maria Aitken, Richard Denning, Vernon Dobtcheff, Raf de la Torre, Katherine Kath, Robert James, Richard Warner, Andrew Keir, Bruce Purchase, Brian Coburn. AAN: John Barry (composer), Vanessa Redgrave.

10. *The Triple Echo* (1972) Directed by Michael Apted. GJ as Alice Charlesworth. With Oliver Reed, Brian Deacon, Anthony May, Gavin Richards, Jenny Lee Wright, Ken Colley, Daphne Heard, Zelah Clarke, Colin Rix, Ioan Meredith.

11. *A Touch of Class* (1972) Directed by Melvin Frank (also producer and co-writer). GJ as Vicki Allessio. With George Segal, Paul Sorvino, Hildegard Neil, Cec Linder, K. Callan, Mary Barclay, Michael Elwyn, Nadim Sawalha, Eve Karpf, Ian Thomspon. AA: Glenda Jackson. AAN: best picture, screenplay (Melvin Frank and Jack Rose), John Cameron (composer), song ('All That Love Went To Waste', with music by George Barrie and lyrics by Sammy Cahn).

12. *Bequest to the Nation* (US title: *The Nelson Affair*) (1973) Directed by James Cellan Jones. GJ as Lady Emma Hamilton. With Peter Finch, Michael Jayston, Anthony Quayle, Margaret Leighton, Dominic Guard, Nigel Stock, Roland Culver, Barbara Leigh-Hunt, Richard Mathews, Liz Ashley, John Nolan, Clelia Matania, Pat Heywood, Stephen Jack.

13. *The Tempter* (1974) Directed by Damiano Damiani. GJ as Sister Geraldine. With Claudio Cassinelli, Lisa Harrow, Adolfo Celi, Arnoldo Foa, Rolf Tasna, Duilio Del Prete, Gabriele Lavia, Francisco Rabal.

14. *The Maids* (1974) Directed by Christopher Miles. GJ as Solange. With Susannah York, Vivien Merchant, Mark Burns.

15. *The Romantic Englishwoman* (1975) Directed by Joseph Losey. GJ as Elizabeth Fielding. With Michael Caine, Helmut Berger, Marcus Richardson, Kate Nelligan, Rene Kolldehof, Michele Lonsdale, Beatrice Romand, Anna Steele,

Nathalie Delon, Bill Wallis, Julie Peasgood, David de Keyser, Phil Brown, Marcella Markham, Lillias Walker, Doris Nolan, Norman Scace, Tom Chatto, Frankie Jordan, Frances Tomelty.

16. *Hedda* (1975) Directed by Trevor Nunn, based on his screenplay. GJ as Hedda. With Patrick Stewart, Peter Eyre, Timothy West, Jennie Linden, Constance Chapman, Pam St Clement. AAN: Glenda Jackson.

17. *The Incredible Sarah* (1976) Directed by Richard Fleischer. GJ as Sarah Bernhardt. With Daniel Massey, Yvonne Mitchell, Douglas Wilmer, Simon Williams, David Langton, John Castle, Edward Judd, Peter Sallis, Rosemarie Dunham, Bridget Armstrong, Margaret Courtenay, Maxwell Shaw, Patrick Newell, Gawn Grainger, Lawrence Douglas, Neil McCarthy, Peter Davidson, Stephan Chase, David Muldowney.

18. *Nasty Habits* (1976) Directed by Michael Lindsay-Hogg. GJ as Sister Alexandra. With Melina Mercouri, Geraldine Page, Sandy Dennis, Anne Jackson, Anne Meara, Susan Penhaligon, Edith Evans, Rip Torn, Eli Wallach, Jerry Stiller, Suzanne Stone, Peter Bromilow, Shane Rimmer, Harry Ditson, Chris Muncke, Oliver Maguire, Alick Hayes, Bill Reimbold, Anthony Forrest, Mike Douglas, Bill Jorgenson, Jessica Savitch, Howard K. Smith.

19. *House Calls* (1978) Directed by Howard Zieff. GJ as Ann Atkinson. With Walter Matthau, Art Carney, Richard Benjamin, Candice Azzara, Dick O'Neill, Thayer David, Anthony Holland, Reva Rose, Sandra Kerns, Brad Dexter, Jane Connell, Lloyd Gough, Gordon Jump, William J. Fiore, Taurean Blacque, Charlie Matthau.

20. *Stevie* (1978) Directed by Robert Enders, who also produced. GJ as Stevie Smith. With Mona Washbourne, Alec McCowen, Trevor Howard, Emma Louise Fox.

21. *The Class of Miss MacMichael* (1978) Directed by Silvio Narizzano. GJ as Conor MacMichael. With Oliver Reed, John Standing, Michael Murphy, Rosalind Cash, Riba Akabusi, Phil Daniels, Patrick Murray, Sylvia O'Donnell, Sharon Fussey, Herbert Norville, Perry Benson, Tony London, Owen Whittaker, Angela Brogan, Victor Evans, Simon Howe, Dayton Brown, Paul Daly, Deirdre Forrest, Stephanie Patterson, Peta Bernard, Judy Wiles, Mavis Pugh, Patsy Byrne, Ian Thompson, Christopher Guinee, Constantin de Goguel, Sally Nesbitt, Sylvia Marriott, Mariane Stone, Pamela Manson, Debbie Morton, John Wreford, Honora Burke.

22. *Lost and Found* (1979) Directed by Melvin Frank (also producer and co-writer). GJ as Tricia Brittenham. With George Segal, Maureen Stapleton, Hollis McLaren, John Cunningham, Paul Sorvino, Kenneth Progue, Janie Sell, Diana Barrington, Leslie Carlson, John Candy, James Morris.

23. *Health* (1979) Directed by Robert Altman (also producer and co-writer). GJ as Isabella Garnell. With James Garner, Lauren Bacall, Carol Burnett, Paul Dooley, Donald Moffat, Henry Gibson, Dick Cavett, Diana Stilwell, MacIntyre Dixon, Alfre Woodard, Ann Ryerson, Georgann Johnson, Allan Nicholls.

24. *Hopscotch* (1980) Directed by Ronald Neame. GJ as Isobel von Schmidt. With Walter Matthau, Sam Waterson, Ned Beatty, Herbert Lom, David Matthau, George Baker, Ivor Roberts, Lucy Saroyan, Severn Darden, George Pravda, Jacquelyn Hyde, Mike Gwilym, Terry Beaver, Ray Charleson, Christopher Driscoll, Michael Cronin, Douglas Dirkson, Ann Haney.

25. *The Patricia Neal Story* (1981) Made-for-TV film. Directed by Anthony Harvey (American sequences) and Anthony Page (British sequences). GJ as Patricia Neal. With Dirk Bogarde, Mildred Dunnock, Ken Kercheval, Jane Merrow, John Reilly. Emmy Award nomination: Glenda Jackson.

26. *Giro City* (1982) Made-for-TV film. Directed by Karl Francis from his own screenplay. GJ as Sophie. With Jon Finch, Kenneth Colley, Emrys Jones, James Donnelly, Bruce Alexander, Karen Archer, Robert Austin, Frank Barker, Gerwyn Baker, David Beames, Colette Barker, James Benson, Graham Berry, Bob Blythe, Norman Caro, Huw Ceredig, Philip Compton, Dermot Crowley, Peter Halliday, Jennifer Hill, Bill Ingrams, Terry Jackson, Sophie Kind, Michel Lees, Alun Lewis, Elizabeth Lynne, Taylor McCauley, Marian McLoughlin, Sharon Morgan, Roger Nott, Robert Pugh, David Quilter.

27. *The Return of the Soldier* (1983) Directed by Alan Bridges. GJ as Margaret. With Alan Bates, Julie Christie, Ann-Margret, Ian Holm, Frank Finlay, Jeremy Kemp.

28. *Sakharov* (1984) Directed by Jack Gold. GJ as Elena Bonner. With Jason Robards, Nicol Williamson, Frank Finlay, Marion Bailey, Michael Bryant, Paul Freeman, Anton Lesser, Anna Massey, Joe Melia, Lee Montague, Jim Norton, Norman Rodway, Elizabeth Spriggs, Eileen Way, Martyn Whitby, Jean Heywood, Bernard Kay, Ralph Nossek, Ron Donachie, Christopher Guinee, Avril Elgar, Tom Wilkinson, Sarah James, Robert Gwilym.

29. *Turtle Summer* (1985) Directed by John Irvin. GJ as Nearer. With Ben Kingsley, Richard Johnson, Michael Gambon, Rosemary Leach, Harriet Walter, Eleanor Bron, Jeroen Kabbe, Nigel Hawthorne, Michael Aldridge. (The second feature film from GJ's United British Artists collective; *Champions* was the first.)

Theatre

(Selective listing; does not include repertory engagements with companies in Crewe, Dundee, Oldham, Watford, Perth, etc.)

1. Worthing Repertory Company, Connaught Theatre, Worthing, Sussex, 1957. Professional stage début. Bit-part as nurse in *Doctor in the House*; Daniel Massey also in cast.

2. Hornchurch Repertory (the Queen's Players), Queen's Theatre, Hornchurch, Essex, 1957. Appeared in two plays. First: *Separate Tables* by Terence Rattigan. Directed by Nancy Poultney. GJ as Jean Stratton and Jean Tanner. With Gwendoline (now Gwen) Watford, Eleanor Darling, Dorothy Gibson, Marion Mathie, Anne Woodward, Sylvia Kay, John Wentworth, Barbara Bolton, Tony Church, Dinsdale Landen. From 18 February to 2 March. Second: *The White Sheep of the Family* by L. du Garde Peach and Ian Hay. Directed by Nancy Poultney. GJ as the maid. With Gwendoline (now Gwen) Watford, Nancy Poultney, James Grant, Geoffrey Russell, John Moore, Hugh Dickinson, Petronella Davies. From 5 to 17 August.

3. *All Kinds of Men* by Alex Samuels. Opened at the Arts Theatre, London, on 19 September 1957. Directed by Robert Mitchell. GJ as Ruby. With Ann Firbank, Patric Doonan, Wilfrid Lawson, Miriam Karlin, Gwen Lewis, Meier Tzelniker, Nancy Nevinson, Golda Casimir, John Nettleton, Jack Lester, Leslie Glazer, Gertan Klauber, John Bay, Anna Welsh, Sylvia Casimir, Deirdre White.

4. *The Idiot* by Jose Ruben, based on the novel by Fyodor Dostoevsky. Ikon Theatre Company. Opened at the Lyric Theatre, Hammersmith, London, on 5 March 1962. Directed and designed by John Crockett. GJ as Alexandra. With Jeffrey Segal, John Woodvine, Christopher Guinee, Peter Wyatt, Penelope Horner, Patrick Godfrey, Paul Curran, Elizabeth Spriggs, Patricia Conolly, Stephanie Bidmead, Sheila Ballantine, Daniel Thorndike, John Ringham, Christopher Burgess, Antonia Pemberton, Barry Wallman, Irene Hamilton, Zena Walker, William Hobbs, John Barry Jones.

5. *Come Back With Diamonds* by Maria Lehmann. Ikon Theatre Company. Opened at the Lyric Theatre, Hammersmith, London, on 21 May 1962. Directed by David Giles. GJ as one of five neighbours. With Brian Phelan, Elizabeth

Spriggs, Sheila Ballantine, Margo Cunningham, Daniel Thorndike, Christopher Burgess, Nora Nicholson, Jeffrey Segal, Patrick Godfrey, Jeremy Conway, Kenneth Warren, Sarah Harter, Patricia Jeffery, Mary Gunn, John Barry Jones, David Ayliff.

6. *Alfie* by Bill Naughton. Opened at the Mermaid Theatre, London, on 19 June 1963, transferring in July to the West End (Duchess Theatre). Directed by Donald McWhinnie. GJ as Siddie. With John Neville, Gemma Jones, David Battley, Arthur Mallen, Norman Wynne, Audine Leith, George Waring, Marcia Ashton, Jerry Verno, Maureen Davis, Edna Landor, Patrick Connor, Alan Townsend, Mary Henefey, Wendy Varnals, Patrick Mower, Margaret Courtenay.

7. Royal Shakespeare Company's Theatre of Cruelty preview, LAMDA Theatre, London, 12 January 1964. RSC Experimental Group. Surrealist revue directed by Peter Brook and Charles Marowitz, comprising brief pieces by a wide variety of authors, among them John Arden, Paul Ableman, Alain Robbe-Grillet, Ray Bradbury, Jean Genet and Shakespeare. GJ, as Christine Keeler and Jacqueline Kennedy, became first serious actress to appear nude on a British stage. With Mary Allen, Jonathan Burn, Richard Dare, Freda Dowie, Rob Inglis, Alexis Kanner, Leon Lissek, Robert Lloyd, Susan Williamson.

8. *The Marat/Sade* (full title: *The Persecution and Assassination of Marat as Performed by the Inmates of the Asylum of Charenton under the Direction of the Marquis de Sade*) by Peter Weiss; English version by Geoffrey Skelton, with verse adaptation by Adrian Mitchell. Directed by Peter Brook. Royal Shakespeare Company. Staged as part of the Theatre of Cruelty season. Opened at the Aldwych Theatre, London, on 20 August 1964; revived November 1965, again at the Aldwych; RSC production then staged at the Martin Beck Theater, New York, on 27 December 1965, with GJ making her Broadway début. GJ as Charlotte Corday. With Clifford Rose, Brenda Kempner, June Baker, Ian Richardson, Michael Williams, Jonathan Burn, Freddie Jones, Elizabeth Spriggs, Robert Lloyd, Clive Revill, Susan Williamson, Patrick Magee, John Steiner, Wyn Jones, Morgan Sheppard, Timothy West, Henry Woolf, Geoffrey Hinsliff, John Harwood, Leon Lissek, Brian Osborn.

9. *The Jew of Malta* by Christopher Marlowe. Royal Shakespeare Company. Staged to mark the 400th anniversary of Marlowe's birth. Opened at the Aldwych Theatre, London, on 1 October 1964. Directed by Clifford Williams. GJ as Bellamira. With Derek Godfrey, Clive Revill, John Harwood, Geoffrey Hinsliff, Leon Lissek, Robert Lloyd, Henry Woolf, Tony Church, Jonathan Burn, Michael Bryant, Morgan Sheppard, Wyn Jones, Michele Dotrice, Ken Wynne, John Nettleton, June Jago, John Steiner, Michael Williams, Paul Dawkins, Bryan Stanyon, Ian Richardson, Doris Hare, Timothy West, Michael Jenkinson.

10. *Love's Labour's Lost* by William Shakespeare. Royal Shakespeare Company. Opened at the Royal Shakespeare Theatre, Stratford-on-Avon, on 7 April 1965. Directed by John Barton. GJ as the Princess of France. With Charles Kay, James Laurenson, Michael Pennington, Charles Thomas, Stanley Lebor, Philip Meredith, Brewster Mason, Katharine Barker, Jessica Claridge, Janet Suzman, Murray Brown, Tim Wylton, David Waller, Patsy Byrne, Marshall Jones, Tony Church, Timothy West.

11. *Puntila* (full title: *Squire Puntila and His Servant Matti*) by Bertolt Brecht. Royal Shakespeare Company. Opened at the Aldwych Theatre, London, on 15 July 1965. Directed by Michel Saint-Denis. GJ as Eva. With Roy Dotrice, Clifford Rose, Davyd Harries, Patrick Magee, Ian Richardson, Patience Collier, John Malcolm, Susan Engel, Jeanette Landis, Carol Raymont, Terence Rigby, Michael Jayston, Ken Wynne, Gabrielle Hamilton, Morgan Sheppard, June Baker, Walter Batalia, John Salmon, Michele Dotrice, John Steiner, John Normington, Penelope Keith, Michael Farnsworth, Iain Blair, Richard Moore, Ian Hogg.

12. *Hamlet* by William Shakespeare. Royal Shakespeare Company. Opened at the Royal Shakespeare Theatre, Stratford-on-Avon, on 19 August 1965. Directed by Peter Hall. GJ as Ophelia. With David Warner, Alan Tucker, Peter Geddis, Jeffery Dench, Donald Burton, Patrick Magee, Brewster Mason, Elizabeth Spriggs, David Waller, Murray Brown, Tony Church, Charles Thomas, Michael Williams, James Laurensen, Tim Wylton, William Squire, Charles Kay, Stanley Lebor, Michael Pennington, John Corvin, Robert Walker, Ted Valentine, Bruce Condell, Robert Lloyd, Marshall Jones.

13. *The Investigation* by Peter Weiss. Royal Shakespeare Company. Opened at the Aldwych Theatre, London, on 21 October 1965. Directed by Peter Brook. GJ as one of the two women readers; the other was Penelope Keith.

14. *US.* A collaboration, from the original text by Denis Cannan, adapted by Michael Kustow and Michael Stott, with lyrics by Adrian Mitchell. Royal Shakespeare Company. Opened at the Aldwych Theatre, London, on 13 October 1966. Directed by Peter Brook. Production was essentially a group effort, though GJ's verbal pyrotechnics dominated the second half. With Eric Allan, Mary Allen, Jeremy Anthony, Hugh Armstrong, Roger Brierley, Noel Collins, Ian Hogg, John Hussey, Mark Jones, Marjie Lawrence, Joanne Lindsay, Leon Lissek, Robert Lloyd, Ursula Mohan, Pauline Munro, Patrick O'Connel, Mike Pratt, Clifford Rose, Morgan Sheppard, Jayne Sofiano, Barry Stanton, Hugh Sullivan, Michael Williams.

15. *The Three Sisters* by Anton Chekhov. Opened at the Royal Court Theatre, London, on 18 April 1967. Directed by William Gaskill. GJ as Masha. With

Marianne Faithfull, Avril Elgar, George Cole, Michael Gwynn, Alan Webb, Marjie Lawrence, Roddy Maude-Roxby, John Shepherd, Peter Russell, John Nettles, Toby Salaman, John Rae, Madoline Thomas, Rosemary McHale, Stuart Mungall.

16. *Fanghorn* by David Pinner. Opened at the Fortune Theatre, London, on 16 November 1967. Directed by Charles Marowitz. GJ as Tamara Fanghorn. With Peter Bayliss, Rachel King, Mary Land, Sydney Bromley.

17. *Collaborators* by John Mortimer. Opened at the Duchess Theatre, London, on 17 April 1973. Directed by Eric Thompson. GJ as Katherine Winter. With John Wood, Joss Ackland, Gloria Connell.

18. *The Maids* by Jean Genet. Opened at the Greenwich Theatre, London, on 14 February 1974. Directed and translated by Minos Volanakis. GJ as Solange. With Susannah York, Vivien Merchant.

19. *Hedda Gabler* by Henrik Ibsen; English version by Trevor Nunn from a literal translation by Kirsten Stenberg Williams. Royal Shakespeare Company. Previewed at the Richmond Theatre, Richmond, Surrey, on 27 February 1975, prior to tour of Australia (Melbourne, Sydney), the United States (Los Angeles, Washington) and Canada (Toronto), with first London performance at the Aldwych Theatre on 17 July 1975. Directed by Trevor Nunn. GJ as Hedda. With Patrick Stewart, Timothy West, Peter Eyre, Constance Chapman, Jennie Linden, Pam St Clement.

20. *The White Devil* by John Webster; adapted by Edward Bond. Opened at the Old Vic, London, on 12 July 1976. Directed by Michael Lindsay-Hogg. GJ as Vittoria Corombona. With Jonathan Pryce, Frances de la Tour, Jack Shepherd, Miriam Margolyes, Patrick Magee.

21. *Stevie* by Hugh Whitemore. Opened at the Vaudeville Theatre, London, on 23 March 1977. Directed by Clifford Williams. GJ as Stevie Smith. With Mona Washbourne, Peter Eyre.

22. *Antony and Cleopatra* by William Shakespeare. Royal Shakespeare Company. Opened at the Royal Shakespeare Theatre, Stratford-upon-Avon, on 4 October 1978, transferring to the Aldwych Theatre, London, on 22 July 1979. Directed by Peter Brook. GJ as Cleopatra. With Alan Howard, Patrick Stewart, John Nettles, Jonathan Pryce, Paul Brooke, Marjorie Bland, David Lyon, John Bowe, Paul Whitworth, Hilton McRae, Dennis Clinton, Paul Webster, Alan Rickman, David Bradley, David Suchet, George Raistrick, Paul Moriarty, Paola Dionisotti, Juliet Stevenson, Philip McGough, Richard Griffiths, Raymond Westwell.

23. *Rose* by Andrew Davies. Opened at the Duke of York's Theatre, London, on 28 February 1980; later opened at the Cort Theater, New York, on 26 March 1981, again with GJ. Directed by Alan Dossor. GJ as Rose. With (London cast) Jean Heywood, Stephanie Cole, Gillian Martell, Tom Georgeson, Diana Davies, Richard Vanstone, David Daker; (New York cast) Jessica Tandy, Beverly May, Margaret Hilton, J. T. Walsh, Guy Boyd, John Cunningham, Don McAllen Leslie, Cynthia Crumlish, Lori Cardille.

24. *Summit Conference* by Robert David MacDonald. Opened at the Lyric Theatre, London, on 28 April 1982. Directed and designed by Philip Prowse. GJ as Eva Braun. With Georgina Hale, Gary Oldman.

25. *Great and Small* by Botho Strauss; translated by David Essinger. Following provincial run in Richmond (Surrey), Leeds, Manchester and Bath, opened at the Vaudeville Theatre, London, on 25 August 1983. Directed by Keith Hack. GJ as Lotte. With Barry Stanton, Marty Cruickshank, Brian Deacon, Robert Morgan, Mark Dignam, Emma Piper.

26. *Strange Interlude* by Eugene O'Neill. Following previews in Croydon and Nottingham, opened at the Duke of York's Theatre, London, on 6 April 1984; opened in New York, again with GJ, in spring 1985. Directed by Keith Hack. GJ as Nina. With Brian Cox, Edward Petherbridge, James Hazeldine, John Phillips.

27. *Phedra* by Jean Racine; translation by Robert David MacDonald specially commissioned for GJ. Lupton Theatre Company. Opened at the Old Vic, London, on 14 November 1984. Directed and designed by Philip Prowse. GJ as Phedra. With Robert Edison, Georgina Hale, Joyce Redman, Tim Woodward.

Television

1. *A Voice in Vision* (1958) Associated Rediffusion (ITV). Live transmission. Produced by Peter Graham Scott. GJ in bit-part as typist who screams. With Lesley Phillips, Gwen Watford.

2. *Dr Everyman's Hour* (1962) Associated Rediffusion (ITV). Live transmission. Produced by Peter Graham Scott. GJ as jury woman; two lines of dialogue.

3. *Let's Murder Vivaldi* by David Mercer (1968) 'Wednesday Play' slot, BBC television. Directed by Alan Bridges; produced by Graeme McDonald. GJ as young housewife. With Gwen Watford, Denholm Elliott.

4. *Elizabeth R* (1971) BBC television. (Shown in United States in 1972 in the 'Masterpiece Theater' slot on Channel 28; and on KCET, Los Angeles.) Produced by Roderick Graham. GJ as Elizabeth I. Six-part serial. Part 1: 'The Lion's Cub' by John Hale (directed by Claude Whatham). Part 2: 'The Marriage Game' by Rosemary Anne Sisson (directed by Herbert Wise). Part 3: 'Shadow in the Sun' by Julian Mitchell (directed by Richard Martin). Part 4: 'Horrible Conspiracies' by Hugh Whitemore (directed by Roderick Graham). Part 5: 'The Enterprise of England' by John Prebble (directed by Roderick Graham). Part 6: 'Sweet England's Pride' by Ian Rodger (directed by Roderick Graham). With Ronald Hines, Daphne Slater, Rachel Kempson, Bernard Hepton, Rosalie Crutchley, John Ronane, Peter Jeffrey. Series won five Emmys, including Best Dramatic Actress award for Glenda Jackson.

5. *The Morecambe and Wise Show* (1971) BBC television. GJ in Ginger Rogers routine: it was this burlesque which led to her being cast in her first film comedy, *A Touch of Class*.

6. *The Muppet Show* (1980) ATV (ITV) Produced by Jim Henson and Jon Stone. GJ as pirate chief, in song-and-dance routine with Fozzie Bear and puppet friends.

7. *The Morecambe and Wise Christmas Show* (1980) Thames Television (ITV). GJ in hello-and-goodbye joke with Eric and Ernie.

8. Glenda Jackson Film Season (1981) BBC television (BBC2). Eight-film season, starting with *Sunday, Bloody Sunday*. Another Glenda Jackson season ran concurrently in the United States on the Bravo cable network.

9. *The Morecambe and Wise Christmas Show* (1982) Thames Television (ITV). GJ in telephone routine with Eric. With Robert Hardy, Rula Lenska, Richard Vernon, Wall Street Crash, Diana Dors, Denis Healey, Jimmy Young, André Previn.

Awards
(as Best Actress)

Films

1970   Variety Club of Great Britain
New York Film Critics

1971   Academy Award (Oscar)
Variety Club of Great Britain
New York Film Critics
National Society of Film Critics (US)

1972   Society of Film and Television Arts (UK)
Academy Award nomination
French Film Academy (Étoile de Cristal)

1973   London *Evening News*

1974   Academy Award (Oscar)

1975   Variety Club of Great Britain

1976   Academy Award nomination

1978   Variety Club of Great Britain

1979   Variety Club of Great Britain

1981   New York Film Critics
National Board of Review of Motion Pictures (US)
Montreal Film Festival

1983   Cannes Film Festival (Distinguished Service to the Cinema award)

Theatre

1966   *Variety* Award (US), Most Promising Actress
New York Drama Critics Circle
Tony nomination

1973   Golden Globe nomination

1981   Tony nomination

Television

1972   Emmy

1981   Emmy award nomination

Honours

1978   *CBE.* Named a Commander of the British Empire in the Queen's Birthday Honours.
D.Litt. Honorary degree from Liverpool University.

Acknowledgements

In researching and writing this biography I have prevailed upon the time and generosity of more than two hundred individuals, many of whom, in one capacity or another, have been associated with Glenda Jackson during her life and professional career – actor colleagues, producers, directors, make-up, wardrobe and design people, cameramen, business associates, screenwriters, journalists, publicists, friends, an enemy or two. To these people, a great many of whom spoke or wrote to me at length, or contributed in various ways to make this book as complete as (within certain limitations) any biography of a living person can be, I extend my gratitude. They are: Ann-Margret, John Austin, Martyn Auty, Bert Bacharach, Richard Barber, Felix Barker, Richard Barkley, David Benedictus, Phillip Bergson, Michael Billington, Rita Black, Ed Blanch, Winfred Blevins, Dirk Bogarde, Helen Bohn, Hilary Bonner, Sally K. Brass, Alan Brien, Sally Brompton, Peter Buckley, Tom Buckley, Patience Bulkeley, Bridget Byrne, Beatrice Campbell, Vincent Canby, Rubin Carson, David Castell, John Castle, Charles Champlin, Chris Chase, Sue Clarke, Minty Clinch, Sidney Cole, Nancy Collins, Clare Colvin, Bruce Cook, John Corry, Michael Graham Cox, Peter Dacre, Barbara Daly, Nigel Davenport, Hunter Davies, Victor Davis, Samantha Dean, John Deighton, Anthea Disney, Vernon Dobtcheff, Paul Donovan, Ken Eastaugh, Henry Ehrlich, Derek Elley, Jane Ellison, Bonnie Estridge, Peter Evans, Trader Faulkner, Sandy Fawkes, Ken Ferguson, Vincent Firth, Gerry Fisher, Guy Flatley, Pamela Flay, Scarth Flett, Julian Fox, David Galligan, George Hadley Garcia, Jane Gaskell, Roderick Gilchrist, James Gilheany, Penelope Gilliatt, Joan Goodman, Martin Goul, Gordon Gow, Richard Grenier, Veronica Groocock, William Hall, Radie Harris, John Heilpern, Margaret Hinxman, Clive Hirschhorn, Veronica Howell, Tom Hutchinson, Catherine Itzin, Barbara Jeffery, Peter Jeffrey, Gregory Jensen, Linda Joffee, Patricia Johnson, Van Johnson, James Cellan Jones, John Jones, T. A. Kalem, Penelope Keith, Walter Kerr, Dick Kleiner, Rhoda Koenig, Herbert Kretzmer, Jack Kroll, Irma Kurtz, Martha Weinman Lear, Lynda Lee-Potter, Barbara Leigh-Hunt, Hugh Leonard, Geoffrey Levy, Adella Lithman, Mary Anne Lloyd, Judy Loe, Pat Longmore, Joseph Losey, Iain F. McAsh, Joseph McBride, Alec McCowen, Peter McEnery, Sue McGinnis, Neil Mackwood, Leonard Maltin, Roderick Mann, Dorothy Manners, Charles Marowitz, R. B. Marriott, Jean Marsh, William Marshall, Daniel Massey, Walter Matthau, Joyce Maynard, Peter Medak, Suzy Menkes, Christopher Miles, Edwin Miller, Russell Miller, Sheridan Morley, Mike Munn, Joy Nelson, John Nettles, Nora Nicholson, Philip Oakes, Robert Osborne, Sally O'Sullivan, Michael Owen, Phyllis Owen, Jeremy Pascall, Barbara Paskin, Garth Pearce, Roy Pickard, Ann Pinkerton, Otto Plaschkes, Peggy Polk, John Preston, Anna Quindlen, Oliver Reed, Rex Reed, Christopher Reeve, Ian Richardson, Fred Robbins, Peter Roberts, Ken Russell, Sue Russell, Peter Saunders, Stephen Schaefer, Peter Graham Scott, George Segal, Vladek Sheybal, Don Short, Milton Shulman, June Southworth, Cecil Smith, David James Smith, Sue Spunner,

Gloria Steinem, David Sterritt, Patrick Stewart, Catherine Stott, Dan Sullivan, Dorothy Summers, Clive Swift, Arthur Thirkell, Jack Tinker, Simon Trussler, Valerie Wade, Alexander Walker, John Walker, Hal Wallis, Christopher Ward, Irving Wardle, Ivan Waterman, Gwen Watford, Timothy West, John Williams, Simon Williams, Douglas Wilmer, Freddie Young, and Donald Zec.

Many other individuals offered much valuable information on the sole understanding that their identity would remain anonymous and, of course, their wishes have been respected.

In Hoylake and West Kirby, Cheshire, location of Glenda Jackson's childhood, many people who knew her then have been of immense help. Mrs D. J. Cheesley, the present headmistress of the West Kirby Grammar School for Girls, was especially cooperative, as were the school's Miss Joyce Harley, Miss Myra Kendrick and Miss Mary Handy, all now retired, who, respectively, taught Glenda Jackson the intricacies of science, English, and physical education (Miss Harley, additionally, was Glenda's form mistress); they all gave me a great deal of their time to talk about the Glenda Jackson that they knew. Mrs Hilda Bethell, who performed with Glenda in the local YMCA Players productions, went out of her way to introduce me to the people in Hoylake and West Kirby who knew Glenda as a girl; she ferried me around, helped to familiarize me with the area, and generally was a godsend. My thanks must also go to Mrs Jill Cumming, who acted with Glenda at the Hoylake YMCA, and to Mrs Phyllis Owen, widow of Warren Owen, the man who first produced Glenda in amateur dramatics and who put her on the path to London and RADA; they both welcomed me into their homes to 'talk Glenda'.

I must also mention the assistance of Jan O'Neill and Peggy Clarke for filling me in on the facts relating to Glenda Jackson's association with the Queen's Theatre in Hornchurch, Essex. Out-of-the-way photographic material was also kindly provided by Sylvia Morris of the Shakespeare Centre Library at Stratford-upon-Avon, and by Robert Gore-Langton of *Plays and Players*. Additionally, the Reference Division of the British Library, London, provided many essential facilities. The *Daily Express* Library, the Library Services department of the British Film Institute, and the BBC Script Library, all in London, and the BBC Written Archives at Caversham Park, Reading, also kindly placed their extensive files at my disposal. In the United States, I would like to thank Val Almendarez, co-ordinator of the National Film Information Service of the Academy of Motion Picture Arts and Sciences, Hollywood, for familiarizing me with the American literature as it relates to Glenda Jackson.

In the process of writing this book I have referred to and in many cases quoted from my interviews with Glenda Jackson which first appeared in the *Guardian*, the *Sun*, the *Christian Science Monitor*, *Woman's Journal*, *Good Housekeeping*, and other publications in Britain and elsewhere. Additionally, for granting permission to quote from the following newspapers and magazines (some of them now discontinued), I am indebted to the respective authors, editors and publishers (British unless otherwise stated): *Advocate* (USA), *Book Digest* (USA), *Boston Globe Magazine* (USA), *Christian Science Monitor* (USA), *Cinema Papers* (Australia), *Cinema TV Today*, *City Limits*, *Cosmopolitan* (USA), *Cue* (USA), *Daily Express*, *Daily Mail*, *Daily Mirror*, *Daily Sketch*, *Daily Telegraph*, *Drama-Logue* (USA), *Entertainment Magazine* (USA), London *Evening News*, London *Evening Standard* (now the *Standard*), *Films and Filming*, *Films Illustrated*, *Film Review*, *Gambit* (USA), *Gossip* (USA), *Guardian*, *Hollywood-Citizen News* (USA), *Hollywood Reporter* (USA), *Honey*, *Look* (USA), *Los Angeles Herald-Examiner* (USA), *Los Angeles Magazine* (USA), *Los Angeles Times* & Syndicate (USA), *Mail on Sunday*, *Miss London*, *Ms* (USA), *National Observer* (USA), *News of the World*, *Newspapers Enterprise Association* (USA), *New York Times* and *New York*

Times Magazine (USA) (copyright © 1966/70/75/76/79/81/82 by the New York Times Company. Reprinted by permission), *Newsweek* (USA), *Now, Observer, Options, Photoplay* (now *Photoplay Movies & Video*), *Plays and Players* (February, June and October 1965; December 1966; June 1967; June 1973; April 1974; September 1975; September 1976; March 1980), *Playgirl* (USA) (© 1976 Author: M. George Haddad), *Radio Times, Redbook* (USA), *Saturday Review* (USA), *Secrets, Seventeen* (USA), *Show* (USA), *Stage, Sun, Sunday Express, Sunday People, Sunday Telegraph* and *Sunday Telegraph Magazine, Sunday Times* (Philip Oakes: 29 September 1968, 30 October 1977; Hunter Davies: 7 March 1971; Veronica Howell: 24 October 1982), *Tatler, Time* (USA), *The Times, TWA Ambassador Magazine* (USA), *Variety* (USA), *Viva* (USA), *What's On, Woman, Woman's Own, Woman's Realm, Woman's World, Women's Wear Daily* (USA), *You: The Mail on Sunday Magazine*.

For permission to quote from their books, I wish to thank the following authors, their executors, and publishers (all published in London, unless stated otherwise): Jonathan Cape Ltd for 'Fire and Ice' by Robert Frost from *The Poetry of Robert Frost*, edited by Edward Connery Lathem; Chatto & Windus Ltd for *An Orderly Man* by Dirk Bogarde; William Collins, Sons & Co. Ltd for *The Mousetrap Man* by Peter Saunders; Hamish Hamilton Ltd for *The Performing World of the Actor* by Clive Swift (material reproduced courtesy of Breslich & Foss, London); Macmillan Co. (New York) for *Big Screen, Little Screen* by Rex Reed and for *Starmaker* by Hal Wallis; New American Library (New York) for *TV Movies* edited by Leonard Maltin; Secker & Warburg Ltd for *Unholy Fools* by Penelope Gilliatt; Sidgwick & Jackson Ltd for *Raising Caine* by William Hall; the Society of Authors as the literary representatives of the Estate of A. E. Housman, and Jonathan Cape Ltd, publishers of A. E. Housman's *Collected Poems*, for the extract from 'To An Athlete Dying Young'; Times Newspapers Ltd for *The Sunday Times Guide to Movies on Television* by Angela and Elkan Allan.

Finally, I wish to extend my heartfelt appreciation to all at Weidenfeld & Nicolson Ltd – John Curtis, my copy editor Alexandra Sulkin and, above all, Alex MacCormick, the most sympathetic and encouraging of editors – for making the writing and production of the book a particularly congenial one. As ever, my wife Zenka typed the manuscript superbly and, along the way, managed to make sense of, and draw my attention to, much that was not always immediately clear or obvious in the final draft: she's an angel incarnate.

Index